CENTURY 21 SHORTHAND DICTIONARY

EDWARD L. CHRISTENSEN, Ph. D.
Graduate School of Management
Brigham Young University

Shorthand Plates Written by
GRACE A. BOWMAN
and
STANFORD D. DeMILLE

R14

Published by
SOUTH-WESTERN PUBLISHING CO.

CINCINNATI   WEST CHICAGO, ILL.   DALLAS   PELHAM MANOR, N.Y.
PALO ALTO, CALIF.   BRIGHTON, ENGLAND

ISBN: 0-538-18140-0

Library of Congress Catalog Card Number: 76-13415

1 2 3 4 5 K 0 9 8 7 6

Printed in the United States of America

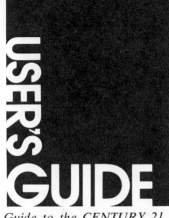

USER'S GUIDE

From the first section, *A Guide to the CENTURY 21 DICTIONARY*, to the timely final section, *International Metric System Symbols in CENTURY 21*, this computerized DICTIONARY is a convenient reference for the teacher, the student, the stenographer, and the secretary.

The DICTIONARY is designed to provide the user quickly with:

- shorthand outlines to four basic vocabularies and all CENTURY 21 texts
- illustrative sounds on which CENTURY 21 outlines are based
- clearly identified Speedforms and derivatives, special abbreviations, and optional contracted outlines based on an abbreviating principle
- dual outlines for different forms of a word with different sounds
- preferred and alternate spellings of key words
- basic theory on which CENTURY 21 outlines are written
- simple, nondecision writing rules of CENTURY 21
- several other useful features — all based upon a communication premise that: *the secretary's primary clues to dictation are the sounds which should be recorded consistently and without hesitation*

Organization of the DICTIONARY

The CENTURY 21 DICTIONARY is composed of three major divisions: (1) A Guide to the CENTURY 21 DICTIONARY, (2) The Business and General Vocabularies, and (3) The Proper Nouns and Tables of Abbreviations.

Division 1 A Guide to the CENTURY 21 DICTIONARY contains the following useful information:

A. Purpose of the DICTIONARY
B. Organization of the DICTIONARY
C. CENTURY 21 Rationale and Theory
  - Significance of Sound
  - Primary Alphabet
  - Derived Alphabet
  - Speedform Rationale
D. CENTURY 21 Writing Rationale
E. Special Features of CENTURY 21

Division 2 The Business and General Vocabularies contain alphabetized words, CENTURY 21 outlines, and special user information:

A. Sources of the DICTIONARY words
B. Approved CENTURY 21 outlines
C. Special Information
  - Preferred and Alternate Spellings
  - Trademarks and Acronyms

Division 3 The Proper Nouns and Tables of Abbreviations contain capitalized words, and lists of abbreviations:

A. Personal and Geographic Names
B. Capitalized Acronyms
C. Tables of Correspondence Abbreviations
D. Special Abbreviations
E. International Metric System Symbols in CENTURY 21

CENTURY 21 Rationale and Theory

Five groups contributed importantly to shaping the premises and principles upon which CENTURY 21 shorthand is based:

- *Shorthand students* — a major segment involved as dropouts and low achievers
- *Vocabulary specialists* — experts concerned with word frequency in areas of communication
- *Practical linguists* — researchers committed to recording word sounds as spoken by the general population

- *Educational psychologists* — scholars dedicated to developing principles of psycho-motor learning
- *Shorthand authorities* — authors engaged in comparative analysis of shorthand systems, 1588–1975

Decreasing student achievement in shorthand and increasing dropout rates (1945–1975) caused general concern in business education. Well-known authorities in learning, in vocabulary, and in word sounds were ignored in both system and text revisions.

Godfrey Dewey,[1] shorthand author and phonetic expert — a man 50 years ahead of his time, warned:

> Word and sound frequencies were indispensable as a first foundation in the scientific study of shorthand problems.

The CENTURY 21 research team studied student problems, vocabularies, word sounds, principles of learning, literature of nearly 300 years of shorthand system experimentation and analysis.

Significance of sound
One basic imperative coming clearly from the studies was an urgent need for a more adequate and consistent adaptation of shorthand to sounds — chiefly the vowels.

Computer studies of vocabulary frequencies for word flow and of dictionaries for word sound brought the CENTURY 21 researchers into contact with two of the foremost names in dictionary simplification: Edward L. Thorndike, noted psychologist from Columbia University, and his co-editor, Clarence L. Barnhart, editor of over a dozen dictionaries with prominent publishers.

Thorndike originated the movement to simplify dictionary definitions and Barnhart spawned the simplifying of dictionary pronunciations. E. R. Moses[2] paid Barnhart this tribute:

It was he (Barnhart) who introduced the schwa to simplify the diacritical system (in dictionary keys) . . . Barnhart also heeded the advice of competent phoneticians in employing current usage in pronunciation.

All major dictionaries, including the *Webster* series, *American Heritage, Random House*, and *World Book* use the Barnhart schwa to designate indistinct sounds.

Simple pronunciation key
Barnhart's complete pronunciation key[3] uses only five markings to indicate the different sounds of the vowels — all easily understood by junior high students.

So closely did the complete pronunciation key parallel the CENTURY 21 *primary alphabet* that the key was adopted as the base for determining the number of primary symbols and their sounds. Below is the simple key to sounds used in writing all English words appearing in the CENTURY 21 DICTIONARY.

Phonetic Base of the CENTURY 21 Primary Alphabet

	As In		As In
a	hat, cap	p	paper, cup
ā	age, face	r	run, try
ã	care, air	s	say, yes
ä	father, far	sh	she, rush
b	bad, rob	t	tell, it
ch	child, much	th	thin, both
d	did, red		then, smooth
e	let, best	u	cup, butter
ē	equal, see	ü	full, put
ér	term, learn	ü	rule, move
f	fat, if	ū	use, music
g	go, bag	ˇv	very, save
h	he, how	w	will, woman
i	it, pin	y	young, yet
ī	ice, five	z	zero, breeze
j	jam, enjoy	zh	measure,
k	kind, seek		seizure
l	land, coal		
m	me, am	Indistinct *schwa* ə represents:
n	no, in	a in career
ng	long, bring	e in taken
o	hot, rock	i in pencil
ō	open, go	o in lemon
ô	order, all	u in supply
oi	oil, voice	
ou	house, out	

---

[1]Godfrey Dewey, *Relative Frequency of English Speech Sounds* (Cambridge: Harvard University Press, 1923), pp. 1–3.

[2]E. R. Moses, Jr., *Phonetics — History and Interpretation* (New York: Prentice-Hall, Inc., 1964), pp. 8–9.

[3]E. L. Thorndike and Clarence L. Barnhart, *High School Dictionary* (Glenview, IL: Scott, Foresman and Co., 1968).

CENTURY 21 Primary Alphabet

Because of the close affiliation to a basic pronunciation key, the CENTURY 21 *primary alphabet* contains all the essential sounds for writing all words.

Note that *ér* requires no special symbol — it is written as sounded: e-r; also, the single *th* symbol represents all sounds of *th*.

<u>Fewer fine distinctions among sounds</u> Prior to the easy-to-use Barnhart pronunciation key, over *70* symbols were used in a dictionary to record *44* sounds. Barnhart's *five* diacritical marks (shown above the vowels in the preceding table) greatly simplify the recognition and writing of all sounds.

The CENTURY 21 *primary alphabet* further simplifies fine differences in sound by writing:

- all sounds of *a* with one symbol
- all sounds of *e* with one symbol
- all sounds of *o* with one symbol
- all sounds of *u* with one symbol

<u>Primary alphabet features</u> Certain unique features of the *primary alphabet* are rooted in two basic guidelines to system development: (1) emphasize consistency and (2) eliminate choice when possible.

Awareness of the following features will aid users of the DICTIONARY.

- No dual symbols (note the *one symbol* by each single or paired alphabet sound)
- Symbols have a single direction (note *one arrow* by each symbol)
- 90% of the symbols facilitate *dominant* direction writing

Curve strokes Straight strokes

<u>Primary alphabet principles</u> A few words have unusual sound sequences that require rules for consistent writing. These five principles apply to the *primary alphabet* vowels:

- Write only the first of two adjacent *e* sounds.

reentry   rēentrē

Primary Alphabet

a[1]		o[1]	
b		oi	
ch		ou	
d		p	
e[1]		r	
f		s-z	
g-j		sh-zh	
h		t	
i		th	
i[2]		u[1]	
k		v-w	
l		y	
m			
n			
ng			

[1] Represents all basic sounds of this vowel

[2] Beginning or ending short i

- Dot the long *i* when it is followed by a basic vowel sound.

triumph   trīumf

- Dot the long *i* of the four basic homophones to make them distinct.

lion   riot
quiet   science

---

v

Two frequently applied principles concern the consistent treatment of short *i* and the neutral (indistinct) *schwa*.

- Do not write the internal short *i* in words.

  pencil   pensl

  illicit   ilisit

- Do not write the internal, indistinct *schwa* sound in words.

  collect   kəlekt

  patron   pātrən

The *primary alphabet*, which contains 27 symbols, carries the burden of shorthand writing in terms of words that are both short and frequent. True, every word in the English language and many foreign words, could be written with the *primary alphabet*; but the outlines for the longer words (1) would be too long and (2) would not take advantage of a shorter way to write repetitive word elements (e.g., *im-* and *-ment*).

<u>Derived alphabet source</u>   Therefore, CENTURY 21 uses a *derived alphabet* (e.g., word beginnings and endings) to make fast and easy the writing of thousands of words in the DICTIONARY. These familiar symbols are derived from the *primary alphabet* in three different ways: (1) as original, unchanged symbols that are assigned new word element sounds, (2) as modified primary symbols, and (3) as combined primary symbols. These three types of *derived alphabet* symbols are shown below.

unchanged as *b*   for *ble*

modified as *nt*   for *nt* (no angle)

combined as *sn*   for *sation*

CENTURY 21 Derived Alphabet

Because of the easy-to-understand features of CENTURY 21 Shorthand, thousands of people in all 50 states have become stenographers, secretaries, and teachers by studying the general spelling and sounds of word elements in CENTURY 21 texts. *They never memorize lists of sounds.*

The fine distinctions in sound (e.g., distinguishing the ending element of fea*ture* from tea*cher*) are of no concern in CENTURY 21. A casual check in any current word dictionary will show why.

The DICTIONARY, like the following derived data, is *for reference only* when one is looking up or verifying an outline, a preferred spelling, or the logic back of a constructed outline, etc.

The *derived alphabet* contains the following single-direction, word-element symbols:

19 word beginnings (4 are disjoined)
30 word endings (21 are disjoined)
12 bends, blends, and ellipses
4 compound word elements
6 proper name elements

To facilitate quick reference by the DICTIONARY user, the following tables present for each derived symbol:

- the classification
- the derived symbol
- the symbol's single direction
- the typical related spellings
- the typical related sounds

"Sounds" in the *derived alphabet* tables that follow refer to those phonetic values of words and word elements found in two closely related dictionary series edited by Clarence L. Barnhart.

E. L. Thorndike and Clarence L. Barnhart (Ed.), *The High School Dictionary* (Glenview, IL: Scott Foresman and Company, 1962 and 1968) Third Edition and Fourth Edition.

Clarence L. Barnhart (Ed. in Chief), *The World Book Dictionary* (Chicago: Field Enterprises Educational Corporation, 1975) Vol. I and II.

Some longer and more technical words appearing in the CENTURY 21 DICTIONARY are found only in the two-volume *World Book Dictionary* which incorporated slight changes of phonetic values in a 1975 updating; consequently, the *e* and *u* sounds continue to be verified by the Third Edition of *The High School Dictionary*.

Word Beginnings — Joined

Word Beginnings — Joined		
Spellings	Sounds	Symbols
al-	ôl	
be-	bi, bə	
com-	kom, kum, kəm	
con-	kon, kun, kən	
de-	di, də	
ex-	eks, egz	
im-	im	
in-	in	
ind-, int-, inv-	ind, int, inv	
per-, pur-	per, pər, per, pir	
pre-	pre, pri	
pro-	pro, prə	
re-	re, ri	
sub-	sub, səb	
un-	un	

To avoid forcing the fine distinctions of sound on a CENTURY 21 learner, stenographer, or secretary, the word beginnings are designed to represent closely related sounds shown in the table. A few illustrations are presented below.

Since *bi* is far more frequent than *bə* as a sound of the word beginning *be-* and since *di* is far more frequent than *də* as a sound of *de-*, only the highly frequent sounds are here illustrated.

because	bikôz	
delay	dilā	

Both *pre* and *pri* are highly frequent sounds of the word beginning *pre-* as *re* and *ri* are the most frequent sounds of *re-*.

prepay	prēpā	
prevent	privent	
rename	rēnām	
receipt	risēt	

Derived alphabet principles In addition to recognizing the sound patterns of word beginnings, the DICTIONARY user should find the following three rules useful in analyzing the construction of an outline with two or more prefixes as well as outlines beginning with *im-* or *in-*.

- A word beginning is consistently written, even though one and two prefixes are added.

process	proses		reprocess	
perceive	pərsēv		unperceiving	

- Write the initial short *i* on *im-* when the *m* immediately precedes any vowel sound.

imagine   imajən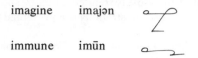

immune   imūn

- Write the initial short *i* only when *in* is part of a one-syllable word.

ink   ingk   inn   in

Word Beginnings — Disjoined

Although the disjoined word beginnings *super-* and *supr-* have a half dozen very closely related sounds, the value *sǖpər* represents most of the words and their frequencies. The most important of the minor sounds is *sǖpr*.

Word Beginnings — Disjoined		
Spellings	Sounds	Symbols
electr-	ilektr	
super-, supr-	sǖpər, sǖpr	
inter-, intr-	intər, intr	
trän-, trans-	tran, trans, tranz	

Likewise, the sound *intər* accounts for most of the *inter-* beginnings with *intr* being fairly frequent. Although established priorities of such word beginnings as *inter-*, *int-*, and *in-* are of use to a dictionary lexicographer, they are of little utility to the general user of the DICTIONARY. Of passing interest is the fact that the three word beginnings above are listed in order of their priority in application. This priority, based upon the underlined portion of the word beginning sounds, is illustrated below.

1. interfere   int**ər**fēr

2. into   int**ü**

3. increase   inkrēs

Whenever a series of words contained adjacent word elements with a common sound (as *d* between *ld* and *d*m* in *seldom*), CENTURY 21 DICTIONARY analysts established logical priorities on the basis of consistency in application, nondecision, and facile writing.

seldom   seldəm

Word Endings — Joined

Word Endings — Joined		
Spellings	Sounds	Symbols
-ble	bl, bəl	
-ful	fủl, fəl	
-gram	gram, grəm	
-graph	graf, grəf	
-ject	jekt, jek jikt, jik	
-ly	lē, li	
-ment, -mant	mənt, ment	
-ther, -thor, -thur	thər, thor	
-sion, -cian -tion, -xion	shən, zhən	

The highly frequent *shən* word ending sound appears in a variety of spelled forms, in addition to the most important ones shown in the preceding table.

Following is an illustration of the dual *-ject* sounds which drop the *t* sound in writing certain derivatives.

deject   dijekt

dejection   dijekshən

<u>Derived alphabet principles</u> Due to space constraint only the two basic rules relating to joined word endings are given here.

- A word ending is consistently written even though one and two suffixes are added.

position   pəzishən

positioned   pəzishənd

- The *lē* sound of the *-ly* word ending is regularly added to words as a loop symbol; when the l sound is present, add only the *ē*.

namely   nāmlē

fully   fúlē

Word Endings — Disjoined

The slight time required to disjoin a word ending produces a distinct and easy-to-transcribe outline element. The word endings, disjoined, are shown for convenience in two tables — Part 1 and Part 2.

Only the most frequent of the closely related sounds are shown in the table for illustration. Note that the əkl sound represents what is heard in three different word elements.

obstacle   obstəkl

medical   medəkl

article   ärtəkl

"Science type" word endings are less frequently used in business dictation, but are useful in writing technical words.

biology   bīoləjē

biologic   bīəlojik

Word Endings — Disjoined Part 1		
Spellings	Sounds	Symbols
-acle, -ical, -icle	əkl, ikl	
-alogy, -ology	aləjē, oləjē, əloj	
-bility	bilətē	
-cation, -casion,	kāshən, kāzhən	
-cher, -ture	chər	
-ed	d, id, t	
-er, -or[1]	ər	
-ety, -ity	ətē	
-hood -ward	húd wərd, wôrd	
-ing	ing	
-ingly	inglē	
-ings	ingz	

[1]Disjoined *-er, -or* with Speedforms and contracted outlines.

ix

A frequent word ending sound, ətē, represents close affinity to normal pronunciation.

security   sikūrətē

society   səsīətē

Derived alpha-bet principles   The word endings -ed and -ous, -us are not applied to single-syllable words such as red, fous, and bus.

A facilitating rule applies here: Two disjoined word endings may be combined where both of the endings remain distinct.

describe[1]   diskrīb

described   diskrībd

regulation   regūlāshən

[1]Single disjoining

Word Endings — Disjoined Part 2		
Spellings	Sounds	Symbols
-ive, -sive, -tive	iv, siv, tiv	
-ous, -us	əs	
-sation, -zation	sāshən, zāshən	
-scribe	skrīb	
-script	skript, skrip	
-ship	ship	
-titude, -titute, -tude	tətüd, tətüt, tüd	
-tual	chù əl, chùel, chùal	
-ulate	ūlāt, ūlit, ùlāt, ūlā, uleţ, ùlā	

The bends   A bend in CENTURY 21 is the curving of either one or two *primary alphabet* symbols to (1) represent a series of related sounds and (2) provide an easier, facile way to write frequently adjacent sounds.

The derivation of a bend is illustrated by the *nd* bend:

n-d   to   *nd*

Bends are found in various positions within words outlines:

indoors render bend

Because of adjacent alphabet sounds, *tm*, *tn* was assigned priority over *nt* (as in *intent*).

intent   intent

Bends		
Spellings	Sounds	Symbols
dm	dəm, dem, dim	
dn	dən, den, din, dn	
tm	təm, tem, tim	
tn	tən, ten, tin, tn	
fr	fər, fėr, fir, fôr, fōr, fr	
gr	gər, gr	
jr	jər, jir	
nd	nd	
nt	nt	
nv	nv	
ld	ld	

The blends   A blend in CENTURY 21 is the merging of two straight *primary alphabet* symbols to (1) represent a series of related sounds and (2) provide an easier, facile way to write frequently adjacent sounds. Note the downward slope of the *nk* (n + k).

x

Blends		
Spellings	Sounds	Symbols
dd	dəd, ded, did	
dt	dət, det, dit	
td	təd, ted, tid	
mm	məm, mem, mim, mum	
mn	mən, men, min, mun	
nk	ngk	

The ellipses   An ellipses in CENTURY 21 is the conversion of two adjacent *primary alphabet* circles to a single oval symbol to provide an easier, facile way to represent both sounds.

y-e   to *ye*   as in *year*

Ellipses		
Spellings	Sounds	Symbols
ya	ya, yā, yä	
ye	ye, yē, yė	
yi	yī	

Compound and Proper Noun Elements

Compound elements   A compound word element in CENTURY 21 is a *primary alphabet* symbol(s) representing the prefix or suffix element of a compound word.

The compound elements are disjoined as prefixes and written above the succeeding part of the outline. Three are disjoined as suffixes, while *self* is always joined as a suffix.

overcome   self-praise

hereunder   myself

Compound Elements — Disjoined		
Spellings	Sounds	Symbols
electric	ilektrik	
over	ōvər	
self	self[1]	
under	undər	

[1]As a suffix, *self* is joined.

Proper noun elements   In CENTURY 21 personal names and proper nouns representing cities and other geographic areas are written with six repetitive word elements. The two beginnings and four endings are applicable to writing proper nouns, since high frequency supports their use.

Proper Noun Elements		
Spellings	Sounds	Symbols
-burg(h), -berg	bėrg, bərg	
-field	fēld	
-port	pórt, pōrt	
-ville	vil	
New	nü, nū	
Saint	sānt	

Speedform rationale   Unlike other shorthand reference books, the DICTIONARY identifies for the user each Speedform and Speedform-related outline, along with all other abbreviated outlines.

As can be seen in the DICTIONARY, the derivatives of the Speedforms extend to hundreds of other outlines. This feature is a direct result of the criteria used in the selection of Speedforms:

- Facility — in recall and writing
- Frequency — of each related word
- Family — in the extent of derivatives
- Phrasing — beyond the most frequent
- Power — or impact on total vocabulary

The nine construction Speedforms multiply the facility, family of derivatives, and power of the original Speedforms.

count	just	serve
form	part	stand
found	present	sure

Because of the pervasive power of the Speedforms, through their derivatives, the number 175 often associated with the Speedforms is not meaningful. Derivatives are sometimes much more frequent than a so-called Speedform. Often overlooked is the fact that a majority of the *natural* CENTURY 21 outlines for the 400 most-used words are both short and facile.

Distinctive and unchanging in form, each Speedform retains its original pattern for the word(s) it represents. They are unlike contracted outlines which are written according to principle, may vary in application in the classroom or on the job, and may involve quite different terminologies.

Writing rationale
CENTURY 21 writing rationale is based on widely accepted premises such as the following, whenever and wherever possible:

- Obtain consistency
- Eliminate choice (decision)
- Avoid complex theory and writing rules
- Remember: "Shorthand writing is more mental than mechanical."

On the basis of these major premises CENTURY 21 researchers developed easy-to-understand and simple-to-apply nondecision writing principles.

- Each alphabet symbol is written in one direction — *no exceptions.*
- All circle vowels cross over (close) the preceding stroke in the dominant direction — *no exceptions.*
- All initial vowels are written on the left side of a straight downstroke — *no exceptions.*
- The direction of each succeeding stroke determines the emerging pattern of the outline — *no exceptions.*
- The first stroke rests on or near the line of writing — exception below.
- If a vowel precedes a consonant downstroke, place the base of the consonant on or near the line of writing — *no exceptions.*

There are a few minor writing guidelines that facilitate consistent writing.

- Two-part outlines are written closely together (as St. Paul).
- Capitalize with a short horizontal stroke.
- A short jog distinguishes consecutive straight strokes.
- Following a horizontal stroke the *u* is turned under.
- An apostrophe is used in outlines representing contractions.
- Place the first word of a phrase on or near the line of writing.

CENTURY 21 features
The internal consistency of the *primary* and *derived alphabet,* of short and simple writing rationale, and of the practical adaptation to the sounds of communication melds together to produce the unique features of CENTURY 21.

These five simple features provide the basic guidelines for understanding the CENTURY 21 system as it relates to learning, teaching, writing, and transcribing. In summary, these five features are:

- Single-direction symbols (nondecision)

- No dual symbols (nondecision)

- All circle vowels join (or cross) other strokes in a uniform direction (nondecision)

- Dominant-direction writing similar to long-hand

- *Primary alphabet* based on a widely used system of word sounds (for the most part, nondecision)

Division 2. Business/General Vocabulary

The CENTURY 21 computerized DICTION-ARY was prepared for several users: (1) the learner in high school and college, (2) the stenographer and secretary in business and government, (3) the secretary in the technical professions, and (4) the teacher who trains secretarial personnel.

Sources for the DICTIONARY The DICTIONARY contains 31,426 entries in its vocabulary division and 2,025 in the proper nouns and abbreviations for a total of 33,451 entries. The most-used phrases, available in CENTURY 21 texts, are not repeated in this compact volume of vocabulary entries.

The sources of the entries in the DICTION-ARY include:

- CENTURY 21 high school/college texts
- *Frequencies of Business Correspondence* — D. J. Perry
- *Basic Vocabulary of Business Writing* — J. E. Silverthorn
- *Present Day American English* — Henry Kučera/W. N. Francis
- *Written Business Office Communication* — Morris Mellinger
- *6,000 Most-Used CENTURY 21 Outlines* — E. L. Christensen/D. J. Perry

Selection Process The selection of words beyond those in the vocabulary-controlled CEN-TURY 21 texts included these considerations:

- Words ending in the consistent, easy CEN-TURY 21 *-ed*, *-ing*, and *-s* were typically deleted, if the root word was present, or replaced by the root word.

- Possessives with *s* endings were omitted, but the word was retained.

- Hyphenated compounds were deleted, but the individual words retained. Essential hyphenated words were retained (such as *self-*, *co-op*, *x-ray*).

- Kučera-Francis list was used selectively beyond the high-frequency entries.

- Other words, such as trademarks, acronyms, and current terms were added.

CENTURY 21 Outlines Outlines in the DICTIONARY were written and edited on the basis of (1) the *primary* and *derived alphabet*, (2) CENTURY 21 unique features, theory, and writing rationale, and (3) a reliable guideline to sound.

Uniquely, each main-vocabulary page of the DICTIONARY presents a ''sound strip'' of about 12 words, giving the sounds with which to check the CENTURY 21 outline. The ''sound strip'' facilitates a check on:

- Theory, such as ''Write beginning and ending schwa,'' or ''Write beginning schwa in adding a prefix'' (see *giveaway*).

- Sound, such as ''Write *m-a-n* in a singular compound'' (see *fireman*), or ''Write *shən* in *-tion* words'' (see *combustion*).

- Dual word sounds, such as occur among verb, noun, and adjective forms of a word (see *separate*).

The DICTIONARY conveniently identifies for the user its special features in the main vocabulary section with these useful techniques:

- Superior figures to left of a word:
  Preferred spelling (see [1]*analogue*)
  Alternate spelling (see [2]*analog*)

- Superior figures to right of a word:
  A trademark (see *zerox*[1])
  Noting an alternate (see *x-ray*[2])

- Acronyms, such as COBOL, appear in both Division 1 and 2, also trademarks

- Derivatives of dual-sound words are arranged in columns (see *appropriate*)

Division 3. Proper Nouns/Abbreviations

The final division of the DICTIONARY is composed of two sections. The first section contains a list of personal and geographic nouns (capitalized) and acronyms — all combined alphabetically.

The second section contains three sets of reference-type abreviations.

- Correspondence abbreviations
- Special abbreviations
- International Metric system symbols

Because of its importance to the user of CENTURY 21 texts, the Proper Nouns and Abbreviations section has an introductory page immediately preceding Division 3.

Sound
Legend The six vowel signs are used in the various editions of the *High School Dictionary* and in the two-volume *World Book Dictionary*. Like all modern dictionaries, the CENTURY 21 DICTIONARY does not use the breve sign because of its high frequency.

The DICTIONARY user will find the Sign Legend useful when checking an unfamiliar word in the "sound strip" at the bottom of each page in the vocabulary division.

Diction-
ary Legend The ten signs in the Dictionary Legend were adopted for the convenience of the user of the CENTURY 21 DICTIONARY.

The user will always know a theory word, because it does not have one of the six circles, triangles, or squares by it. Each abbreviated word is identified as indicated in the legend — no time-wasting surprises. The last four signs have been explained previously in the USER'S Guide.

Sound Legend			
Sign	**Name**	**Pronounced**	**Illustration**
—	macron	(mākron)	see: sē
••	dieresis	(dīerəsis)	sue: sü
~	tilde	(tildə)	air: ãr
•	dot	(dot)	term: tėrm
^	circumflex	(sėrkəmfleks)	horse: hôrs
⌄	breve	(brēv)	pin: pin[1]

[1]Because of high frequency, the breve sign is always deleted: therefore, *a vowel without a sign has a short sound.*

Dictionary Legend	
Sign	**Meaning**
○	Speedform
⊙	Speedform related
△	Abbreviation or correspondence form
⚠	Abbreviation or correspondence form related
□	Contracted form
⊡	Contracted form related
[1]adapter	Preferred spelling
[2]adaptor	Alternate spelling
alternate v.;a.;n.	Verb, adjective, noun
Marian[1]	Footnote

—Edward L. Christensen

a ○

aback

abandon

abandoned

abandonment

abase

abasement

abate

abatement

abbey

abbreviate

abbreviated

abbreviating

abbreviation

abbreviations

abdomen

abdominal

abduct

abduction

aberrant

aberrate

aberration

abet

abeyance

abhor

abhorrent

abide

abilities

ability

abject

ablaze

able ○

ably ⊙

abnormal

abnormalities

abnormality

abnormally

aboard

abode

abolish

abolishment

abolition

abolitionist

abominable

aboriginal

aborigine

abort

abortion

abortive

abound

abounds

about ○

above

aboveground ⊙

abovementioned

abrasion

abrasions

abrasive

abrasives

abreast

abridge

abridgment

abroad

abrogate

abrupt

abruptly

abruptness

abscess

absence

absences

absent
a.; v.

absentee

absenteeism

absentees

absenting

absently

absolute

absolutely

absoluteness

absolution

absorb

absorbed

absorbent

absorbing

---

absorbs	academics	accessory
absorption	academies	accident
absorptive	academy	accidental
abstain	accede	accidentally
abstainer	acceded	accidents
abstainers	acceding	acclaim
abstention	accelerate	acclaimed
abstract	accelerated	acclamation
abstraction	accelerating	acclimatize
abstractionist	acceleration	accolade
abstractor	accelerator	accommodate
abstractors	accelerometer	accommodated
abstracts	accent	accommodates
abstruse	accentuate	accommodating
absurd	accentuated	accommodation
absurdity	accept ○	accommodations
abundance	acceptability ○	accompanied ○
abundant	acceptable ○	accompanies ○
abundantly	acceptably ○	accompaniment ○
abuse	acceptance ○	accompaniments ○
abuses	acceptances ○	accompanist ○
abusive	accepted ○	accompanists ○
abut	accepting ○	accompany ○
abutment	accepts ○	accompanying ○
abutting	access	accomplice
abysmal	accessibility	accomplish
abyss	accessible	accomplished
academe	accession	accomplishes
academic	accessorial	accomplishing
academically	accessories	accomplishment

accomplishments	accrued	achievement
accord ○	accrues	achievements
accordance ⊙	accruing	achieving
accorded ⊙	accumulate	acid
according ⊙	accumulated	acidic
accordingly ⊙	accumulates	acidity
accordion ⊙	accumulating	acids
accordions ⊙	accumulation	acknowledge
accords ⊙	accumulations	acknowledged
accost	accumulative	acknowledges
account ⊙	accumulator	acknowledging
accountability ⊙	accuracies	acknowledgment
accountable ⊙	accuracy	acknowledgments
accountancy ⊙	accurate	acme
accountant ⊙	accurately	acne
accountants ⊙	accusation	acorn
accounted ⊙	accuse	acoustic
accounting ⊙	accused	acoustical
accounts ⊙	accuses	acoustically
accouter	accusing	acoustics
accouterment	accustom ⊙	acquaint
accredit	accustomed ⊙	acquaintance
accreditation	ace	acquaintances
accredited	acetate	acquaintanceship
accrediting	acetone	acquainted
accrete	acetonemia	acquainting
accretion	acetylene	acquaints
accrual	ache	acquiesce
accruals	achieve	acquiescence
accrue	achieved	acquire

acquired	activation ⊙	¹adapter
acquires	active ⊙	adapting
acquiring	actively ⊙	²adaptor
acquisition	activism ⊙	add
acquisitions	activities ⊙	added
acquisitive	activity ⊙	addenda
acquisitiveness	actor	addendum
acquit	actress	addict
acquittal	acts	addiction
acquittance	actual	adding
acre	actuality	addition
acreage	actually	additional
acreages	actuarial	additionally
acres	actuaries	additions
acrid	actuary	additive
acrobat	actuate	additives
acrobatic	actuated	address
acronym	actuates	addressed
acropolis	acumen	addressee
across	acute	addresser
acrylic	acutely	addressers
act	ad	addresses
acted	adage	addressing
acting	adagio	adds
action	adamant	adduce
actions	adapt	ade
activate ⊙	adaptability	adenoid
activated ⊙	adaptable	adenoidectomy
activates ⊙	adaptation	adenoids
activating ⊙	adapted	adept

adequacy	adjuncts	admissions
adequate	adjust ⊙	admit
adequately	adjustable ⊙	admits
adhere	adjusted ⊙	admittance
adhered	adjuster ⊙	admitted
adherence	adjusters ⊙	admittedly
adherent	adjusting ⊙	admitting
adheres	adjustment ⊙	admix
adhesion	adjustments ⊙	admixture
adhesive	adjusts ⊙	admonish
adhesives	adjutant	admonition
ad hoc	administer ⊙	adobe
adieu	administered ⊙	adolescence
adios	administering ⊙	adolescent
adjacent	administers ⊙	adolescents
adjectival	administration ⊙	adopt
adjective	administrations ⊙	adopted
adjoin	administrative ⊙	adopting
adjoining	administratively ⊙	adoption
adjoins	administrator ⊙	adoptions
adjourn	administrators ⊙	adoptive
adjourned	admirable	adopts
adjourning	admirably	adorable
adjournment	admiral	adore
adjudge	admiralty	adorn
adjudged	admiration	adrenal
adjudicate	admire	adrift
adjudication	admired	adroit
adjudicatory	admissible	adroitness
adjunct	admission	ads

adsorb	advertised ⊙	aerate
adsorbed	advertisement ⊙	aerating
adulate	advertisements ⊙	aeration
adulation	advertiser ⊙	aerator
adult	advertisers ⊙	aerial
adulterate	advertises ⊙	aero
adulthood	advertising ⊙	aerobe
adults	advice ⊙	aerobic
ad valorem	advices ⊙	aerodynamic
advance ⊙	advisability ⊙	aerodynamics
advanced ⊙	advisable ⊙	aeronautical
advancement ⊙	advise ⊙	aeronautics
advancements ⊙	advised ⊙	aerosol
advances ⊙	advisedly ⊙	aerosolize
advancing ⊙	advisee ⊙	aerospace
advantage ⊙	advisees ⊙	aesthetic
advantageous ⊙	advisement ⊙	aesthetics
advantageously ⊙	¹adviser ⊙	afar
advantages ⊙	¹advisers ⊙	affable
advent	advises ⊙	affair
adventure	advising ⊙	affairs
adventurer	²advisor ⊙	affect ⊙
adventurous	²advisors ⊙	affectation ⊙
adverb	advisory ⊙	affected ⊙
adverbial	advocacy	affecting ⊙
adversary	advocate	affectingly ⊙
adverse	advocated	affection ⊙
adversely	advocates	affectionate ⊙
adversity	advocating	affectionately ⊙
advertise ⊙	aegis	affections ⊙

adulation	adult	advent	adventure	adverb	adverbial	adversary	aegis	aerial	aeronautical	aerosol	affable
ajülāshən	ədult	advent	advenchər	advèrb	advèrbēəl	advərserē	ējis	ārēəl	ārənôtəkl	ārəsol	afəbl

affective ⊙	affront	agents
affects ⊙	afield	ager
affiance	afire	agers
affiant	aflame	ages
affidavit	afloat	agglomerate
affidavits	afoot	agglomeration
affiliate	aforementioned	agglutinate
affiliated	aforesaid	agglutination
affiliates	aforethought	aggravate
affiliating	afoul	aggravation
affiliation	afraid	aggregate
affiliations	aft	aggregating
affinity	after ⊙	aggress
affirm	afterglow ⊙	aggression
affirmation	aftermath ⊙	aggressive
affirmations	afternoon ⊙	aggressively
affirmative	afternoons ⊙	aggressiveness
affirmatively	afterward ⊙	aggressor
affirmed	afterwards ⊙	aggressors
affix	again	aggrieve
affixed	against	aghast
affixing	agate	agile
afflict	agates	agilely
affliction	age	agility
afflicts	aged	aging
affluence ⊙	ageless	agitate
affluent	agencies	agitator
afford	agency	agleam
afforded	agenda	agnostic
affords	agent	ago

agonize	ailerons	airman
agony	ailing	airmen
agrarian	ailment	airmobile
agree	ailments	airpark
agreeable	aim	airplane
agreeableness	aimed	airplanes
agreeably	aiming	airport
agreed	aimless	airports
agreeing	aims	airship ☉
agreement	air	airshipping ☉
agreements	airborne	airships ☉
agrees	airbrush	airspace
agribusiness ☉	airbus	airstrip
agricultural ☉	aircraft	airway
agriculturalist ☉	airdrop	airways
agriculturalists ☉	aired	airworthiness ☉
agriculturally ☉	airfield	airworthy ☉
agriculture ☉	airflow	airy
agronomist	airfoil	aisle
agronomy	airframe	aisles
ague	airhouse	ajar
ahead	airless	akin
aid	airlift	alabaster
aide	airline	à la carte
aided	airliner	alacrity
aides	airlines	alarm
aiding	airlock	alarmed
aids	airmail	alarming
ail	airmailed	alarmingly
aileron	airmailing	alarmist

alarms	align	alleviating
alas	aligned	alleviation
albacore	alignment	alley
album	alignments	alleyway
albumin	aligns	alliance
albums	alike	alliances
alchemy	alimony	allied
alcohol	aliquot	alligator
alcoholic	alive	alliterate
alcoholism	alkali	alliteration
alcove	alkaline	alliterative
alderman	alkalis	allocable
aldermen	all	allocate
alert	allay	allocated
alerted	allegation	allocates
alerting	allegations	allocating
alertly	allege	allocation
alertness	alleged	allocations
alerts	allegedly	allot
alfalfa	alleges	allotment
alga	allegiance	allotments
algae	allegoric	allotted
algebra	allegorical	allow
ALGOL	allegory	allowable
alibi	allegro	allowance
alien	allergic	allowances
alienate	allergies	allowed
alienating	allergy	allowing
alienation	alleviate	allows
alight	alleviated	alloy

allude		already		alumna	
allure		also		alumnae	
allurement		altar		alumni	
allusion		alter		alumnus	
allusive		alteration		alveolar	
allusiveness		alterations		alveoli	
ally		altercate		alveolus	
alma mater		altercation		always	
alma maters		altered		am ○	
almanac		altering		amalgamate	
almanacs		alternate		amalgamation	
		v.; a., n.			
almighty		alternately		amandine	
almond		alternates		amanuensis	
		v.; n.			
almost		alternating		amass	
aloft		alternation		amateur	
alone		alternations		amateurish	
aloneness		alternative		amateurs	
along		alternatively		amaze	
alongside		alternatives		amazed	
aloof		alternator		amazement	
aloofness		alternators		amazing	
aloud		although		amazingly	
alpha		altimeter		amazon	
alphabet		altitude		ambassador	
alphabetic		altitudes		ambassadorship	
alphabetical		alto		amber	
alphabetically		altogether		ambidextrous	
alphabetize		altruism		ambiguity	
alphabetized		altruistically		ambiguous	
alpine		aluminum		ambition	

ambitions		amid		amplified	
ambitious		amidst		amplifier	
ambitiously		amiss		amplify	
ambivalence		amity		amplitude	
ambivalent		ammonia		amply	
amble		ammonium		amputate	
ambler		ammunition		amputated	
ambrosia		among		amputation	
ambrosial		amongst		amulet	
ambulance		amoral		amuse	
ambulances		amorality		amusement	
ambulate		amorous		amusements	
ambulates		amorphous		amusingly	
ambulatory		amortization		an ○	
ambush		amortizations		anachronism	
amen		amortize		anaconda	
amenable		amortized		anagram	
amend		amortizing		anal	
amendatory		amount ○		analgesia	
amended		amounted ⊙		analgesic	
amending		amounting ⊙		²analog	
amendment		amounts ⊙		analogous	
amendments		ampere		analogously	
amenities		amperes		¹analogue	
amenity		ampersand		analogy	
amethyst		amphibian		²analyse	
amethystine		amphibious		analyses	
amiable		amphitheater		analysis	
amicable		ample		analyst	
amicably		amplification		analysts	

analytic	anemia	annal
analytical	anemic	annals
analytically	anent	anneal
[1]analyze	anesthesia	annealed
analyzed	anesthetic	annealing
analyzer	anesthetics	annex
analyzes	anesthetist	annexation
analyzing	anesthetize	annexations
anarchic	anew	annexed
anarchical	angel	annihilate
anarchist	anger	annihilation
anarchy	angle	anniversaries
anastomosis	angles	anniversary
anatomic	angling	annotate
anatomical	angriest	announce ○
anatomically	angrily	announced ⊙
anatomy	angry	announcement ⊙
ancestor	anguish	announcements ⊙
ancestral	angular	announcer ⊙
ancestry	angulation	announcers ⊙
anchor	animal	announces ⊙
anchorage	animals	announcing ⊙
anchored	animate	annoy
	v.; a.	
anchors	animated	annoyance
anchovy	animation	annoyed
ancient	animism	annoying
ancillary	animosity	annual
and ○	anion	annually
anecdotal	anionic	annuitant
anecdote	ankle	annuities

annuity	anterior	antiperspirants
annul	anthem	antiphon
annular	anthology	antipode
annulment	anthracite	antipollution
annum	anthrax	antipoverty
annunciate	anthropological	antiquarian
anode	anthropologist	antiquary
anodize	anthropology	antiquate
anomalous	antibiotic	antiquated
anomaly	antibiotics	antique
anonymity	antibody	antiques
anonymous	antic	antiquity
another	anticipate	antiseptic
answer	anticipated	antiserum
answerable	anticipates	antislavery
answered	anticipating	antisubmarine
answerer	anticipation	antithesis
answering	anticipations	antithetical
answers	anticipatory	antithyroid
ant	antidiscrimination	antitrust
antagonism	antidote	antler
antagonist	antifreeze	antlers
antagonistic	antifreezes	anvil
antagonize	antifriction	anxiety ⊙
ante	antigen	anxious ⊙
anteater	antimonopoly	anxiously ⊙
antecedent	antineoplastic	any ⊙
antelope	antiparty ⊙	anybody ⊙
antenna	antipathy ⊙	anyhow ⊙
antennae	antiperspirant	anymore ⊙

anyone ⊙		apothecary		appetite	
anyplace ⊙		appall		appetizer	
anything ⊙		appalling		appetizers	
anytime ⊙		appallingly		applaud	
anyway ⊙		appanage		applauded	
anywhere ⊙		apparatus		applause	
apart ⊙		apparel		apple	
apartheid ⊙		apparent		apples	
apartment ⊙		apparently		appliance	
apartments ⊙		apparition		appliances	
apathetic		appeal		applicability	
apathy		appealed		applicable	
aperture		appealing		applicant	
apex		appeals		applicants	
aphid		appear		application	
apiece		appearance		applications	
apocalypse		appearances		applicator	
apocalyptic		appeared		applied	
apogee		appearing		applies	
apologetic		appears		appliqué	
apologetically		appease		apply	
apologies		appeasement		applying	
apologist		appellant		appoint	
apologize		appellate		appointed	
apologized		append		appointee	
apology		appendage		appointees	
apostate		appendectomy		appointing	
apostle		appended		appointive	
apostolic		appendix		appointment	
apostrophe		appestat		appointments	

appoints		apprised		apricot	
apportion		approach		a priori	
apportioned		approachable		apron	
apportioning		approached		aprons	
apportionment		approaches		apropos	
appraisal		approaching		apt	
appraisals		appropriate *v.; a.*		aptitude	
appraise		appropriated		aptitudes	
appraised		appropriately		aptly	
appraisement		appropriateness		aptness	
appraiser		appropriation		aqua	
appraisers		appropriations		aquanaut	
appraises		approvable		aqueduct	
appraising		approval		aqueducts	
appreciable ⊙		approvals		aqueous	
appreciably ⊙		approve		arable	
appreciate ○		approved		arbiter	
appreciated ⊙		approves		arbitrarily	
appreciates ⊙		approving		arbitrary	
appreciating ⊙		approvingly		arbitrate	
appreciation ⊙		approximate ○		arbitration	
appreciative ⊙		approximated ⊙		arbitrator	
appreciatively ⊙		approximately ⊙		arbor	
apprehend		approximates ⊙		arboreal	
apprehension		approximating ⊙		arc	
apprehensive		approximation ⊙		arcade	
apprehensively		approximations ⊙		arch	
apprentice		appurtenance		archaeological	
apprenticeship		appurtenances		archaeologist	
apprise		appurtenant		archaeology	

archaic		argued		armory	
archangel		arguing		armpit	
archbishop		argument		arms	
archdiocese		argumentation		army	
arched		arguments		aroma	
archer		argyle		aromatic	
archery		arid		arose	
arches		aridity		around	
architect □		aright		arousal	
architects □		arise		arouse	
architectural □		arisen		aroused	
architecture □		arises		arraign	
architectures □		arising		arrange	
archive		aristocracy		arranged	
archives		aristocrat		arrangement	
archivist		aristocratic		arrangements	
arcology		arithmetic		arranges	
arctic		arithmetical		arranging	
ardency		arm		array	
ardent		armament		arrear	
ardor		armature		arrearage	
arduous		armchair		arrearages	
are ○		armchairs		arrears	
area		armed		arrest	
areas		armful		arrested	
aren't ○		armhole		arrester	
arena		armies		arrests	
argon		armistice		arrival	
argot		armor		arrivals	
argue		armored		arrive	

archivist	arcology	arduous	area	argument	argumentation	aristocratic	armature	aroma	aromatic	arrearage
ärkəvist	ärkoləjē	ärjúəs	ārēə	ärgūmənt	ärgūmentāshən	əristəkratik	ärməchər	ərōmə	ərəmatik	ərērij

arrived	artifice	ashamed
arrives	artificer	ashen
arriving	artificial	ashes
arrogance	artificiality	ashore
arrogant	artificially	aside
arrogantly	artillery	asinine
arrogate	artisan	ask
arrow	artist	askance
arrowhead	artistic	asked
arroyo	artistically	askew
arsenate	artistry	asking
arsenic	artists	asks
arson	artless	asleep
art	arts	asocial
arterial	as ○	asparagus
arteries	asbestos	aspect
arteriolar	ascend	aspects
arteriole	ascendancy	aspen
artery	ascension	asphalt
artesian	ascent	asphaltic
artful	ascertain	aspirant
artfully	ascertained	aspirants
arthritis	ascertaining	aspiration
article	ascetic	aspirations
articles	asceticism	aspire
articulate	ascribe	aspirin
articulated	ascribed	aspiring
articulation	asepsis	assail
artifact	aseptic	assailant
artifacts	ash	assassin

assassinate		assign		assortment	
assassination		assigned		assortments	
assault		assignee		assuage	
assay		assignees		assume	
assemblage		assigning		assumed	
assemble		assignment		assumes	
assembled		assignments		assuming	
assembler		assignor		assumption	
assembles		assigns		assumptions	
assemblies		assimilate		assurance ⊙	
assembling		assimilation		assurances ⊙	
assembly		assist		assure ⊙	
assemblyman		assistance		assured ⊙	
assent		assistant		assuredly ⊙	
assented		assistants		assureds ⊙	
assert		assistantship		assures ⊙	
asserted		assistantships		assuring ⊙	
assertion		assisted		asterisk	
assertive		assisting		asterisks	
asserts		assists		asteroid	
assess		associate ⊙		asthma	
assessed		associated ⊙		asthmatic	
assessing		associates ⊙		asthmatics	
assessment		associating ⊙		astonish	
assessments		association ⊙		astonishingly	
assessor		associations ⊙		astonishment	
assessors		associative ⊙		astound	
asset		associatively ⊙		astounding	
assets		assort		astray	
assiduity		assorted		astride	

astringency	atom	attempting
astringent	atomic	attempts
astringents	atoms	attend
astro	atonal	attendance
astronaut	atonally	attendant
astronauts	atone	attendants
astronomer	atonement	attended
astronomical	atop	attendee
astronomy	atrocious	attendees
astrophysics	atrociously	attending
astute	atrocity	attends
astuteness	atrophy	attention ○
asunder	attach	attentive
asylum	attaché	attentively
asymmetric	attached	attest
asymmetrically	attaches	attested
asymmetry	attaching	attesting
at ○	attachment	attic
ate	attachments	attire
atheist	attack	attitude
atheistic	attacker	attitudes
athlete	attacking	attorney
athletes	attacks	attorneys
athletic	attain	attract
athletically	attainable	attracted
athletics	attained	attracting
atlas	attaining	attraction
atlases	attainment	attractions
atmosphere	attempt	attractive
atmospheric	attempted	attractively

attractiveness		audits		authorize	
attracts		auger		authorized	
attributable		augment		authorizes	
attribute		augmented		authorizing	
attributed		aunt		authors	
attributes		aunts		authorship	
attrition		aural		autist	
attune		aurally		autistic	
atypical		aurora		auto	
auburn		auspice		autobiographic	
auction		auspices		autobiography	
auctioneer		auspicious		autoclave	
auctions		austere		autoclaved	
audacity		austerity		autocode	
audibility		authentic		autocollimator	
audible		authentically		autocracy	
audibly		authenticate		autocrat	
audience		authentication		autocratic	
audiences		authenticity		autograph	
audio		author		autographs	
audit		authored		autoloader	
audited		authoring		automate	
auditing		authoritarian		automated	
audition		authoritarianism		automates	
auditions		authoritative		automatic	
auditor		authoritatively		automatically	
auditorium		authorities		automating	
auditoriums		authority		automation	
auditors		authorization		automobile	
auditory		authorizations		automobiles	

automotive	avers	aware	
autonomic	averse	awareness	
autonomous	aversion	awash	
autonomy	avert	away	
autopsy	averted	awe	
autos	aviary	awful	
autotransformer ⊙	aviation	awfully	
autumn	aviator	awfulness	
auxiliaries	avid	awhile ⊙	
auxiliary	avidity	awkward	
avail	avidly	awkwardly	
availability	avocado	awning	
available	avocation	awnings	
availing	avoid	awoke	
avails	avoidance	awry	
avalanche	avoided	ax	
avarice	avoiding	axes	
avaricious	avow	axial	
avenge	await	axiom	
avenue	awaiting	axiomatic	
avenues	awaits	axis	
aver	awake	axle	
average	awaken	axles	
averaged	award	azalea	
averages	awarded	azaleas	
averaging	awarding		
averment	awards		

B

babe
babies
baby
baccalaureate
bachelor
bachelors
back
backache
backbend
backbone
backdrop
backed
backer
background ☉
backgrounds ☉
backhand
backhaul
backhoe
backhoes
backing
backlash
backlog
backpack
backpacking

backs
backscatter
backside
backslide
backstage
backstitch
backup
backward
backwards
backwater
backwoods
bacon
bacteria
bacterial
bactericide
bad
bade
badge
badger
badges
badly
badminton
badness
baffle
bag
bagatelle
baggage
bagged
bagger
baggers

bagging
baggy
bags
bail
bailiff
bailout ☉
bait
baits
bake
baked
baker
bakeries
bakers
bakery
baking
balance
balanced
balances
balancing
balconies
balcony
bald
baldness
bale
baleful
baler
bales
balk
ball
ballad

| baccalaureate | backhand | backwoods | bacterial | bactericide | badminton | bagatelle | bagger | bailiff | balance | ballad |
| bakəlôrēit | bakhand | bákwŭdz | baktirēəl | baktirəsīd | badmintn | bagətel | bagər | bālif | baləns | baləd |

B

ballast	bane	barbarous
ballasts	baneful	[1]barbecue
ballerina	bang	[2]barbeque
ballet	banged	barber
ballets	bangle	bard
ballistic	banish	bare
balloon	banishment	barefoot
balloons	banister	barely
ballot	banjo	barest
balloting	bank	bargain
ballots	banker	bargaining
ballplayer	bankers	bargains
ballroom	banking	barge
balls	bankrupt	barges
ballute	bankruptcies	baritone
balsam	bankruptcy	barium
balustrade	banks	bark
ban	banner	barker
banal	banners	barkers
banalize	banquet	barking
banana	banquets	barley
bananas	banter	barn
band	baptism	barnyard
bandage	baptismal	barometer
bandit	baptistery	barometric
bandoleer	baptize	baron
bands	bar	baroness
bandstand ⊙	barb	baronial
bandwagon	barbarian	barony
bandy	barbaric	baroque

barrack	basing	baths
barrage	basins	bathtub
barred	basis	baton
barrel	bask	batt
barréled	basket	battalion
barrels	basketball	batten
barren	baskets	batter
barricade	bass	batteries
barricades	basset	battery
barrier	basswood	batting
barriers	baste	battle
barring	bastings	battlefield
barrow	bastion	battleground ⊙
bars	bat	battlement
bartender	batch	battles
basal	batches	batts
basally	bate	bawd
base	bateau	bawdy
baseball	bated	bawl
baseballs	bates	bawls
based	bath	bay
baseman	bathe	bayonet
basement	bathed	bays
basements	bather	bazaar
bases	bathhouse	be ○
bashful	bathhouses	beach
basic	bathing	beaches
basically	bathrobe	beachhead
basics	bathroom	beacon
basin	bathrooms	bead

beadle	beautifully	bedsore
beaker	beautify	bedsores
beam	beautifying	bedspread
beamed	beauty	bedspreads
beamer	beaver	bedspring
beaming	beavers	bedstraw
beams	becalm	bedtime ⊙
bean	became	bedway
beans	because	bedways
bear	beck	bee
beard	beckon	beebread
bearer	become	beech
bearers	becomes	beef
bearing	becoming	beefsteak
bearings	bed	beefy
bearish	bedazzle	beehive
bears	bedazzlement	been ○
beast	bedbug	beep
beat	bedded	beer
beaten	bedding	beeswax
beatific	bedfast	beet
beatification	bedlam	beetle
beating	bedpan	beetles
beatitude	bedpost	beets
beatnik	bedraggle	befall
beats	bedridden	befit
beau	bedroom	befog
beauteous	bedrooms	before
beautification	beds	beforehand
beautiful	bedside	befuddle

beg	belatedly	belonged
began	belch	belonging
beget	belfry	belongings
beggar	belie	belongs
begin	belief	beloved
beginner	beliefs	below
beginning	believable	belt
beginnings	believably	belts
begins	believe	bemoan
begot	believed	bench
begotten	believer	benches
beguile	believes	bend
begun	believing	bending
behalf	belittle	bends
behave	bell	beneath
behavior	bellboy	benediction
behavioral	bellboys	benefactor
behaviorally	bellhop	benefactors
behaviors	bellicose	beneficent
behead	bellicosity	beneficial
behind	belligerence	beneficiaries
behold	belligerent	beneficiary
behoove	belligerently	benefit
behooves	bellman	benefited
beige	bellow	benefiting
being ⊙	bells	benefits
beings ⊙	bellwether	benevolence
bel	bellwethers	benevolent
belabor	belly	benign
belated	belong	bent

benzene	bet	biased
bequeath	betide	bib
bequeathed	betray	bible
bequest	betrayal	bibles
bequests	betrayer	biblical
berate	betroth	bibliographical
bereave	betrothal	bibliographies
bereavement	bets	bibliography
bereft	better	bicameral
beret	betterment	bicarbonate
beriberi	betterments	biceps
berm	betting	bicker
berms	between	bicycle
berry	bevel	bicycles
berth	beveled	bicycling
berths	beverage	bid
beseech	beverages	bidder
beset	bevy	bidders
beside	bewail	bidding
besides	beware	bide
besiege	bewilder	bidirectional ⊙
besieged	bewildered	bids
besieger	bewilderingly	[1]biennia
besmirch	bewilderment	biennial
bespeak	bewitch	biennium
best	beyond	[2]bienniums
bestial	bezel	bifocal
bestow	biannual	big
bestowal	biannually	bigger
bests	bias	biggest

bigot	binational	bipartisan ⊙
bigotry	bind	biplane
bike	binder	birch
bikes	binders	bird
bilateral	binding	birdie
bile	bindings	birds
bilge	bing	birth
bilinear	bingo	birthday
bilingual	binocular	birthdays
bilk	bins	birthplace
bill	biochemical	birthright
billboard	biochemistry	biscuit
billboards	biocontrol ⊙	bishop
billed	biographer	bison
billet	biographic	bisque
billeting	biographical	bit
billets	biographies	bite
billfold	biography	bites
billfolds	biologic	bits
billiard	biological	bitten
billing	biologically	bitter
billings	biologist	bitterest
billion	biologists	bitterly
billionaire	biology	bitterness
billions	biomathematics ⊡	bittersweet
billow	biomedical	bituminous
bills	biopsies	bivouac
bimonthly	biopsy	biweekly
bin	biosynthesis	bizarre
binary	biotechnology	black

blackberry	blast	blessing
blackbird	blasted	blessings
blackboard	blasting	blest
blacked	blatancy	[2]bleu
blacken	blatant	blew
blackjack	blaze	blight
blackmail	blazer	blimp
blackmailer	blazon	blind
blackness	bleach	blindfold
blackout ⊙	bleacher	blindly
blacksmith	bleak	blindness
blackstrap	bleakly	blinds
blacktop	blear	blindstitch
bladder	bleary	blindstitched
blade	bleat	blink
blades	bleb	blinker
blame	bled	blip
blamed	bleed	bliss
blames	bleeding	blissful
blanch	bleedings	blissfully
bland	bleeds	blister
blandly	blemish	blithe
blank	blemishes	blithely
blanket	blend	blitz
blankets	blended	blizzard
blanks	blender	bloat
blare	blending	blob
blaspheme	blends	block
blasphemous	bless	blockade
blasphemy	blessed	blocked

blanket	blaspheme	blasphemous	blatancy	bleacher	blear	bleu	blindstitch	bliss	blissfully	blithe	blizzard
blangkit	blasfēm	blasfəməs	blātnsē	blēchər	blēr	blü	blīndstich	blis	blisfəlē	blīth	blizərd

blocker	blubber	boards
blockhouse	bludgeon	boast
blocking	¹blue	boastful
blocks	bluegill	boastfully
blocky	blueprint	boastings
blond	blueprints	boat
blood	blues	boater
bloodhound	bluff	boaters
bloodiest	bluffs	boathouse
bloodless	bluish	boating
bloodshed	blunder	boatload
bloodshot	blunderings	boatman
bloodstain	blunders	boatmen
bloody	blunt	boats
bloom	blunter	boatswain
blooming	bluntly	bob
blooms	bluntness	bobbin
blossom	blur	bobwhite
blot	blurry	bode
blotter	blurt	bodice
blotters	blurting	bodied
blouse	blush	bodies
blouses	bluster	bodily
blow	blustery	body
blower	boa	bodyguard
blowers	board	bodysuit
blowing	boarded	bog
blown	boarder	bogey
blowout ☉	boarding	boggle
blows	boardman	boggy

bogus	bond	bookish
boil	bondage	bookkeeper
boiled	bonded	bookkeepers
boiler	bondholder	bookkeeping
boilers	bondholders	booklet
boiling	bonding	booklets
boisterous	bonds	bookplate
bold	bondsman	bookplates
bolder	bone	books
boldest	bones	bookseller
boldly	bonfire	booksellers
boldness	bong	bookshelf
bolero	boniface	bookshop
bologna	bon jour	bookstore
bolster	bonnet	bookstores
bolstered	bonus	boom
bolt	bonuses	boomerang
bolts	bony	booms
bomb	booby	boon
bombard	book	boondoggle
bombarding	bookbinder	boondoggling
bombast	bookbinding	boost
bombastic	bookcase	booster
bomber	bookcases	boosters
bombing	bookdealer	boosting
bombings	bookdealers	boosts
bombproof	booked	boot
bombs	booker	booth
bona fide	booking	booths
bonanza	bookings	bootlegger

boots		bothered		bourgeois	
bootstrap		bothering		bourgeoisie	
booty		bothers		bout	
borax		bothersome		bouts	
border		bottle		bovine	
bordereau		bottled		bow *n., v.; n., v.*	
bordering		bottleneck		bowel	
borderland		bottlenecks		bowels	
borderline		bottler		bower	
borders		bottlers		bowers	
bore		bottles		bowl	
boredom		bottom		bowler	
borer		bottomless		bowling	
born		bottoms		bowls	
borne		bough		bowman	
borough		bought		bowstring	
borrow		boulder		box	
borrowed		boulevard		boxcar	
borrower		bounce		boxcars	
borrowers		bound		boxed	
borrowing		boundaries		boxer	
borrows		boundary		boxes	
bosom		bounded		boxing	
boss		boundless		boy	
bosses		bounds		boycott	
botanical		bountiful		boyhood	
botanist		bounty		boyish	
botany		bouquet		boys	
both		bouquets		brace	
bother		bourbon		braced	

bracelet	brands	breakdowns ⊙
bracelets	brandy	breaker
braces	brash	breakers
bracing	brass	breakfast
bracket	brassiere	breakfasts
bracketed	brassieres	breaking
brackets	brassy	breaks
brackish	brat	breakthrough
brad	bravado	breakup
brag	brave	breakwater
braggart	bravely	breast
braggarts	braver	breastwork ⊙
braid	bravery	breath
brain	bravest	breathalyzer
brains	bravo	breathe
brainstorm	brawl	breather
brainstorming	bray	breathiness
brainwash	brazen	breathing
brainy	brazenly	breathless
brake	brazenness	breathlessly
brakes	brazier	breathtaking
braking	breach	bred
bramble	bread	breed
bran	breadth	breeder
branch	breadwinner	breeders
branches	break	breeding
brand	breakable	breeds
branded	breakage	breeze
branding	breakaway	breezy
brandish	breakdown ⊙	brethren

braggart	brassiere	bravado	bravest	bravo	brazenness	brazier	breakaway	breakwater	breathiness	breathless
bragərt	brəzēr	brəvädō	brāvist	brävō	brāznnis	brāzhər	brākə(a)wā	brākwôtər	brethēnis	brethlis

breve	brigade	broadcast
brevity	brigades	broadcaster
brew	brigadier	broadcasters
brewer	bright	broadcasting
breweries	brighten	broadcastings
brewery	brighter	broadcasts
bribe	brightest	broadcloth
bribery	brightly	broaden
brick	brightness	broadened
brickbat	brilliance	broadening
brickbats	brilliant	broader
bricklayer	brilliantly	broadest
bricks	brim	broadhead
bridal	brimful	broadloom
bride	brindle	broadlooms
bridegroom	bring	broadly
bridesmaid	bringing	broadside
bridge	brings	broadsides
bridgehead	brink	broadway
bridges	brioche	brocade
bridgework ⊙	brisk	broccoli
bridle	briskly	brochure ⊙
brief	briskness	brochures ⊙
briefed	bristle	broil
briefer	bristles	broiler
briefest	brittle	broilers
briefing	broach	broke
briefings	broached	broken
briefly	broad	brokenly
briefs	broadbrim	broker

brokerage	browse	buckram
brokers	browsed	buckshot
bromide	bruise	buckskin
bronchi	bruises	buckwheat
bronchial	bruising	bud
bronchiole	brunch	buddies
bronchus	brunt	buddy
bronco	brush	budge
bronze	brushed	budget
brooch	brushes	budgetary
brood	brushing	budgeted
brooder	brusque	budgeting
brooders	brusquely	budgets
broody	brutal	buds
brook	brutalist	buff
brooks	brutality	buffalo
broom	brutalize	buffer
brooms	brutally	buffers
broomstick	brute	buffet n.; n., v.
broth	bubble	buffoon
brother	bubbled	buffs
brotherhood	bubbles	bug
brother-in-law ⊙	bubbletop	buggies
brotherly	bubbly	buggy
brothers	buck	bugle
brought	buckboard	bugler
brow	bucket	bugs
brown	buckets	build
browned	bucking	builder
browning	buckle	builders

building		bundle		burlapped	
buildings		bundled		burlaps	
builds		bundles		burlesque	
built		bungalow		burly	
bulb		bungle		burn	
bulbs		bunion		burned	
bulge		bunk		burner	
bulging		bunker		burners	
bulk		bunny		burning	
bulkhead		bunt		burnish	
bulky		buoy		burns	
bull		buoyancy		burnt	
bulldoze		buoyant		burrow	
bulldozer		burden		burrows	
bullet		burdened		bursar	
bulletin		burdens		bursars	
bulletins		burdensome		bursitis	
bullock		bureau		burst	
bulls		bureaucracy		bursting	
bully		bureaucrat		bury	
bulwark		bureaucratic		bus	
bum		bureaucrats		buses	
bumblebee		bureaus		bush	
bump		burgeon		bushel	
bumper		burglar		bushels	
bumpers		burglarproof		bushes	
bumping		burglary		bushing	
bumps		burial		bushings	
bun		buried		busier	
bunch		burlap		busiest	

busily	butchery	butylenes
business ⊙	butler	butyrate
businesses ⊙	butt	buxom
businesslike ⊙	butter	buy
businessman ⊙	butterfat	buyer
businessmen ⊙	butterfly	buyers
bust	buttermilk	buying
bustard	butternut	buys
buster	buttery	buzz
bustle	button	by ⊙
busy	buttonhole	bye
but	buttons	bygone
butadiene	buttress	bylaw
butane	butts	bylaws
butcher	butylene	byword

C

cab

cabana

cabaret

cabbage

cabin

cabinet

cabinets

cabins

cable

cablegram

cables

caboose

cache

cachet

cackle

cactus

cadaver

cadaverous

caddie

cadence

cadenza

cadet

cadmium

cadre

cafe

cafeteria

cafeterias

cage

cagey

caisson

cake

cakes

calamitous

calamity

calcification

calcified

calcify

calcite

calcium

calculate

calculated

calculates

calculating

calculation

calculations

calculator

calculators

calculi

calculus

calendar

calendars

calf

calfskin

caliber

calibrate

calibration

calico

caliper

caliph

calisthenic

[1]calk

calking

call

callback

called

caller

callers

calligrapher

calligraphy

calling

callous

callously

calls

calm

calmer

calmest

calmly

calmness

caloric

calorie

calories

calorimeter

calumny

calve

C

calves	canal	cankerworms
calypso	canals	canned ⊙
cam	canary	canner ⊙
camaraderie	cancel	cannery ⊙
cambric	¹canceled	cannibal
came	¹canceling	canning ⊙
camel	cancellation	cannon
camellia	cancellations	cannot ⊙
camellias	²cancelled	canny
cameo	²cancelling	canoe
camera	cancels	canoes
cameraman	cancer	canon
cameramen	candelabra	canons
cameras	candelabrum	canopy
camouflage	candid	cans ⊙
camp	candidacy	can't ⊙
campaign	candidate	canteen
campaigner	candidates	canto
campaigning	candidly	canton
campaigns	candle	cantor
camper	candlelight	canvas
campers	candles	canvass
campfire	candlestick	canvassed
campground ⊙	candor	canvasser
camping	candy	canvassing
camps	cane	canyon
campsite	canine	canyons
campus	canister	cap
campuses	canker	capabilities
can ○	cankerworm	capability

capable	captain	carboy
capably	captaincy	carboys
capacious	captains	carburetor
capacities	caption	carcass
capacitor	captioned	carcasses
capacitors	captioning	card
capacity	captions	cardboard
cape	captivate	cardiac
caper	captive	cardinal
capillary	captivity	carding
capita	captor	cardiogram
capital	capture	cardiograph
capitalism	captured	cardiology
capitalist	captures	cardiopulmonary
capitalistic	capturing	cardiovascular
capitalization	caput	carditis
capitalize	car	cards
capitalized	caramel	care
capitalizes	[1]carat	cared
capitalizing	caravan	careen
capitals	caraway	career
capitol	carbide	careers
capitulate	carbine	carefree
capitulation	carbohydrate	careful
capping	carbon	carefully
caprice	carbonate	careless
capricious	carbonize	carelessly
caps	carbonized	carelessness
capstan	carbonizing	cares
capsule	carbons	caress

caretaker	carrot	cases
cargo	carrots	casework ⊙
cargoes	carry	caseworker ⊙
caricature	carrying	cash
caries	cars	cashed
carload	cart	cashew
carloads	cartage	cashier
carlot	carte blanche	cashiers
carman	cartel	cashing
carmen	carter	cashmere
carmine	cartilage	casing
carnal	cartographic	casings
carnival	cartographical	casino
carol	cartography	cask
carouse	carton	casket
carp	cartons	cassette
carpenter	cartoon	cassock
carpenters	cartoonist	cast
carpentry	cartoons	castanet
carpet	cartridge	caste
carpeted	cartridges	caster
carpeting	carts	casters
carpets	cartwheel	castigate
carport	carve	castigation
carports	carver	casting
carriage	carvings	castings
carried	cascade	castle
carrier	case	castoff
carriers	caseharden	castoffs
carries	casehardened	castor

casts	categorically	cause
casual	categories	caused
casually	categorize	causes
casualties	categorized	causing
casualty	category	cauterize
cat	cater	caution
cataclysm	caterer	cautioned
cataclysmic	catering	cautious
catalog	caterpillar	cautiously
cataloged	caterpillars	cavalcade
cataloging	caters	cavalier
catalogs	catfish	cavalry
catalyst	catgut	cavalryman
catalytic	catharsis	cavalrymen
catapult	cathedral	cave
catastrophe	catheter	caveat
catastrophes	cathode	caveat emptor
catastrophic	catkin	cavern
catastrophically	²catsup	cavernous
catatonia	cattle	caverns
catch	cattleman	caviar
catchall	cattlemen	cavities
catcher	caucus	cavity
catches	caught	cavort
catching	cauliflower	cay
¹catchup	²caulk	cayenne
catchword	caulking	cease
catchy	causal	ceased
catechism	causation	ceaseless
categorical	causative	ceaselessly

ceases		censorship		ceramic	
cedar		censure		ceramics	
cede		census		cereal	
ceil		cent		cereals	
ceiled		centenary		cerebellum	
ceiling		centennial		cerebral	
ceilings		center		cerebrate	
celebrant		centered		ceremonial	
celebrate		centering		ceremonially	
celebrated		centerline		ceremonies	
celebrating		centerpiece		ceremonious	
celebration		centers		ceremoniously	
celebrity		centigrade		ceremony	
celerity		centimeter		cerise	
celery		centimeters		certain	
celestial		central		certainly	
cell		centrality		certainty	
cellar		centralization		certificate ○	
cellars		centralize		certificated ⊙	
cellist		centralized		certificates ⊙	
cello		centrally		certification ⊙	
cellophane		centric		certifications ⊙	
cells		centrifugal		certified ⊙	
cellular		centrifugally		certifies ⊙	
cellulose		centrifuge		certify ○	
cement		centrist		certifying ⊙	
cements		cents		certitude	
cemetery		centum		cervical	
censor		centuries		cervix	
censorial		century		cesium	

cessation	champions	char
chafe	championship	character
chaff	chance	characteristic □
chagrin	chancel	characteristically □
chain	chancellor	characteristics □
chains	chancery	characterization
chair	chances	characterize
chaired	chandelier	characterized
chairing	chandler	characters
chairman ○	change ○	charbroil
chairmanship ○	changeable ○	charcoal
chairmen ○	changed ○	charge
chairperson	changeover ○	chargeable
chairs	changes ○	charged
chairwoman	changing ○	charges
chaise	channel	charging
chalk	channeled	chariot
challenge	channels	charisma
challenged	chant	charitable
challenges	chantey	charitably
challenging	chaos	charities
challis	chaotic	charity
chamber	chap	charlatan
chambermaid	chapel	charm
chambers	chapels	charmer
chambray	¹chaperon	charming
chamois	²chaperone	charmingly
champ	chaplain	charred
champagne	chapter	chart
champion	chapters	charted

charter		checkbook		chemistry	
chartered		checked		chemists	
charting		checker		chemotherapy	
charts		checkers		cherish	
chase		checking		cherished	
chasing		checkoff		cherries	
chasm		checkout ⊙		cherry	
chassis		checkpoint		cherub	
chaste		checkpoints		cherubim	
chastise		checks		chess	
chastisement		checkup		chest	
chastity		checkups		chestnut	
chat		cheek		chests	
chateau		cheekbone		chew	
chats		cheer		chews	
chatted		cheerful		chic	
chattel		cheerfully		chicanery	
chattels		cheerfulness		chick	
chatter		cheering		chicken	
chatting		cheery		chickens	
chatty		cheese		chicks	
chauffeur		cheesecloth		chide	
chauffeurs		cheeses		chided	
cheap		chef		chief	
cheaper		chefs		chiefly	
cheapest		chemical		chieftain	
cheaply		chemically		chilblain	
cheat		chemicals		child	
cheating		chemise		childbirth	
check		chemist		childhood	

chasm	chassis	chaste	chastity	chateau	chauffeur	cheerfulness	cheeses	chemotherapy	chic	chicanery	chide
kazəm	chasē	chāst	chastətē	shatō	shōfər	chērfəlnis	chēzəz	kemōtherəpē	shēk	shikānərē	chīd

childish		chloride		chores	
childishly		chlorinate		chortle	
childishness		chlorinated		chorus	
childless		chlorine		chose	
childlike		chlorophyll		chosen	
children		chloroprene		chow	
chili		chock		chowder	
chill		chocolate		christen	
chilled		choice		chromatic	
chilly		choices		chromatographic	
chime		choicest		chromatography	
chimney		choir		chrome	
chimneys		choke		chromed	
chimpanzee		choked		chromic	
chin		chokes		chromium	
china		cholera		chronic	
chine		cholesterol		chronically	
chinless		choose		chronicle	
chip		chooses		chronicler	
chipboard		choosing		chronological	
chipped		chop		chronologically	
chipper		chopper		chronologist	
chiropractic		choppy		chronology	
chiropractor		choral		chrysanthemum	
chirp		chord		chubby	
chisel		chore		chuck	
chiseling		choreograph		chuckhole	
chivalrous		choreographer		chuckholes	
chivalry		choreographic		chuckle	
chive		choreography		chug	

---

chum		circuits		citizen	
chunk		circular		citizenry	
chunks		circularization		citizens	
chunky		circularize		citizenship	
church		circularized		citron	
churches		circularizing		citrus	
churchman		circulars		city	
churchmen		circulate		citywide	
churn		circulated		civic	
churned		circulates		civil	
churning		circulating		civilian	
chute		circulation		civilians	
chutes		circulator		civility	
cider		circulators		civilization	
cigar		circulatory		civilizational	
cigarette		circumference		civilize	
cigarettes		circumscribe		clad	
ciliate		circumscription		claim	
cinch		circumspect		claimable	
cinder		circumstance □		claimant	
cinema		circumstances ▣		claimants	
cinematic		circumvent		claimed	
cipher		circus		claiming	
circle		cistern		claims	
circled		citation		clairvoyance	
circles		citations		clairvoyant	
circling		cite		clam	
circuit		cited		clamber	
circuitous		cities		clammy	
circuitry		citing		clamor	

churchman	cigarette	cipher	circuitry	circular	circumference	circumspect	cistern	civilian	claimant
chẻrchmən (man)	sigəret	sīfər	sẻrkətrē	sẻrkūlər	sẻrkumfərəns	sẻrkəmspekt	sistərn	səvilyən	klāmənt

clamoring	classics	cleans
clamorous	classification	cleanse
clamp	classifications	cleanup
clamps	classified	clear
clamshell	classifier	clearance
clamshells	classifies	clearances
clan	classify	cleared
clandestine	classifying	clearer
clang	classmate	clearest
clank	classmates	clearing
clannish	classroom	clearinghouse
clap	classrooms	clearly
claret	classwork ☉	clearness
clarification	clatter	clears
clarified	clause	cleat
clarifier	clauses	cleavage
clarifies	claustrophobia	cleave
clarify	clavier	cleaver
clarifying	claw	cleft
clarinet	claws	clemency
clarity	clay	clement
clash	clays	clench
clasp	clean	clergy
class	cleaned	clergyman
classed	cleaner	clergymen
classes	cleaners	cleric
classic	cleanest	clerical
classical	cleaning	clerk
classically	cleanliness	clerks
classicist	cleanly	clever

clandestine	clannish	claret	classicist	clavier	cleanliness	clearance	clearness	cleavage	clergyman
klandestən	klanish	klarət	klasəsist	kləvēr	klenlēnis	klērəns	klērnis	klēvij	klérjēmən (man)

cleverly		clipped		closures	
cleverness		clipper		clot	
cliché		clippers		cloth	
click		clipping		clothback	
client		clippings		clothe	
clientele		clips		clothes	
clients		clique		clotheshorse	
cliff		cloak		clothesline	
cliffs		cloakroom		clothier	
climactic		clobber		clothing	
climate		clock		cloths	
climax		clocks		cloud	
climb		clockwise		cloudburst	
climber		clockwork ☉		clouded	
climbers		clod		cloudless	
climbing		clog		clouds	
climbout ☉		cloister		cloudy	
clime		close		clout	
clinch		closed		clove	
clincher		closely		clover	
cline		closeness		cloverleaf	
cling		closeout ☉		clown	
clinger		closer		cloy	
clinging		closes		club	
clinic		closest		clubhouse	
clinical		closet		clubs	
clinically		closets		cluck	
clinician		closing		clue	
clinics		closings		clumsily	
clip		closure		clumsy	

clung	coat	coddle
cluster	coated	code
clutch	coating	coded
clutches	coatings	codefendant
clutter	coats	codes
cluttered	coattail	codfish
coach	coax	codicil
coaches	coaxial	codicils
coaching	cob	codification
coachman	cobalt	codify
coachmen	cobble	coding
coadjust ☉	cobblestone	coefficient
coadjuster ☉	COBOL	coefficients
coadjusters ☉	cobra	coerce
coagulate	cobs	coercion
coagulation	cobweb	coercive
coal	cocaine	coexist
coalesce	cochairman ☉	coexistence
coalescence	cochairmen ☉	coffee
coalescent	cock	coffer
coals	cockatoo	coffin
coarse	cockpit	cog
coarsely	cockroach	cogent
coarseness	cocktail	cogitate
coast	cocktails	cogitation
coastal	cocky	cognac
coaster	cocoa	cognate
coasters	coconut	cognitive
coasting	cocoon	cognizance
coastline	cod	cognizant

cohere	collaborating	collects
coherence	collaboration	colleen
coherent	collaborator	college
cohesion	collage	colleges
cohesive	collapse	collegian
cohort	collapsible	collegiate
coif	collapsing	collet
coiffure	collar	collide
coiffures	collarbone	collided
coil	collard	collie
coils	collards	collision
coin	collate	collisions
coincide	collateral	colloquial
coincidence	collating	colloquy
coincident	collation	collude
coincidental	collator	collusion
coins	collators	collusive
coinsurance ☉	colleague	cologne
coinsure ☉	colleagues	colon
coke	collect	colonel
colby	collected	colonels
cold	collectibility	colonial
colder	collectible	colonialism
coldest	collecting	colonic
coldly	collection	colonies
coldness	collections	colonist
cole	collective	colonize
colin	collectively	colonnade
coliseum	collector	colons
collaborate	collectors	colony

color	combining	commandment
coloration	combo	commandments
colored	combs	commando
colorful	combustible	commands
coloring	combustion	commemorate
colorings	come	commemorative
colorist	comeback	commence
colorless	comedian	commenced
colors	comedy	commencement
colossal	comely	commencements
colossus	comes	commences
colostomy	comet	commencing
colt	comfort	commend
columbine	comfortable	commendable
column	comfortably	commendation
columnar	comforter	commendations
columnist	comforts	commendatory
columnists	comic	commended
columns	comical	commending
comb	comically	commensurate
combat	coming	comment
combatant	comings	commentary
combating	comma	commentator
combed	command	commentators
combination	commandant	commented
combinations	commanded	commenting
combine	commandeer	comments
combined	commander	commerce
combines	commanders	commercial
combing	commanding	commercialism

commercialization	commonly	commuters
commercialize	commonplace	commuting
commercially	commonwealth	compact
commercials	commonwealths	compactly
commingle	commotion	companies ⊙
commiserate	communal	companion
commissary	commune	companionable
commission	communicable	companions
commissioned	communicate	companionship
commissioner	communicated	companionway
commissioners	communicates	company ○
commissioning	communicating	comparability
commissions	communication	comparable
commit	communicational	comparative
commitment	communications	comparatively
commitments	communicative	compare
committed	communicator	compared
committee ○	communion	compares
committeeman ⊙	communiqué	comparing
committeemen ⊙	communism	comparison
committees ⊙	communist	comparisons
committeewoman ⊙	communistic	compart ⊙
committing	communities	compartment ⊙
commode	community	compartments ⊙
commodities	commutate	compass
commodity	commutating	compassion
commodore	commutation	compassionate
common	commute	compassionately
commoner	commuted	compatibility
commonest	commuter	compatible

compatriot	complacent	complicates
compel	complain	complication
compelled	complainant	complications
compelling	complained	complicity
compendium	complainer	complied
compensable	complaining	compliment
compensate	complains	complimentary
compensated	complaint	complimented
compensating	complaints	complimenting
compensation	complaisance	compliments
compensatory	complaisant	comply
compete	complement	complying
competence	complementary	component
competency	complemented	components
competent	complementing	comport
competently	complements	comportment
competing	complete	compose
competition	completed	composed
competitive	completely	composer
competitively	completeness	composite
competitiveness	completes	composition
competitor	completing	compositional
competitors	completion	compost
compilation	complex	composure
compilations	complexion	compote
compile	complexities	compound
compiled	complexity	compounded
compiler	compliance	compounding
compiling	complicate	compounds
complacency	complicated	comprehend

comprehension	computerese	conception
comprehensive	computerization	concepts
comprehensively	computerize	conceptual
comprehensiveness	computerized	conceptualize
compress	computers	concern
compressed	computes	concerned
compresses	computing	concerning
compressibility	comrade	concerns
compressible	comradeship	concert *v.; a., n.*
compression	comsat	concerted
compressive	con	concertina
compressor	concave	concerto
compressors	conceal	concerts *v.; n.*
comprise	concealed	concession
comprised	concealment	concessionaire
comprises	concede	concessional
comprising	conceded	concessions
compromise	conceit	conciliate
compromises	conceivable	conciliator
comptroller ⊙	conceivably	conciliatory
compulsion	conceive	concise
compulsive	conceived	concisely
compulsively	concentrate	conciseness
compulsory	concentrated	conclave
computation	concentrating	conclaves
computational	concentration	conclude
computations	concentrations	concluded
compute	concentrative	concludes
computed	concentric	concluding
computer	concept	conclusion

conclusions	condition ☉	conferees
conclusive	conditional ☉	conference
conclusively	conditioned ☉	conferences
concoct	conditioner ☉	conferred
concord	conditioners ☉	conferring
concordance	conditioning ☉	confess
concordant	conditions ☉	confession
concourse	condole	confessional
concrete	condolence	confessions
concretely	condolences	confessor
concur	condominium	confide
concurred	condominiums	confided
concurrence	condone	confidence
concurrent	conducive	confidences
concurrently	conduct	confident
concurring	conducted	confidential
concussion	conducting	confidentiality
condemn	conductive	confidentially
condemnation	conductor	confidently
condemnatory	conductors	configuration ☉
condemned	conducts	configure ☉
condemning	conduit	confine
condensate	cone	confined
condensation	cones	confinement
condense	confectionery	confines
condensed	confederacy	confining
condenser	confederate	confirm
	a., n.; v.	
condensers	confederation	confirmation
condescend	confer	confirmations
condescension	conferee	confirmatory

confirmed	congenial	conjunction □
confirming	congeniality	conjure
confirms	congenital	connect
confiscate	congest	connected
confiscatory	congested	[1]connecter
conflagration	congestion	connecting
conflict	congestive	connection
conflicting	congratulate	connections
conflicts	congratulated	connective
confluence	congratulation	[2]connector
confluent	congratulations	[2]connectors
conform ☉	congratulatory	connects
conformation ☉	congregate	connive
conformational ☉	congregated	connoisseur
conformed ☉	congregation	connoisseurs
conforming ☉	congregational	connotation
conformist ☉	congregations	connote
conformity ☉	congress	conquer
conforms ☉	congresses	conquering
confound ☉	congressional	conqueror
confounded ☉	congressman	conquest
confront	congressmen	cons
confrontation	congresswoman	consanguine
confronted	congruence	consanguinity
confronting	congruent	conscience
confuse	conic	conscientious
confused	conjectural	conscientiously
confusing	conjecture	conscientiousness
confusion	conjoin	conscious
congeal	conjugate	consciously

consciousness	consideration ⊙	consort
conscript	considerations ⊙	consortium
consecrate	considered ⊙	conspicuous
consecration	considering ⊙	conspicuously
consecutive	considers ⊙	conspiracy
consecutively	consign	conspirator
consensus	consigned	conspire
consent	consignee	conspired
consented	consignees	constable
consequence	consigning	constancy
consequences	consignment	constant
consequent	consignments	constantly
consequential	consist	constellation
consequently	consisted	consternation
conservation ⊙	consistency	constituency
conservationist ⊙	consistent	constituent
conservatism ⊙	consistently	constituents
conservative ⊙	consisting	constitute
conservatively ⊙	consists	constituted
conservatives ⊙	consolation	constitutes
conservator ⊙	console	constituting
conservatory ⊙	consoles	constitution
conserve ⊙	consolidate	constitutional
conserves ⊙	consolidated	constitutions
conserving ⊙	consolidating	constrain
consider ○	consolidation	constraint
considerable ⊙	consolidations	constraints
considerably ⊙	consonance	constrict
considerate ⊙	consonant	constriction
considerately ⊙	consonantal	constrictor

construct ○	consuming	contemplative
constructed ⊙	consummate *a.; v.*	contemporaries
constructing ⊙	consummated	contemporary
construction ⊙	consummately	contempt
constructional ⊙	consummation	contemptible
constructions ⊙	consumption	contemptuous
constructive ⊙	consumptive	contend
constructively ⊙	contact ○	contender
constructor ⊙	contacted ⊙	contends
construe	contacting ⊙	content
construed	contactor ⊙	contention
consul	contacts ⊙	contentment
consular	contagion	contents
consulate	contagious	contest
consult	contain ○	contestable
consultant	contained ⊙	contestant
consultants	container ⊙	contestants
consultation	containerization ⊙	contested
consultations	containers ⊙	contests
consultative	containing ⊙	context
consulted	containment ⊙	contiguous
consulting	contains ⊙	continence
consults	contaminate	continent
consumable	contaminated	continental
consume	contamination	contingencies
consumed	contemplate	contingency
consumer	contemplated	contingent
consumerism	contemplates	continuable
consumers	contemplating	continual
consumes	contemplation	continually

continuance		contrary		convalescent	
continuation		contrast		convect	
continue		contrasted		convection	
continued		contrasting		convector	
continues		contravention		convene	
continuing		contribute ⊙		convened	
continuity		contributed ⊙		convenience ⊙	
continuous		contributes ⊙		conveniences ⊙	
continuously		contributing		convenient ⊙	
continuum		contribution ⊙		conveniently ⊙	
contort		contributions ⊙		convening	
contortion		contributor ⊙		convent	
contour		contributors ⊙		convention ⊙	
contours		contributory ⊙		conventional ⊙	
contraband		contrite		conventionality ⊙	
contract ⊙		contrivance		conventionalize ⊙	
contracted ⊙		contrive		conventionally ⊙	
contracting ⊙		control ⊙		conventions ⊙	
contraction ⊙		controllable ⊙		converge	
contractor ⊙		controlled ⊙		conversant	
contractors ⊙		controller ⊙		conversation	
contracts ⊙		controllers ⊙		conversational	
contractual ⊙		controlling ⊙		conversations	
contradict		controls ⊙		converse	
contradicted		controversial		conversely	
contradiction		controversy		conversion	
contradictory		contuse		conversions	
contralto		contusion		convert	
contraption		convalesce		converted	
contrarily		convalescence		converter	

converters		cook		coordinates	
convertibility		cooked		coordinating	
convertible		cookery		coordination	
convertibles		cookies		coordinator	
converting		cooking		coordinators	
converts		cookware		coowner	
convex		cooky		coowners	
convexity		cool		cope	
convey		coolant		copied	
conveyance		cooled		copier	
conveyances		cooler		copiers	
conveyed		coolest		copies	
conveying		cooling		coping	
conveyor		coolly		copious	
conveys		coolness		copiously	
convict		coon		copper	
convicted		coop		copy	
conviction		co-op		copyholder	
convictions		cooper		copying	
convince		cooperate		copyreader	
convinced		cooperated		copyreaders	
convinces		cooperating		copyright	
convincing		cooperation		copyrighted	
convincingly		cooperative		copyrights	
convocation		cooperatively		copywriter	
convoy		cooperatives		copywriters	
convulse		cooperator		coquette	
convulsion		co-ops		coral	
convulsive		coordinate		cord	
convulsively		coordinated		cordial	

cordiality	corpsmen	correspondingly ⊙
cordially △	corpulence	corresponds ⊙
cordon	corpulent	corridor
cords	corpus	corridors
corduroy	corpuscle	corroborate
core	corpuscular	corroborated
cork	corral	corrode
corker	correct	corroding
corkscrew	corrected	corrosion
corn	correctible	corrosive
cornea	correcting	corrugate
corner	correction	corrugated
corners	correctional	corrugation
cornerstone	corrections	corrupt
cornet	corrective	corruptible
cornfield	correctly	corruption
cornucopia	correctness	corsage
corollary	correlate	cortege
corona	correlated	cortex
coronary	correlates	cortical
coronation	correlating	cortisone
coroner	correlation	cosecant
corporal	correlations	co-sign
corporate	correlative	cosigned
corporation	correspond ○	cosigner
corporations	corresponded ⊙	cosigners
corporeal	correspondence ○	cosmetic
corps	correspondent ⊙	cosmetics
corpse	correspondents ⊙	cosmic
corpsman	corresponding ⊙	cosmologist

cornea	cornucopia	corona	corporeal	corpulent	corpuscle	correct	corroborate	corrosion	corrupt	cortex
kôrnēə	kôrnəkōpēə	kərōnə	kôrpôrēəl	kôrpūlənt	kôrpusl	kərekt	kərobərāt	kərōzhən	kərupt	kôrteks

cosmology	council	countersignature ⊙
cosmopolitan	councilman	countersigned ⊙
cosmopolitanism	councilmen	countersink ⊙
cosmos	councils	counties ⊙
co-sponsor	counsel	counting ⊙
co-sponsored	counseled	countless ⊙
cost	counseling	countries
costing	counselor	country
costings	counselors	countryman
costly	counsels	countrymen
costs	count ⊙	countryside
costume	counted ⊙	counts ⊙
costumes	countenance ⊙	county ⊙
costwise	counter ⊙	coup
cosy	counteract ⊙	coupe
cot	counterattack ⊙	couple
cotillion	counterbalance ⊙	coupled
cottage	counterbalanced ⊙	coupler
cottages	counterclaim ⊙	couplers
cotter	counterclockwise ⊙	couples
cotton	counterfeit ⊙	couplings
cottons	countermand ⊙	coupon
cottontail	countermove ⊙	coupons
couch	countermoves ⊙	courage
couches	counteroffensive ⊙	courageous
cougar	counterpart ⊙	courier
cougars	counterparts ⊙	course
cough	counterpoint ⊙	courses
could	counters ⊙	court
couldn't	countersign ⊙	courteous

courteously		covetous		craft	
courtesies		covetousness		crafts	
courtesy		covey		craftsman	
courthouse		cow		craftsmanship	
courtier		coward		craftsmen	
courting		cowardice		crafty	
courtliness		cowardly		crag	
courtly		cowboy		craggy	
courtroom		cower		cram	
courts		cowhide		crammed	
courtship		cowl		cramp	
courtyard		cowling		cramped	
cousin		cowman		cranberry	
cove		co-worker ☉		crane	
covenant		co-workers ☉		cranes	
covenants		cows		cranial	
cover		cox		crank	
coverage		coy		crankcase	
coverages		coyness		cranky	
coverall		coyote		cranny	
coveralls		cozier		crash	
covered		cozy		crashes	
covering		crab		crashing	
coverings		crack		crass	
coverlet		crackdown ☉		crassness	
covers		cracker		crate	
covert		cracking		crated	
covertly		crackle		crater	
covet		crackling		crates	
coveted		cradle		crating	

crave	credenza	crescendo
craven	credenzas	crescent
craving	credibility	cresol
crawl	credible	crest
crawls	credibly	crestfallen
crayon	credit	crevice
crayons	creditable	crew
craze	credited	crewel
crazily	crediting	crewman
crazy	creditor	crewmen
creak	creditors	crews
cream	credits	crib
creamer	credo	cricket
creamery	credulity	cried
creamy	credulous	cries
crease	credulousness	crime
create	creed	crimes
created	creeds	criminal
creates	creek	criminality
creating	creeks	criminals
creation	creep	criminologist
creations	creeper	criminology
creative	creeping	crimson
creatively	creeps	cringe
creativeness	cremate	crinkle
creativity	creole	cripple
creator	creosote	crippled
creature	creosoted	crippling
credential	crepe	crises
credentials	crept	crisis

crisp	crossed	cruelly
crisply	crosses	cruelty
crispness	crossing	cruise
crisscross	crossings	cruiser
criteria	crossover	cruises
criterion	crossply	cruising
critic	crossroad	crumb
critical	crosstie	crumble
critically	crossties	crumbling
criticism	crosswalk	crumbs
criticisms	crosswise	crummy
criticize	crossword	crump
criticized	croton	crumple
criticizing	crouch	crunch
critics	crow	crupper
critique	crowd	crusade
critter	crowded	crusader
croak	crowder	crush
crock	crowding	crushable
crockery	crowds	crushed
crocket	crown	crusher
crocodile	crucial	crushing
crony	crucially	crust
crook	crucible	crutch
crooked	crucify	crutches
croon	crude	crux
crop	crudely	cry
crops	crudest	crying
cross	crudity	crypt
crossbar	cruel	cryptic

cryptograph	cult	curbing
cryptographic	cultist	curbs
crystal	cultivate	curd
crystalline	cultivated	curdle
crystallite	cultivating	cure
crystallization	cultivation	cured
crystallize	cultural	cures
crystallizing	culturally	curfew
crystals	culture	curing
cub	cultured	curio
cubage	cultures	curiosity
cubbyhole	culver	curious
cube	culvert	curiously
cubes	cumbersome	curl
cubic	cum laude	curler
cubicle	cumulate	curling
cubism	cumulative	curly
cubist	cumulus	currant
cucumber	cunning	currants
cudgel	cunningly	currencies
cue	cup	currency
cuff	cupboard	current
cuisine	cupboards	currently
cull	cupful	currents
culled	cur	²curricula
culling	curable	curricular
culminate	curative	curriculum
culminates	curator	¹curriculums
culmination	curb	curry
culprit	curbed	curse

cursory	customarily ⊙	cutworm
curt	customary ⊙	cutworms
curtail	customer ⊙	cybernate
curtailed	customers ⊙	cybernation
curtailment	customize ⊙	cybernetics
curtain	customized ⊙	cycle
curtains	customs ⊙	cycles
curtly	cut	cyclic
curvature	cutaway	cyclical
curve	cutback	cyclist
curved	cutbacks	cyclone
curves	cute	cyclones
cushion	cutin ⊙	cylinder
cushioncraft	cutins ⊙	cylinders
cushioned	cutlass	cylindrical
cushioning	cutlery	cynic
cushions	cutlet	cynical
cusp	cutoff	cynically
cuss	cutout ⊙	cynicism
custard	cutover	cypress
custodial	cuts	cyst
custodian	cutter	cytology
custodians	cutters	cytoplasm
custody	cutting	czar
custom ⊙	cuttings	

D

dab	damp	darkest
dabble	dampen	darkness
dachshund	dampened	darling
dad	dampness	darn
dads	dams	dart
daffodil	damsite	darts
daguerreotype	dance	dash
dailies	dancer	data
daily	dancers	date
daintily	dances	dated
dainty	dancing	dateline
dairies	dandelion	dates
dairy	dandily	dating
dairyman	dandy	datum
dais	danger	daub
daisy	dangerous	daughter
dale	dangerously	daughter-in-law ⊙
dam	dangers	daughters
damage	dangle	daunt
damaged	dangling	dauntless
damages	dank	dauphin
damaging	dapper	dawn
damask	dapple	day
dame	darcy	daybreak
	dare	daydream
	daredevil	daylight
	daring	daylights
	dark	days
	darken	daytime ⊙
	darker	daze

dazzle	deanery	debtor
dazzling	deans	debtors
deacon	dear	debts
deacons	dearer	debug
deactivate ☉	dearest	debugging
deactivated ☉	dearly	debunk
deactivation ☉	dearth	debut
dead	deary	debutante
deaden	death	decade
deadhead	deathbed	decadence
deadliest	deathless	decadent
deadline	deaths	decades
deadlines	deathward	decal
deadliness	debark	decalcify
deadlock	debarkation	decals
deadly	debatable	decant
deadwood	debate	decathlon
deaf	debated	decay
deafen	debating	decease
deafness	debauch	deceased
deal	debauchery	decedent
dealer	debenture	decedents
dealers	debentures	deceit
dealership	debilitate	deceitful
dealerships	debility	deceive
dealing	debit	deceived
dealings	debits	decelerate
deals	debonair	deceleration
dealt	debris	decency
dean	debt	decent

decently	declare	decree
decentralization	declared	decreed
decentralize	declares	decrement
decentralized	declaring	decry
deception	declination	dedicate
deceptive	decline	dedicated
deceptively	declined	dedicating
decertify ⊙	declines	dedication
decide	declining	dedications
decided	declivity	deduce
decides	decode	deduct
deciding	decompose	deducted
decimal	decomposition	deductibility
decipher	decontrol ⊙	deductible
deciphered	decontrolled ⊙	deductibles
deciphering	décor	deducting
decision	decorate	deduction
decisional	decorated	deductions
decisions	decorates	deductive
decisive	decorating	dee
decisively	decoration	deed
decisiveness	decorations	deeded
deck	decorative	deeds
decking	decorator	deem
decks	decorators	deemed
declaim	decorum	deep
declamatory	decrease	deepen
declaration	decreased	deeper
declarations	decreases	deepest
declarative	decreasing	deeply

deer	defense	definitively
deerskin	defenseless	deflate
deerstalker	defenses	deflation
dees	defensible	deflect
deface	defensive	deflection
defacement	defensiveness	deflections
defacing	defer	defocus
defat	deference	defoliant
defatted	deferent	defoliants
default	deferment	defoliate
defaulted	deferral	defoliated
defaulting	deferred	deform ☉
defaults	defiance	deformation ☉
defeat	defiant	deformational ☉
defeated	defiantly	deformed ☉
defeating	deficiencies	deformities ☉
defeatism	deficiency	deformity ☉
defeatist	deficient	defraud
defeats	deficit	defrauding
defect	deficits	defray
defection	definable	defrost
defective	define	defroster
defects	defined	deft
defend	defines	deftness
defendant	defining	defunct
defendants	definite	defuse
defended	definitely	defuser
defender	definition	defy
defenders	definitions	degenerate
		v.; a., n.
defending	definitive	degeneration

---

defeatist	defect	defend	defenseless	defensiveness	defer	defiant	definition	defoliant	defoliate	defunct
difḗtist	difékt	difénd	difénslis	difénsivnis	difė́r	difíənt	defəníshən	difṓlēənt	difṓlēāt	difúngkt

degradable	delegation	delinquents □
degradation	delete	delirium
degrade	deleted	deliver ○
degree	deleting	deliverable ⊙
degreed	deletion	deliverance ⊙
degrees	deletions	delivered ⊙
degression	deliberate *v.; a.*	deliverer ⊙
dehumanize	deliberately	deliverers ⊙
dehydrate	deliberating	deliveries ⊙
dehydrated	deliberation	delivering ⊙
dehydrating	deliberations	delivers ⊙
dehydration	delicacies	delivery ⊙
dehydrogenation	delicacy	dell
deification	delicate	delouse
deify	delicately	delta
deign	delicatessen	delude
deity	delicatessens	deluded
deject	delicious	deluge
dejected	deliciously	deluged
dejectedly	delight	delusion
dejection	delighted	deluxe
delay	delightful	delve
delayed	delightfully	delving
delaying	delimit	demagogue
delays	delineate	demand
delectate	delineated	demanded
delectation	delineation	demanding
delegate	delinquencies □	demandingly
delegated	delinquency □	demands
delegates	delinquent □	demarcate

demarcation	demonstrative ⊡	denominator
demean	demonstratives ⊡	denote
demeanor	demonstrator ⊡	denotes
dement	demonstrators ⊡	denoting
demineralization	demoralization	denounce
demineralize	demoralize	denouncing
demise	demote	dense
democracy	demotion	densest
democrat	demotions	densified
democratic	demount	densify
democratization	demountable	density
democratize	demur	dent
democrats	demure	dental
demographer	demurrage	dented
demographic	demurrer	dentifrice
demography	den	dentist
demolish	denature	dentistry
demolished	denatured	dentists
demolishing	denial	dents
demolition	denied	denture
demon	denier	denude
demonstrable ⊡	denies	denunciation
demonstrably ⊡	denim	deny
demonstratable ⊡	denims	denying
demonstrate ⊡	denominate	deodorant
demonstrated ⊡	denominated	deodorants
demonstrates ⊡	denomination	deodorize
demonstrating ⊡	denominational	deodorizer
demonstration ⊡	denominationally	depart ⊙
demonstrations ⊡	denominations	departed ⊙

departing ⊙	deplore	depreciation ▫
department ⊙	deplores	depredate
departmental ⊙	deploy	depredation
departmentalize ⊙	deployed	depress
departmentalized ⊙	deployment	depressant
departments ⊙	deport	depressed
departs ⊙	deportee	depressing
departure	depose	depressingly
departures	deposed	depression
depend	deposes	depressions
dependability	deposit	deprivation
dependable	depositary	deprive
depended	deposited	deprived
dependence	depositing	depth
dependency	deposition	depths
dependent	depositions	deputize
dependents	depositor	deputy
depending	depositories	derail
depends	depositors	derange
depersonalization	depository	derangement
depersonalize	deposits	derby
depict	depot	derelict
depicting	deprave	dereliction
depiction	depravity	deride
depicts	deprecate	derision
deplete	deprecatory	derisive
depleted	depreciable ▫	derisively
depletion	depreciate ▫	derivation
deplorable	depreciated ▫	derivative
deplorably	depreciating ▫	derive

derived	deserve ☉	desperado
derives	deserved ☉	desperate
dermatologic	deserves ☉	desperately
dermatologist	deserving ☉	desperation
dermatology	design	despise
derogate	designate	despite
derogatory	designated	despoil
derrick	designates	despoiler
dervish	designating	despond
desalt	designation	despondence
descend	designations	despondency
descendant	designed	despondent
descendent	designer	despot
descending	designers	despotism
descent	designing	dessert
describe	designs	desserts
described	desirability	destination
describes	desirable	destinations
describing	desire	destine
description	desired	destined
descriptions	desires	destiny
descriptive	desiring	destitute
desecrate	desirous	destroy
desecration	desist	destroyed
desegregate	desk	destroyer
desegregation	desks	destroyers
desensitize	desolate _v.; a._	destroying
desert _n., v.; a., n._	desolation	destroys
deserted	despair	destruct
desertion	despairingly	destruction

destructive	determinable	devastated
desultory	determinant	devastating
detach	determination	devastation
detachable	determinative	develop ○
detaching	determine	developed ⊙
detachment	determined	developer ⊙
detail	determines	developers ⊙
detailed	determining	developing ⊙
detailing	determinism	development ⊙
details	deterministic	developmental ⊙
detain	deterred	developments ⊙
detainer	deterrence	develops ⊙
detaining	deterrent	deviance
detect	detest	deviant
detectable	detestable	deviate
detected	destestation	deviates
detecting	detonate	deviation
detection	detonator	deviations
detective	detonators	device
detector	detour	devices
détente	detract	devil
detention	detracted	devilish
deter	detractor	devious
detergency	detriment	devise
detergent	detrimental	devised
detergents	devaluate ⊙	devisee
deteriorate	devaluation ⊙	devises
deteriorating	devalue ⊙	devising
deterioration	devalued ⊙	devoid
determinability	devastate	devote

devoted	dial	dictator
devotee	dialect	dictators
devoting	dialectic	dictatorship
devotion	dialectical	diction
devotional	dialectically	dictionaries
devour	dialed	dictionary
devourer	dialogue	dictum
devout	dials	did
devoutly	dialysis	diddle
dew	dialyze	didn't
dewdrop	diameter	die
dexter	diameters	died
dexterity	diametric	dies
dextrose	diametrically	diesel
diabetes	diamond	diet
diabetic	diamonds	dietary
diabolic	diaper	dietetic
diabolical	diaphragm	²dietician
diagnosable	diarrhea	²dieticians
diagnose	diary	dieting
diagnosed	diathermy	¹dietitian
diagnoses	diazo	diets
diagnosis	dice	differ
diagnostic	dichotomy	difference
diagnostician	dictate	differences
diagonal	dictated	different
diagonally	dictates	differentiability
diagram	dictating	differentiable
diagrammatic	dictation	differential
diagrams	dictational	differentials

differentiate	dignitary	din
differentiated	dignity	dine
differentiating	digress	diner
differentiation	digs	diners
differently	dike	dinette
differing	dilapidate	dinettes
differs	dilate	dingy
difficult ⊙	dilated	dining
difficulties ⊙	dilation	dinner
difficulty ⊙	dilatory	dinners
diffidence	dilemma	dinnertime ⊙
diffident	diligence	dinnerware
diffuse	diligent	diocesan
diffuser	diligently	diocese
diffusion	dill	diode
dig	dilute	diodes
digest	diluted	dioxide
digested	dilution	dip
digester	dim	diphtheria
digestible	dime	diploma
digesting	dimension	diplomacy
digestive	dimensional	diplomas
digests	dimensionally	diplomat
digger	dimensions	diplomatic
digging	diminish	dipole
digit	diminished	dipper
digital	diminishes	dipping
digits	diminution	dire
dignify	dimly	direct ⊙
dignitaries	dimmer	directed ⊙

directing ☉	disadvantage ☉	disarrange
direction ☉	disadvantaged ☉	disarray
directional ☉	disadvantages ☉	disassemble
directionality ☉	disaffect ☉	disassembly
directions ☉	disaffected ☉	disassociate ☉
directive ☉	disaffection ☉	disassociation ☉
directiveness ☉	disaffiliate	disaster
directives ☉	disaffiliation	disasters
directivity ☉	disagree	disastrous
directly ☉	disagreeing	disband
directness ☉	disagreement	disbanded
director ☉	disallow	disbar
directorate ☉	disallowance	disbarment
directories ☉	disallowed	disbelief
directors ☉	disappear	disbelieve
directorship ☉	disappearance	disburse
directory ☉	disappeared	disbursed
directs ☉	disappearing	disbursement
dirge	disappears	disbursements
dirigible	disappoint	disbursing
dirigibles	disappointed	²disc
dirt	disappointing	discard
dirty	disappointment	discarded
disabilities	disappointments	discern
disability	disapprobation	discernible
disable ☉	disapproval	discharge
disabled ☉	disapprove	discharged
disables ☉	disapprovingly	discharges
disabling ☉	disarm	discharging
disabuse	disarmament	disciple

discipleship	discordantly	discretionary
disciplinary	discount ⊙	discriminate v.; a.
discipline	discountable ⊙	discriminating
disciplined	discounted ⊙	discrimination
disciplines	discounting ⊙	discriminatory
disciplining	discounts ⊙	discursive
disclaim	discourage	discursiveness
disclaimer	discouraged	discuss ⊙
disclose	discouragement	discussant ⊙
disclosed	discourages	discussed ⊙
discloses	discouraging	discusses ⊙
disclosing	discourse	discussing ⊙
disclosure	discourteous	discussion ⊙
discolor	discourteously	discussions ⊙
discomfort	discourtesies	disdain
discomforts	discourtesy	disdainful
disconcert	discover	disease
disconnect	discovered	diseased
disconnected	discoverer	diseases
disconnecting	discoveries	disembark
discontent	discovering	disembarkation
discontinuance	discovers	disembody
discontinue	discovery	disemploy ⊙
discontinued	discredit	disengage
discontinues	discreet	disenroll
discontinuing	discreetly	disentangle
discontinuities	discrepancies	disfavor
discontinuity	discrepancy	disfigure ⊙
discord	discrete	disfigured ⊙
discordant	discretion	disgrace

disgraceful	dislocation	disparate
disgruntle	dislocations	disparities
disguise	dislodge	disparity
disgust	disloyal	dispassion
disgusted	disloyalty	dispassionate
dish	dismal	dispassionately
disharmony	dismally	dispatch
dishearten	dismay	dispatched
dishes	dismember	dispatcher
dishevel	dismemberment	dispatchers
dishonest	dismiss	dispatches
dishonesty	dismissal	dispatching
dishonor	dismissed	dispel
dishwasher	dismissing	dispensary
dishwashers	dismount	dispensation
dishwater	disobedience	dispense
disillusion	disobedient	dispenser
disinclination	disobey	dispensers
disincline	disorder ⊙	dispensing
disinfectant	disordered ⊙	dispersal
disintegrate	disorderliness ⊙	dispersant
disintegration	disorderly ⊙	dispersants
disinter	disorders ⊙	disperse
disinterest ⊙	disorganization ⊙	dispersed
disinterested ⊙	disorganize ⊙	dispersing
disjoint	disorganized ⊙	dispersion
¹disk	disorient	displace
disks	disown	displaced
dislike	disparage	displacement
dislocate	disparagement	display

displayed	disregarding ⊙	disservice ⊙
displayer	disrepair	dissident
displaying	disreputable	dissimilar
displays	disrepute	dissimulate
displease ⊙	disrespect ⊙	dissimulation
displeased ⊙	disrobe	dissipate
displeasing ⊙	disrupt	dissipated
displeasure	disrupted	dissipator
disposable	disruption	dissociate
disposal	disruptions	dissociation
disposals	disruptive	dissolution
dispose	dissatisfaction ⊙	dissolve
disposed	dissatisfactions ⊙	dissolved
disposing	dissatisfied ⊙	dissolves
disposition	dissatisfy ⊙	dissolving
dispossess	dissect	dissonance
dispossessed	dissecting	dissuade
dispossession	dissection	distal
disproportion	dissections	distance
disproportionate a.; v.	dissector	distances
disprove	dissects	distant
disputable	dissemble	distantly
dispute	disseminate	distaste
disputed	disseminated	distasteful
disputes	dissemination	distastefully
disqualify	dissension	distend
disquiet	dissent	distension
disquietude	dissenter	distill
disregard ⊙	dissertation	distillation
disregarded ⊙	dissertations	distilled

disposal	disposition	dispute	disquietude	disrepute	dissertation	dissimilar	dissonance	distension	distill
dispōzl	dispəzishən	dispūt	diskwīətüd	disripūt	disərtāshən	disimələr	disənəns	distenshən	distil

distiller	distributed ⊙	diverge
distillery	distributes ⊙	divergence
distinct ⊙	distributing ⊙	divergent
distinction ⊙	distribution ⊙	diverse
distinctions ⊙	distributions ⊙	diversification
distinctive ⊙	distributive ⊙	diversified
distinctively ⊙	distributor ⊙	diversify
distinctiveness ⊙	distributors ⊙	diversion
distinctly ⊙	distributorship ⊙	diversionary
distinctness ⊙	distributorships ⊙	diversions
distinguish ⊙	district	diversity
distinguishable ⊙	districts	divert
distinguished ⊙	distrust	diverted
distinguishes ⊙	distrustful	diverting
distinguishing ⊙	disturb	divest
distort	disturbance	divestiture
distorted	disturbed	divide
distortion	disturber	divided
distortions	disturbing	dividend □
distract	disturbingly	dividends □
distractedly	disunion	divider
distractible	disunite	dividers
distracting	ditch	divides
distraction	ditches	dividing
distractions	ditto	divination
distraught	ditty	divine
distress	diurnal	divinely
distressed	divan	diving
distressing	dive	divinity
distribute ⊙	diver	divisible

division	doctrine	doll
divisional	doctrines	dollar
divisions	document	dollars
divisive	documentary	dollies
divorce	documentation	dolls
divorced	documenting	dolly
divorcee	documents	dolphin
divorcees	dodge	dolt
divulge	dodger	doltish
divulged	doe	domain
divulges	does	dome
divulging	doesn't	domestic
dizzily	doff	domestically
dizziness	doffed	domesticate
dizzy	dog	domesticity
do	doggedly	domestics
docile	dogging	domicile
dock	doghouse	domiciled
docket	dogma	domiciliary
docketed	dogmatic	dominance
docking	dogmatically	dominant
docks	dogmatism	dominantly
dockside	dogs	dominate
doctor △	dogtrot	dominated
doctoral △	doing	domination
doctorate △	doings	domineer
doctors △	dolce	domineering
doctrinaire	doldrums	dominion
doctrinal	dole	domino
doctrinally	doleful	don

donate		dossier		downgrade ⊙	
donated		dot		downgraded ⊙	
donating		dots		downgrades ⊙	
donation		double		downhill ⊙	
donations		doubled		downing ⊙	
done		doubles		downpour ⊙	
donkey		doubling		downright ⊙	
donnybrook		doubloon		downstairs ⊙	
donor		doubloons		downstream ⊙	
donors		doubly		downswing ⊙	
don't		doubt		downtime ⊙	
[2]donut		doubted		downtown ⊙	
doom		doubtful		downtrend ⊙	
door		doubtfully		downtrodden ⊙	
doorbell		doubtingly		downturn ⊙	
doorknob		doubtless		downward ⊙	
doorman		doubts		downwards ⊙	
doormen		dough		downwind ⊙	
doors		[1]doughnut		downy ⊙	
doorstep		doughnuts		dowry	
doorway		dour		doze	
dope		dourly		dozen	
dormancy		douse		dozens	
dormant		dove		dozer	
dormitories		dovetail		drab	
dormitory		dowel		draft	
dorsal		dower		drafted	
dosage		down ○		draftee	
dose		downcast ⊙		drafting	
doses		downfall ⊙		drafts	

draftsman	drastically	dregs
draftsmen	draught	drench
drafty	draughty	dress
drag	draw	dressed
dragger	drawback	dresser
dragging	drawbridge	dressers
dragnet	drawee	dresses
dragon	drawer	dressing
dragoon	drawers	dressings
drain	drawing	dressy
drainage	drawings	drew
drained	drawl	dribble
drains	drawn	dried
drake	draws	drier
drama	dread	dries
dramatic	dreadful	drift
dramatical	dreadfully	drifted
dramatically	dream	drill
dramatist	dreamboat	drilled
dramatization	dreamed	drilling
dramatize	dreamer	drillings
dramatized	dreamless	drills
drank	dreamlessly	drink
drape	dreams	drinker
draped	dreamy	drinking
draper	dreariness	drinks
draperies	dreary	drip
drapery	dredge	drive
drapes	dredging	drivable
drastic	dreg	driven

driver	drug	duel
drivers	druggist	duels
drives	druggists	dues
driveway	drugs	duet
driveways	drugstore	duffel
driving	drum	dug
drizzle	drummer	dugout ⊙
drizzly	drums	dugouts ⊙
drone	drunk	duke
drones	drunken	dull
droop	drunkenness	duller
drop	dry	dullest
droplet	dryer	dullness
dropout ⊙	dryers	dully
dropouts ⊙	drying	duly
dropped	dryly	dumb
dropper	dryness	dumbbell
dropping	dual	dummy
droppings	dualism	dump
drops	dub	dumped
dross	dubious	dumping
drought	duchess	dumpling
drove	duck	dumplings
drover	ducks	dumps
drown	duct	dun
drowse	ductile	dune
drowsily	ducts	dunes
drowsy	dud	dungaree
drudge	dude	dungarees
drudgery	due	dunk

duns	dusted	dyers
dupe	dusting	dyes
duplex	dustless	dying
duplexes	dusty	dynamic
duplicate *v.; a., n.*	duties	dynamical
duplicated	dutiful	dynamically
duplicates *v.; n.*	dutifully	dynamics
duplicating	duty	dynamite
duplication	dwarf	dynamo
duplicator	dwell	dynamos
duplicators	dweller	dynast
durability	dwellers	dynastic
durable	dwelling	dynasty
duration	dwellings	dysentery
durations	dwelt	dysfunction
duress	dwindle	dyspepsia
during	dye	dyspeptic
dusk	dyed	dystrophy
dusky	dyeing	
dust	dyer	

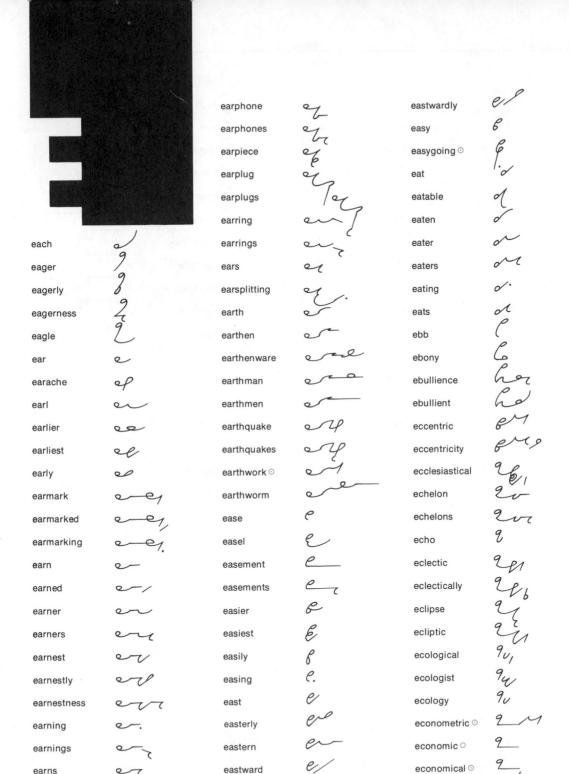

each	earphone	eastwardly
eager	earphones	easy
eagerly	earpiece	easygoing ☉
eagerness	earplug	eat
eagle	earplugs	eatable
ear	earring	eaten
earache	earrings	eater
earl	ears	eaters
earlier	earsplitting	eating
earliest	earth	eats
early	earthen	ebb
earmark	earthenware	ebony
earmarked	earthman	ebullience
earmarking	earthmen	ebullient
earn	earthquake	eccentric
earned	earthquakes	eccentricity
earner	earthwork ☉	ecclesiastical
earners	earthworm	echelon
earnest	ease	echelons
earnestly	easel	echo
earnestness	easement	eclectic
earning	easements	eclectically
earnings	easier	eclipse
earns	easiest	ecliptic
	easily	ecological
	easing	ecologist
	east	ecology
	easterly	econometric ☉
	eastern	economic ☉
	eastward	economical ☉

eagerness	earlier	earnest	earring	earrings	earthquake	easiest	eastern	eccentric	echelon	eclectic	eclipse
ēgərnis	érlēər	érnist	ērring	ērringz	érthkwāk	ēzēist	ēstərn	eksentrik	eshəlon	eklektik	iklips

economically ☉	editorialist	effervesce
economics ☉	editorially	effervescence
economies ☉	editorials	efficacious
economist ☉	editors	efficacy
economists ☉	editorship	efficiency
economize ☉	educate ☉	efficient
economizing ☉	educated ☉	efficiently
economy ☉	educating ☉	effluent
ecstasy	education ☉	effort
ecumenical	educational ☉	effortless
ecumenism	educationally ☉	effortlessly
ecumenist	educations ☉	efforts
eddy	educator ☉	egalitarian
edema	educators ☉	egalitarianism
edge	eel	egg
edges	eerie	eggnog
edging	eerily	eggs
edgy	efface	eggshell
edible	effect ☉	ego
edict	effected ☉	egotism
edification	effecting ☉	egotist
edifice	effective ☉	egress
edify	effectively ☉	eighth
edit	effectiveness ☉	either
edited	effects ☉	ejaculate
editing	effectual ☉	eject
edition	effectuate ☉	ejected
editions	effectuation ☉	ejection
editor	effeminacy	eke
editorial	effeminate	eking

E

ekistics	electricity	elegance
elaborate a.; v.	electrics	elegant
elaborately	electrification	elegantly
elaboration	electrified	elegy
elapse	electrify	element
elapsed	electrifying	elemental
elastic	electro	elementary
elasticity	electrocardiogram	elements
elate	electrocardiograph	elephant
elation	electrocute	elephantine
elbow	electrocution	elevate
elder	electrode	elevated
elderly	electrodynamic	elevating
eldest	electroencephalogram	elevation
elect ○	electrolysis	elevations
elected ⊙	electrolyze	elevator
electing ⊙	electromagnet	elevators
election ⊙	electron	elf
elections ⊙	electronic	elfin
elective ⊙	electronically	elicit
electives ⊙	electronics	elicited
elector ⊙	electrophoresis	eligibility
electoral ⊙	electroplate	eligible
electorate ⊙	electroplating	eligibles
electors ⊙	electros	eliminate
electric	electroshock	eliminated
electrical	electrostatic	eliminates
electrically	electrotherapist	eliminating
electrician	electrotherapy	elimination
electricians	elects ⊙	eliminations

elite	emasculation	emboss
elk	embank	embossed
elks	embankment	embossing
ellipse	embankments	embrace
ellipsis	embargo	embraced
ellipsoid	embargoes	embroider
elliptical	embark	embroidery
elm	embarking	embroil
elms	embarrass	embroilment
elongate	embarrassed	embryo
elongation	embarrassing	embryonic
elope	embarrassingly	emcee
eloquence	embarrassment	emerald
eloquent	embassy	emeralds
eloquently	embattle	emerge
else	embed	emerged
elsewhere ⊙	embellish	emergence
elucidate	ember	emergencies
elucidation	embers	emergency
elude	embezzle	emergent
elusion	embezzled	emerges
elusive	embezzlement	emerging
elusiveness	embitter	emery
em	emblem	emigrant
emaciate	emblematic	emigrate
emanate	emblems	emigrated
emanation	embodied	emigration
emancipate	embodiment	eminent
emancipation	embody	eminently
emasculate	embolden	emissary

emission	employers ⊙	encampment
emissions	employing ⊙	encase
emit	employment ⊙	encased
emitted	employments ⊙	enchant
emmer	employs ⊙	enchantingly
emotion	empower	enchantment
emotional	emptied	encircle
emotionalism	emptier	enclave
emotionally	empties	enclose ⊙
emotions	emptiness	enclosed ⊙
empathy	empty	encloses ⊙
emperor	emptying	enclosing ⊙
emphasis	emulate	enclosure ⊙
emphasize	emulsified	enclosures ⊙
emphasized	emulsifier	encode
emphasizes	emulsify	encoding
emphasizing	emulsifying	encomium
emphatic	emulsion	encompass
emphatically	en	encompasses
emphysema	enable ⊙	encompassing
empire	enabled ⊙	encore
empires	enables ⊙	encounter ⊙
empirical	enabling ⊙	encountered ⊙
empirically	enact	encountering ⊙
employ ⊙	enacted	encounters ⊙
employability ⊙	enaction	encourage
employed ⊙	enactment	encouraged
employee ⊙	enamel	encouragement
employees ⊙	encamp	encourages
employer ⊙	encamped	encouraging

emission	emit	emphysema	empirical	emptier	empty	en	encircle	encode	encomium	encompass	encore	encourage
imishən	imit	emfəsēmə	empirəkl	emptēər	emptē	en	ensèrkl	enkōd	enkōmēəm	enkumpəs	ängkôr	enkèrij

encouragingly	endorser	engaged
encroach	endorsers	engagement
encroachment	endorsing	engagements
encrust	endosperm	engaging
encumber	endow	engagingly
encumbrance	endowed	engender
encumbrances	endowment	engendered
encyclopedia	endowments	engine
encyclopedias	ends	engineer
encyclopedic	endurable	engineered
end	endurance	engineering
endanger	endure	engineers
endangered	endured	engines
endangering	enduringly	engrave
endear	enemies	engraved
endearment	enemy	engraver
endeavor	energetic	engraving
endeavored	energetically	engravings
endeavoring	energies	engross
endeavors	energize	engulf
ended	energy	enhance
ending	enervate	enhanced
endings	enervation	enhancement
endless	enforce	enhances
endlessly	enforceable	enhancing
endogamy	enforced	enigma
endorse	enforcement	enjoin
endorsed	enforcer	enjoinder
endorsement	enforcing	enjoined
endorsements	engage	enjoins

enjoy	enriched	entered
enjoyable	enrichment	entering
enjoyed	enroll	enterprise
enjoying	enrolled	enterprises
enjoyment	enrollee	enterprising
enjoys	enrollees	enterprisingly
enlarge	enrolling	enters
enlarged	enrollment	entertain
enlargement	enrollments	entertained
enlarging	enrolls	entertainer
enlighten	en route	entertainers
enlightening	ensconce	entertaining
enlightenment	ensemble	entertainment
enlist	enshrine	enthrall
enlisted	enshrined	enthrone
enlistee	ensign	enthused
enlisting	ensile	enthusiasm □
enlistment	enslave	enthusiasms □
enliven	enslavement	enthusiast □
enmesh	ensue	enthusiastic □
enmity	ensuing	enthusiastically □
enologist	ensure ◎	enthusiasts □
enology	ensuring ◎	entice
enormity	entail	enticed
enormous	entailed	enticement
enormously	entails	enticing
enough ○	entangle	entire
enrage	entanglement	entirely
enrapture	entanglements	entirety
enrich	enter	entitle

entitled	enunciation	epidemiological
entitles	envelope ○	epidemiology
entitling	envelopes ⊙	epidermis
entity	enveloping ⊙	epigram
entomb	enviable	epigrammatic
entomologist	enviably	epigraph
entomology	envied	epilepsy
entourage	envies	epileptic
entrance n.; v.	envious	epilogue
entrances n.; v.	enviously	epiphysis
entranceway	environ	episode
entrant	environment	episodes
entrants	environmental	epistemology
entreat	environmentalist	epistle
entree	environs	epitaph
entrees	envisage	epithet
entrench	envision	epitome
entrepreneur	envisioned	epitomize
entrepreneurs	envoy	epoch
entries	envy	epochal
entropy	enzymatic	epoxy
entrust	enzyme	epsilon
entrusted	enzymes	equal
entrusting	ephemeral	equaled
entry	epic	[1]equaling
entwine	epicenter	equality
enumerate	epicure	equalization
enumerated	epicycle	equalize
enumeration	epidemic	equalized
enunciate	epidemics	equalizer

equalizes	eradicate	erudition
equalizing	eradication	erupt
²equalling	erasable	erupted
equally	erase	eruption
equals	erased	escalate
equanimity	eraser	escalation
equate	erasers	escalator
equation	erasing	escalators
equations	erasure	escapade
equator	erasures	escape
equatorial	erect	escaped
equidistant	erected	escapee
equidistantly	erecting	escapes
equilibrium	erection	escapist
equine	erode	escheat
equinox	erosion	escheats
equip ○	erotic	eschew
equipment ⊙	erotically	escort
equipments ⊙	err	escrow
equipped ⊙	errand	escrows
equipping ⊙	errands	escutcheon
equitable	errata	esoteric
equitably	erratic	especial ○
equity	erratically	especially ⊙
equivalence	erroneous	espionage
equivalent	erroneously	esplanade
equivalents	error	espousal
equivocal	errors	espouse
equivocate	ersatz	espousing
era	erudite	esprit

equanimity	equate	equatorial	equinox	equitable	equivalence	eradicate	eʀ	errand	errata	erroneous	erupt
ēkwənimətē	ikwāt	ēkwətôrēəl	ēkwənoks	ekwətəbl	ikwivələns	iradəkāt	ėr	erənd	ərätə	ərōnēəs	irupt

esprit de corps	estrangement	evade
esquire	et cetera △	evader
esquires	etch	evaders
essay	etchings	evaluate ⊙
essayist	eternal	evaluated ⊙
essence	eternity	evaluates ⊙
essential	ethane	evaluating ⊙
essentially	ether	evaluation ⊙
essentials	ethereal	evaluations ⊙
establish ○	ethic	evaluative ⊙
established ⊙	ethical	evangelical
establishes ⊙	ethically	evangelism
establishing ⊙	ethics	evangelist
establishment ⊙	ethnic	evaporate
establishmentarian ⊙	ethos	evaporation
establishments ⊙	ethyl	evaporator
estate ⊙	ethylene	evasion
estates ⊙	etiquette	evasive
esteem	etymological	evasiveness
esteemed	etymologist	even
esthetic	etymology	evening
esthetics	eugenic	evenings
estimate	eugenics	evenly
estimated	eulogize	event ○
estimates	eulogizer	eventful ⊙
estimating	eulogy	eventfully ⊙
estimation	euphemism	events ⊙
estimations	eureka	eventual ⊙
estimator	evacuate	eventuality ⊙
estrange	evacuation	eventually ⊙

esprit de corps — esprē dəkôr
essential — əsenshəl
esteem — estēm
esthetic — esthetik
eternity — itérnətē
ethereal — ithirēəl
etiquette — etəket
eugenics — ūjeniks
eureka — ūrēkə
evacuate — ivakūāt
evasive — ivāsiv

ever ○	evolved	exasperating
everglade ⊙	ewe	exasperation
evergreen ⊙	ewes	excavate
everlasting ⊙	exacerbate	excavation
everlastingly ⊙	exacerbation	excavations
every ⊙	exact	exceed
everybody ⊙	exacting	exceeded
everyday ⊙	exactitude	exceeding
everyone ⊙	exactly	exceedingly
everything ⊙	exaggerate	exceeds
everywhere ⊙	exaggerated	excel
evict	exaggerating	excelled
eviction	exaggeration	excellence
evidence	exalt	excellency
evidenced	exaltation	excellent
evidences	exam	excellently
evident	examination	excelsior a.; n.
evidentiary	examinations	except
evidently	examine	excepted
evil	examined	excepting
evils	examinee	exception
evince	examiner	exceptional
evinced	examiners	exceptionally
evocation	examines	exceptions
evocative	examining	excerpt
evoke	example	excerpts
evolution	examples	excess
evolutionary	exams	excessive
evolutionist	exasperate	excessively
evolve	exasperated	ex-chairman ⊙

exchange ☉	excrete	exercised
exchangeable ☉	excretion	exercises
exchanged ☉	excruciate	exercising
exchanger ☉	excursion	exert
exchanges ☉	excursions	exerted
exchanging ☉	excusable	exerting
exchequer	excuse	exertion
excise	excused	exhale
excision	excuses	exhaust
excitability	execute	exhausted
excitable	executed	exhaustible
excite	executing	exhaustion
excited	execution	exhaustive
excitedly	executioner	exhaustively
excitement	executions	exhibit
exciting	executive	exhibited
excitingly	executives	exhibiting
exclaim	executor	exhibition
exclamation	executors	exhibitions
exclude	executrix	exhibitor
excluded	exemplar	exhibitors
excludes	exemplary	exhibits
excluding	exemplifies	exhilarate
exclusion	exemplify	exhort
exclusions	exempt	exhortation
exclusive	exempted	exhumation
exclusively	exempting	exhume
exclusiveness	exemption	exigency
excommunicate	exemptions	exigent
excoriate	exercise	exile

exist		expansiveness		expenditure	
existed		expatriate		expenditures	
existence		expatriation		expends	
existent		expatriations		expense ○	
existential		expect ○		expenses ⊙	
existing		expectable ⊙		expensive ⊙	
exists		expectancy ⊙		experience ○	
exit		expectant ⊙		experienced ⊙	
exits		expectantly ⊙		experiences ⊙	
exodus		expectation ⊙		experiencing ⊙	
ex officio		expectations ⊙		experiential ⊙	
exonerate		expected ⊙		experientially ⊙	
exoneration		expectedly ⊙		experiment	
exorbitance		expecting ⊙		experimental	
exorbitant		expects ⊙		experimentally	
exorcise		expediency		experimentation	
exorcism		expedient		experimented	
exothermic		expedite		experimenter	
exotic		expedited		experimenting	
expand		expedites		experiments	
expandable		expediting		expert	
expanded		expedition		expertise *n.; v.*	
expander		expeditions		expertly	
expanding		expeditious		experts	
expanse		expeditiously		expiate	
expansion		expel		expiation	
expansionary		expend		expiration	
expansions		expendable		expirations	
expansive		expended		expire	
expansively		expending		expired	

expires	explosion	expressway
expiring	explosions	expressways
explain	explosive	expropriate
explained	explosively	expropriation
explaining	explosives	expulsion
explains	exponent	expulsive
explanation	exponential	expunge
explanations	export	expurgate
explanatory	exported	expurgation
explicable	exporter	exquisite
explicate	exporters	exquisitely
explicit	exporting	extant
explicitly	exports	extemporaneous
explicitness	expose	extempore
explode	exposed	extend
exploded	exposit	extended
exploding	exposition	extending
exploit	expositor	extends
exploitation	expository	extension
exploiter	exposure	extensions
exploiting	expound	extensive
exploitive	express	extensively
exploration	expressed	extent
exploratory	expresses	extenuate
explore	expressing	extenuating
explored	expression	exterior
explorer	expressionless	exterminate
explorers	expressions	extermination
explores	expressive	external
exploring	expressly	externalization

explicable	exploratory	exponent	exposition	expository	expulsion	expunge	extant	extenuate	exterior
eksplƏkƏbl	eksplôrƏtôrē	ekspōnƏnt	ekspƏzishƏn	ekspozƏtôrē	ekspulshƏn	ekspunj	ekstant	ekstenūät	ekstirēƏr

externalize	extraordinary	exuberantly
externally	extrapolate	exude
extinct	extrapolation	exult
extinction	extras	exultant
extinguish	extrasensory	exultantly
extinguisher	extravagance	exultation
extirpate	extravagant	ex-wife
extol	extravaganza	eye
extort	extravehicular	eyeball
extortion	extreme	eyebrow
extra	extremely	eyed
extract	extremes	eyeglass
extracted	extremist	[2]eyeing
extracting	extremity	eyelash
extraction	extricate	eyelet
extractor	extrinsic	eyelid
extracurricular	extrovert	eyepiece
extradite	extrude	eyes
extradition	extruder	eyesight
extralegal	extrusion	eyewitness
extraneous	exuberance	[1]eying
extraordinarily	exuberant	

F

fable	
fabric	
fabricate	
fabricated	
fabricating	
fabrication	
fabricator	
fabricators	
fabrics	
fabulous	
facade	
face	
faced	
facedown ⊙	
faceless	
faces	
facet	
facetious	
facets	
facial	
facile	
facilitate	
facilitates	
facilitating	

facilities	
facility	
facing	
facings	
facsimile	
fact ⊙	
faction	
factor	
factorial	
factories	
factors	
factory	
facts ⊙	
factual ⊙	
facture	
factures	
facultative	
faculties	
faculty	
fad	
fade	
faded	
fading	
fail	
failed	
failing	
fails	
failure	
failures	
faint	

faintest	
faintly	
fair	
fairer	
fairest	
fairground ⊙	
fairgrounds ⊙	
fairly	
fairness	
fairs	
fairway	
fairways	
fairy	
faith	
faithful	
faithfully	
faiths	
fake	
faker	
falcon	
fall	
fallacies	
fallacious	
fallacy	
fallen	
fallible	
falling	
fallout ⊙	
fallow	
falls	

---

false		fans		fascinatingly	
falsehood		fantasies		fascination	
falsely		fantasize		fascism	
falsify		fantasizes		fascist	
falsifying		fantastic		fashion	
falsity		fantastically		fashionable	
falter		fantasy		fashioned	
fame		far		fashions	
famed		faraway		fast	
familial		farce		fasten	
familiar		farcical		fastened	
familiarity		fare		fastener	
familiarize		fares		fasteners	
familiarizing		farm		fastenings	
familiarly		farmed		faster	
families		farmer		fastest	
family		farmers		fastidious	
famine		farmhouse		fat	
famous		farming		fatal	
fan		farmland		fatalist	
fanatic		farms		fatalities	
fanatical		farther		fatality	
fanaticism		farthest		fatally	
fancier		fascia		fate	
fanciers		¹fasciae		fateful	
fancies		²fascias		father	
fanciful		fascicle		father-in-law ⊙	
fancy		fascinate		fatherland	
fanfare		fascinated		fatherly	
fang		fascinating		fathers	

fathom	fears	fedora
fatigue	fearsome	fee
fatten	feasibility	feeble
fatter	feasible	feebly
fatty	feast	feed
fatuous	feat	feedback
faucet	feather	feeder
fault	featherbed	feeders
faulted	featherbedding	feeding
faults	featheredge	feedings
faulty	feathertop	feeds
fauna	featherweight	feedstock
faux pas	feathery	feedstocks
favor	feature	feel
favorable	featured	feeler
favorably	featureless	feeling
favored	features	feelings
favoring	featuring	feels
favorite	fecund	fees
favorites	fecundity	feet
favoritism	fed	feign
favors	federal	feint
fawn	federalism	felicitous
fealty	federalist	felicity
fear	federalize	feline
feared	federally	fell
fearful	federate a., n.; v.	fellow
fearfully	federated	fellows
fearless	federation	fellowship
fearlessly	federations	fellowships

felon	ferryboat	fiancé
felony	fertile	fiasco
felt	fertility	fiat
felts	fertilization	fiber
female	fertilize	fiberboard
females	fertilizer	fiberglass
feminine	fertilizers	fibers
femininity	fervent	fibrosis
feminism	fervently	fibrous
feminist	fervor	fiche
femur	fester	fickle
fen	festival	fiction
fence	festive	fictional
fences	festivities	fictitious
fencing	festivity	fiddle
fender	fetch	fiddlestick
fennel	fete	fidelities
ferment	fetid	fidelity
fermentation	fetish	fidget
fermented	fettle	fidgety
fermenter	feud	fiduciary
fern	feudal	field
ferocious	feudalism	fielder
ferociously	feudalistic	fielding
ferocity	fever	fields
ferret	feverish	fieldwork ☺
ferric	feverishly	fiend
ferrier	few	fiendish
ferries	fewer	fierce
ferry	fewest	fiercely

fierceness		filing		finally	
fiercest		filings		finals	
fiery		fill		finance	
fife		filled		financed	
fifth		filler		finances	
fig		fillers		financial	
fight		filling		financially	
fighter		fillings		financier	
fighters		fills		financing	
fighting		filly		finch	
fights		film		find	
figment		films		finder	
figs		filmstrip		finding	
figurative ⊙		filmstrips		findings	
figuratively ⊙		filmy		finds	
figure ⊙		filter		fine	
figured ⊙		filtering		fined	
figures ⊙		filters		finely	
figurine ⊙		filth		fineness	
figurines ⊙		filthy		finer	
figuring ⊙		filtrate		fines	
filament		filtration		finest	
filch		fin		finger	
file		final		fingernail	
filed		finale		fingernails	
filer		finalist		fingerprint	
files		finality		fingerprinted	
filial		finalize		fingerprinting	
filibuster		finalized		fingerprints	
filigree		finalizing		fingers	

fingertip	fireworks ☉	fitfully
fingertips	firing	fitness
finial	firings	fits
finick	firm	fitted
finicky	firmed	fittest
finis	firmer	fitting
finish	firmly	fittings
finished	firmness	fix
finisher	firms	fixed
finishers	first	fixing
finishes	firsthand	fixture
finishing	firstly	fixtures
finite	firth	fizzle
fir	fiscal	fizzled
fire	fish	flag
firearm	fisher	flagellate
firearms	fisheries	flagellation
firecracker	fisherman	flagged
fired	fishermen	flagpole
firelight	fishery	flagrant
fireman	fishhook	flagrantly
firemen	fishing	flags
fireplace	fishyback	flail
fireplaces	fission	flair
firepower	fist	flake
fireproof	fists	flaky
fireproofing	fistula	flamboyant
fires	fistulas	flamboyantly
fireside	fit	flame
firework ☉	fitful	flameproof

flames	flatness	flesh
flaming	flatten	fleshy
flamingo	flatter	flew
flammable	flattered	flex
flange	flattering	flexibility
flanger	flatteringly	flexible
flanges	flattery	flexibly
flank	flattest	flexing
flannel	flatulence	[2]flexion
flannels	flatware	flexural
flap	flaunt	flexure
flapper	flavor	flick
flapping	flavoring	flicker
flaps	flavorings	flier
flare	flavors	fliers
flash	flaw	flies
flashback	flawless	flight
flashed	flawlessly	flights
flasher	flax	flightworthy ⊙
flashes	flaxen	flimsy
flashing	flaxseed	flinch
flashings	flea	fling
flashlight	fleck	flint
flashy	[1]flection	flip
flask	fled	flippant
flat	fledge	flipper
flatcar	flee	flirt
flatcars	fleet	flirtation
flatiron	fleetest	flirtatious
flatly	fleeting	float

floater	flounder	fluorescent
floating	flour	fluoridate
floats	flourish	fluoridation
flock	flours	fluoride
flocks	flout	fluorinate
flog	flow	fluorine
flood	flowage	flurry
flooded	flower	flush
flooding	flowerpot	flushed
floodlight	flowers	fluster
floodlights	flowing	flute
floods	flown	flutist
floodwater	flows	flux
floor	flu	fly
floorboard	fluctuate	flyer
floored	fluctuating	flyers
flooring	fluctuation	flying
floorman	fluctuations	flyleaf
floors	flue	foal
flop	fluency	foam
floppy	fluent	foamed
flora	fluently	foams
floral	fluff	foamy
florid	fluffy	fob
florist	fluid	focal
florists	fluidity	focally
floss	fluids	focus
flotation	flung	focused
flotilla	fluoresce	focusing
flounce	fluorescence	fodder

foe	fondly	footsteps
fog	fondness	footstool
foggy	food	footwear
foible	foods	footwell ⊙
foil	foodstuff	footwork ⊙
foist	foodstuffs	fop
fold	fool	foppish
folded	foolhardy	for
folder	fooling	forage
folders	foolish	foray
folding	foolishly	forbade
foldout ⊙	foolishness	forbear
foliage	foolproof	forbearance
folio	foot	forbid
folk	footage	forbidden
folklore	football	forbidding
folks	footbridge	force
folksy	footfall	forced
follies	foothill	forceful
follow	foothills	forcefully
followed	foothold	forceps
follower	footing	forces
followers	footings	forcible
following	footman	forcibly
follows	footnote	forcing
folly	footpad	ford
foment	footpath	fore
fomentation	footprint	forearm
fond	footprints	forearmed
fonder	footstep	forebear

foil	foliage	folk	foment	fomentation	foolhardy	footage	footstool	for	forage	foray	forbearance	forbid
foil	fōlēij	fōk	fōment	fōmentāshən	fülhärdē	fůtij	fůtstül	fôr	fôrij	fôrā	fôrbārəns	fərbid

forebode	forerunner	forgetful
forecast	foresee	forgetfulness
forecasted	foreseeable	forgetting
forecaster	foreseen	forging
forecasters	foresees	forgive
forecasting	foreshorten ☉	forgiven
forecasts	foreshortened ☉	forgiveness
foreclose	foreshortening ☉	forgot
foreclosure	foresight	forgotten
forefather	foresighted	fork
forefeet	forest	forks
forefinger	forestall	forlorn
forefoot	forested	form ☉
forefront	forestry	formal ☉
forego ☉	forests	formalities ☉
foregoing ☉	foretell	formality ☉
foregone	forethought	formalize ☉
foreground ☉	forever ☉	formalized ☉
forehead	forewarn	formalizing ☉
foreign	forewarning	formally ☉
foreigner	foreword	format ☉
foreknowledge	forfeit	formation ☉
foreknown	forfeited	formations ☉
foreleg	forfeiture	formative ☉
foreman	forgave	formats ☉
foremen	forge	formed ☉
foremost	forged	former ☉
forenoon	forgeries	formerly ☉
forensic	forgery	formidable ☉
forepart ☉	forget	formidably ☉

forming ☉	forum	fountains
forms ☉	forums	fourfold
formula ☉	forward	foursome
formulaic ☉	forwarded	fourth
formulas ☉	forwarder	fowl
formulate ☉	forwarders	fowler
formulated ☉	forwarding	fox
formulating ☉	forwards	foyer
formulation ☉	fossil	fraction
forsake	foster	fractional
forsaken	fostered	fractionate
forswear	fostering	fractionation
fort	fought	fractions
forte a., n.; n.	foul	fractious
forth	foulest	fracture
forthcoming	fouling	fractured
forthright	foully	fractures
forthrightly	found ☉	fragile
forthrightness	foundation ☉	fragment
forthwith ☉	foundational ☉	fragmentary
fortification	foundations ☉	fragmentation
fortified	founded ☉	fragments
fortifies	founder ☉	fragrance
fortify	foundering ☉	fragrant
fortitude	founders ☉	frail
fortress	founding ☉	frailest
fortunate	foundling ☉	frame
fortunately	foundry ☉	framed
fortune	fountain	framer
fortunes	fountainhead	framers

frames	freak	frenetic
framework ⊙	freakish	frenzy
framing	freckle	frequencies
franc	free	frequency
franchise	freeboot	frequent
franchised	freebooter	frequently
franchises	freed	fresco
franchising	freedom	fresh
frank	freehand	freshen
franked	freehold	fresher
frankest	freeholder	freshest
frankfurter	freeing	freshly
frankfurters	freely	freshman
frankly	freeman	freshmen
frankness	freer	freshness
franks	frees	fret
frantic	freest	friable
frantically	freethinking ⊙	friar
fraternal	freeway	friction
fraternally	freeways	frictional
fraternities	freeze	fried
fraternity	freezer	friend
fraternize	freezers	friendless
fraternizing	freezes	friendliness
fraud	freezing	friendly
fraudulent	freight	friends
fraught	freighter	friendship
fray	freighters	friendships
frayed	freighting	frieze
frazzle	freights	fright

frighten	frosty	fulfilled
frightened	froth	fulfilling
frightening	frothy	fulfillment
frighteningly	frown	fulfills
frightful	froze	full
frightfully	frozen	fullback
frigid	frugal	fuller
frill	frugality	fullest
fringe	frugally	fullness
fritter	fruit	fully
frivolity	fruitful	fulminate
frivolous	fruitfully	fulsome
frizzle	fruition	fumble
fro	fruitless	fume
frock	fruitlessly	fumes
frog	fruits	fun
frolic	frustrate	function
from ○	frustrating	functional
front	frustration	functionalism
frontage	frustrations	functionally
frontal	fry	functionary
frontier	frying	functioned
frontiers	fudge	functioning
frontiersman	fuel	functions
frontiersmen	fueled	fund
fronts	fueling	fundamental
frost	fuels	fundamentalist
frostbite	fugitive	fundamentally
frostbitten	fugitives	fundamentals
frosts	fulfill	funded

funding	furnaces	fury
funds	furnish	fuse
funeral	furnished	fuselage
fungicide	furnisher	fuser
fungicides	furnishers	fusers
fungus	furnishes	fusible
funnel	furnishing	fusing
funnier	furnishings	fusion
funniest	furniture	fuss
funny	furor	fusses
fur	furring	fussy
furbish	furrow	futile
furious	further	futility
furiously	furtherance	future
furl	furthered	futures
furlong	furthering	futurist
furlough	furthermore ☉	fuzz
furloughed	furtive	fuzzy
furnace	furtively	

G

gabardine	galena	gangway
gabardines	gall	gantlet
gable	gallant	gap
gadfly	gallantry	gaps
gadget	gallery	garage
gadgetry	galley	garages
gadgets	gallium	garb
gag	gallon	garbage
gaiety	gallonage	garble
gaily	gallons	garden
gain	gallop	gardener
gained	gallows	gardeners
gainer	gallstone	gardenia
gainful	galvanic	gardening
gainfully	galvanize	gardens
gaining	galvanized	gargle
gains	galvanizing	garish
gait	gambit	garishness
gaited	gamble	garlic
gaiter	gambler	garment
gala	gambles	garments
galax	gambling	garner
galaxy	game	garrison
gale	games	garrulous
	gamma	garter
	gamut	garters
	gander	gas
	gang	gaseous
	gangplank	gases
	gangster	gash

gasification	gay	generalization
gasket	gaze	generalizations
gasketed	gazelle	generalize
gaskets	gazette	generalized
gaslight	gazetteer	generally
gasoline	gazettes	generals
gasp	gazing	generate
gastrectomy	gear	generated
gastric	geared	generates
gastrointestinal	gearing	generating
gastronomy	gearless	generation
gate	gears	generations
gates	gee	generator
gateway	geese	generators
gateways	gel	generic
gather	gelatin	generosity
gathered	gem	generous
gatherer	gemlike	generously
gatherers	gems	genesis
gathering	gemstone	genetic
gatherings	gender	geneticist
gaudy	gene	genial
gauge	genealogical	genius
gauges	genealogist	geniuses
gaunt	genealogy	genteel
gauntlet	general	gentile
gauze	generalist	gentility
gave	generalists	gentle
gawk	generality	gentleman
gawky	generalizable	gentlemen △

gentleness	germs	giddiness
gentler	gerontology	giddy
gently	gerund	gift
gentry	gerundial	gifted
genuine	gestate	gifts
genuinely	gestation	giftwrap
genus	gesture	giftwraps
geocentric	gestures	gig
geochemistry	get	gigantic
geographer	getaway	gigging
geographic	gets	giggle
geographical	getter	gill
geographically	getters	gilt
geography	getting	gimmick
geologic	geyser	gimmicks
geological	geysers	gin
geologist	ghastly	ginger
geologists	ghetto	gingerly
geology	ghettos	gingham
geometrical	ghost	gird
geometrically	ghostly	girder
geometry	ghoul	girdle
geophysical	giant	girl
geopolitical	giants	girlhood
geriatric	gib	girlish
geriatrics	gibbon	girls
germ	gibbons	girt
germane	gibe	girth
germinal	giblet	girts
germinate	gibs	gist

give		glaze		globulin	
giveaway		glazed		gloom	
giveaways		glazer		gloomily	
given		glazing		gloomy	
giver		gleam		glorification	
givers		gleaming		glorify	
gives		glean		glorious	
giving		gleaned		glory	
glacier		glee		gloss	
glad		gleeful		glossary	
gladden		gleefully		glossy	
gladiator		glen		glottal	
gladly		glib		glottis	
glamorize		glibly		glove	
glamorized		glide		glover	
glamorous		glider		gloves	
glamour		glides		glow	
glance		gliding		glower	
glancing		glimmer		*n.; n., v.*	
gland		glimpse		glowing	
glands		glimpses		glucose	
glandular		glint		glue	
glare		glisten		glued	
glaringly		glistening		gluer	
glass		glitter		gluing	
glasses		gloat		glum	
glassine		global		glumly	
glassware		globe		glut	
glassy		globes		glutting	
glaucoma		globetrotter		glutton	
				glycerin	

glycerol	golfer	governing ⊙
glycol	golfing	government ⊙
gnarl	gondola	governmental ⊙
gnarled	gondolas	governmentally ⊙
gnash	gone	governments ⊙
gnaw	good ⊙	governor ⊙
gnome	goodies ⊙	governors ⊙
go ⊙	goodly ⊙	governs ⊙
goad	goodness ⊙	gown
goal	goods ⊙	gowns
goals	goodwill ⊙	grab
goat	goody ⊙	grace
goats	goose	graced
gobble	gore	graceful
god	gorge	gracefully
goddess	gorgeous	graces
godless	gory	gracious
godlike	gospel	graciously
gods	gossamer	graciousness
godsend ⊙	gossip	gradation
goes ⊙	got	grade
goggle	gotten	graded
going ⊙	gouge	grader
goings ⊙	gourd	graders
goiter	gourmet	grades
gold	gourmets	gradient
golden	gout	grading
goldfish	govern ⊙	gradual
goldsmith	governed ⊙	gradually
golf	governess ⊙	graduate ⊙

graduated ☉	grandstand ☉	grasped
graduates ☉	grange	grasping
graduating ☉	granger	grass
graduation ☉	granite	grasses
graduations ☉	granny	grassland
graffiti	grant	grassy
graffito	granted	grate
graft	grantee	grateful
graham	grantees	gratefully
grain	granting	gratefulness
grains	grantor	gratification
gram	grantors	gratified
grammar	grants	gratify
grammarian	granular	gratifying
grammatic	granulate	gratifyingly
grammatical	granulated	gratis
grammatically	granulation	gratitude
grams	granule	gratuities
granary	grape	gratuitous
grand	grapefruit	gratuitously
grandchild	grapes	gratuity
grandeur	grapevine	grave
		a., n., v.; a.
grandfather	graph	gravedigger
grandfathers	graphic	gravel
grandiloquent	graphically	gravely
grandiose	graphite	graven
grandly	graphs	graver
grandmother	grapple	graves
grandmothers	grappling	gravest
grandparent	grasp	gravestone

graveyard	greeted	grisly
gravitation	greeting	grist
gravitational	greetings	grit
gravity	gregarious	gritting
gravy	grenade	gritty
gray	grew	grizzle
graybeard	grey	grizzly
graze	greyhound	groan
grazing	grid	grocer
grease	grief	grocers
greases	grievance	grocery
greasy	grievances	grog
great ○	grievant	groggy
greatcoat ⊙	grieve	groin
greater ⊙	grieved	groom
greatest ⊙	grievous	groomed
greatly ⊙	grill	groove
greatness ⊙	grills	groover
greats ⊙	grim	grooves
greed	grimace	grope
greedily	grimly	gross
greedy	grin	grossed
green	grind	grossly
greenest	grinder	grotesque
greenhouse	grinding	grotesquely
greenish	grindings	ground ○
greenly	grindstone	grounded ⊙
greens	grip	grounder ⊙
greenwood	gripper	grounding ⊙
greet	grips	groundkeeper ⊙

groundkeepers ⊙	gruesome	guided
groundless ⊙	gruff	guideline
groundman ⊙	gruffly	guidelines
groundmen ⊙	grumble	guidepost
grounds ⊙	grunt	guides
groundwork ⊙	guarantee	guiding
group	guaranteed	guild
grouped	guaranteeing	guile
grouping	guarantees	guileless
groupings	guaranties	guilt
groups	guarantor	guiltiness
grout	guaranty	guiltless
grouting	guard	guilty
grove	guarded	guinea
grovel	guardian	guise
groves	guardians	guitar
grow	guardianship	guitarist
grower	guards	guitarists
growers	guardsman	guitars
growing	gubernatorial	gulf
growl	guerrilla	gulfs
grown	guess	gull
grows	guessed	gullet
growth	guessing	gullible
grub	guesswork ⊙	gully
grubbiness	guest	gulp
grubby	guests	gum
grudge	guidance	gummed
grudgingly	guide	gummy
gruel	guidebook	gumption

gums	guru	gymnast
gun	gush	gymnastic
gunfight	gusher	gymnastics
gunfighter	gusset	gynecological
gunfire	gust	gynecologist
gunman	gusto	gynecology
gunmen	gusty	gyp
gunner	gutter	gypsum
gunny	guttering	gypsy
gunpowder	guttural	gyrate
guns	guy	gyration
gunsmith	guys	gyro
gunwale	guzzle	gyroscope
gunwales	gym	
gurgle	gymnasium	

	hailstorm	halves
	hair	ham
	haircut	hamburger
	hairdo	hamlet
	hairdos	hammer
	haired	hammering
habeas corpus	hairline	hammers
haberdashery	hairpin	hammock
habit	hairstyle	hamper
habitable	hairy	hampered
habitant	halation	hand
habitants	halazone	handbag
habitat	hale	handball
habits	hales	handbill
habitual	half	handbills
habitually	halfback	handbook
hack	halfway	handbooks
hacking	hall	handclasp
hackle	hallmark	handcraft
hackney	hallow	handcuff
hacksaw	halls	handed
had	hallucinate	handful
haddock	hallway	handgun
hadn't	hallways	handhold
haggard	halo	handicap
haggardly	halt	handicapped
haggle	halted	handicaps
haggling	halter	handicraft
hail	haltingly	handicraftsman
hailed	halve	handier

handiest	hangar	harbors
handily	hanger	hard
handing	hangers	hardboard
handiwork ⊙	hanging	harden
handkerchief	hangman	hardened
handkerchiefs	hangover	hardener
handle	hank	hardening
handled	hanker	harder
handler	hanks	hardest
handlers	hansom	hardhat
handles	haphazard	hardly
handling	hapless	hardness
handout ⊙	haploid	hardship
handouts ⊙	happen	hardships
handrail	happened	hardstand ⊙
hands	happening	hardware
handshake	happenings	hardwood
handsome	happens	hardwoods
handsomely	happenstance	hardworking ⊙
handsomer	happier	hardy
handspike	happiest	hare
handspray	happily	hark
handstand ⊙	happiness	harm
handwork ⊙	happy	harmful
handwriting	harangue	harmless
handwritten	haranguing	harmlessly
handy	harass	harmonious
handyman	harassed	harmoniously
handymen	harassment	harmonization
hang	harbor	harmonize

H

harmonizes	hatching	haystack
harmony	hatchway	haywire
harness	hate	hazard
harp	hateful	hazardous
harpist	hating	hazards
harpoon	hatred	haze
harpsichord	hats	hazel
harrow	hatter	hazelnut
harsh	haughtily	hazy
harsher	haughty	he ○
harshly	haul	head
harshness	haulage	headache
harvest	hauled	headaches
harvested	hauler	headboard
harvester	haulers	headdress
harvesting	hauling	headed
has ○	haunch	header
hash	haunt	headers
hasn't ⊙	have ○	headgear
hasp	haven	heading
hasps	havens	headings
haste	haven't ⊙	headland
hasten	having ⊙	headless
hastened	havoc	headlight
hastily	haw	headlights
hasty	hawk	headline
hat	hawker	headlines
hatch	hawkish	headmaster
hatcher	hawks	headphone
hatchet	hay	headquarter □

headquartered ▢	heart	heaviest
headquarters ▢	heartache	heavily
heads	heartaches	heaviness
headstand ☉	heartbeat	heavy
headstone	heartbreak	heavyweight
headstrong	hearten	hectic
headwall	heartened	he'd ☉
headwater	heartening	hedge
headwaters	heartfelt	hedonism
headway	hearth	hedonistic
headwork ☉	hearthside	heed
heady	heartiest	heeded
heal	heartily	heedless
healed	heartless	heel
healer	hearts	heels
health	heartwood	heft
healthful	hearty	hefty
healthfulness	heat	hegemony
healthier	heated	height
healthiest	heatedly	heighten
healthily	heater	heightened
healthy	heaters	heights
heap	heathen	heir
hear	heather	heirs
heard	heating	held
hearer	heave	helicopt
hearing	heaven	helicopter
hearings	heavenly	helicopters
hears	heavenward	heliocentric
hearsay	heavier	heliotrope

helipad	hens	hermit
heliport	hepatitis	hernia
helium	her	herniate
he'll ☉	herald	hero
hello	heralds	heroes
helm	herb	heroic
helmet	herbicide	heroically
helmets	herbicides	heroine
help	herd	heroism
helped	herds	heron
helper	here	herpetologist
helpers	hereabout ☉	herpetology
helpful	hereabouts ☉	herring
helpfully	hereafter ☉	herringbone
helpfulness	hereby ☉	hers
helping	hereditary	herself
helpless	heredity	he's ☉
helplessly	herein ☉	hesitance
helplessness	hereinafter ☉	hesitancy
helpmate	hereinbefore ☉	hesitant
helps	hereof ☉	hesitantly
hem	here's ☉	hesitate
hemisphere	heresy	hesitated
hemorrhage	heretic	hesitatingly
hemorrhoid	hereto	hesitation
hemorrhoids	heretofore	heterogeneity
hems	hereunder	heterogeneous
hen	hereunto	hew
hence	herewith ☉	hex
henceforth	heritage	hexagon

hexagonal	hike	hiring
hexameter	hikes	his ○
heyday	hiking	hiss
hiatus	hilar	histochemistry
hiccup	hilarious	histology
hickory	hilarity	historian
hid	hill	historic
hidden	hills	historical
hide	hillside	historically
hideous	hilly	histories
hideously	hilt	historiography
hideout ⊙	hilum	history
hierarch	him	histrionic
hierarchy	himself	hit
high	hind	hitch
higher	hinder *v.; a.*	hither
highest	hindered	hitherto
highland	hindrance	hits
highlight	hinge	hitter
highlighted	hinges	hitting
highlighting	hint	hive
highlights	hinterland	hoard
highly	hinting	hoarse
highness	hints	hoarsely
highroad	hip	hoarseness
highway	hippodrome	hoax
highwayman	hire	hobbies
highways	hired	hobble
hijack	hirelings	hobby
hijacker	hires	hobo

hock	holy	homogenize
hockey	holystone	homogenized
hod	homage	hone
hoe	home	honed
hog	homecoming	honest
hogan	homefolk	honestly
hogs	homeland	honesty
hogshead	homeless	honey
hoist	homelike	honeybee
hold	homely	honeycomb
holder	homemade	honeymoon
holders	homemaker	honeymooner
holding	homemaking	honeysuckle
holdings	homeowner	hong
holdout ☉	homeowners	honing
holdover	homeroom	honor
holds	homes	honorable
holdup	homesick	honorably
hole	homesickness	honorarium
holes	homesite	honorary
holiday	homespun	honored
holidays	homestead	honoring
holiness	homesteader	honors
hollow	homeward	hood
hollowness	homework ☉	hoodlum
holly	homicidal	hoods
hollyhock	homicide	hoof
holocaust	homogeneity	hook
holography	homogeneous	hooked
holster	homogeneously	hooker

hookup	horrify	hostile
hookups	horror	hostility
hookworm	hors d'oeuvre	hosting
hoop	horse	hostler
hoot	horseback	hosts
hop	horseflesh	hot
hope ⊙	horsehair	hotbed
hoped ⊙	horseless	hotel
hopeful ⊙	horseman	hotels
hopefully ⊙	horsemanship	hothouse
hopefulness ⊙	horsemen	hotly
hopeless ⊙	horseplay	hotter
hopelessly ⊙	horsepower	hottest
hopelessness ⊙	horses	hound
hopes ⊙	horseshoe	hour ⊙
hoping ⊙	horsewoman	hourly ⊙
hopper	hose	hours ⊙
hoppers	hoses	house
horde	hosiery	houseboat
horizon	hospitable	housebreaker
horizons	hospital ⊙	housebroken
horizontal	hospitality ⊙	housecleaning
horizontally	hospitalization ⊙	housecoat
hormone	hospitalize ⊙	housed
horn	hospitalized ⊙	household
horns	hospitals ⊙	householder
horoscope	host	householders
horrible	hostage	housekeeper
horribly	hostelry	housekeepers
horrid	hostess	housekeeping

housemother	human	hundred
houser	humane	hundreds
houses	humanely	hundredth
housewares	humanism	hundredweight
housewife	humanist	hung
housewives	humanistic	hunger
housework ⊙	humanitarian	hungering
housing	humanitarians	hungrier
hovel	humanities	hungry
hover	humanity	hunk
hovercraft	humanize	hunt
hovertrain	humanly	hunter
how ⊙	humans	hunters
however ⊙	humble	hunting
howl	humbly	hurdle
howsoever ⊙	humid	hurdles
hub	humidification	hurl
hubbub	humidify	hurler
huckster	humidity	hurricane
hucksterism	humiliate	hurricanes
huddle	humiliating	hurried
hue	humiliation	hurriedly
huff	humility	hurry
hug	hummock	hurt
huge	humor	hurtful
hula	humorist	hurting
hulk	humorous	hurtle
hull	hump	hurts
hulls	hunch	husband
hum	hunches	husbandry

---

husbands	hydrogen	hyphen
hush	hydrogenate	hyphenate
husk	hydrologic	hypnosis
huskily	hydrology	hypnotic
huskiness	hydrolysis	hypnotically
husky	hydrophobia	hypnotize
hustle	hydroplane	hypoallergenic
hustler	hydrospace	hypocrisy
hut	hydrostatic	hypocrite
huts	hydrostatics	hypocritical
hybrid	hyena	hypodermic
hybridize	hygiene	hypodermics
hybridizer	hygienist	hypothalamic
hybridizers	hymn	hypotheses
hydrant	hymns	hypothesis
hydrants	hyperactive ☉	hypothesize
hydraulic	hyperactivity ☉	hypothetical
hydraulically	hyperbole	hypothyroid
hydro	hyperbolic	hypothyroidism
hydrocarbon	hyperbolically	hysteria
hydrocarbons	hypertension	hysteric
hydrochloride	hyperthyroid	hysterical
hydroelectric	hypertrophy	hysterics

I	
ice	
icebox	
icer	
icicle	
icicles	
icing	
icon	
iconoclasm	
iconoclast	
icy	
I'd ⊙	
idea	
ideal	
idealism	
idealist	
idealistic	
idealists	
idealization	
idealize	
ideally	
ideals	
ideas	
ideation	

ideational	
identical	
identically	
identifiable	
identification	
identifications	
identified	
identifier	
identifies	
identify	
identifying	
identity	
ideological	
ideologist	
ideology	
idiom	
idiomatic	
idiosyncrasy	
idiot	
idiotic	
idiotically	
idle	
idleness	
idler	
idly	
idol	
idolatry	
idolize	
idyl	
idyllic	

if ○	
igloo	
ignite	
ignited	
ignition	
ignorance	
ignorant	
ignore	
ignored	
ignores	
ignoring	
ileum	
iliac	
ill	
I'll ⊙	
illegal	
illegally	
illegible	
illegitimacy	
illegitimate	
illicit	
illiteracy	
illiterate	
illness	
illnesses	
illogical	
ills	
illuminate	
illuminated	
illuminating	

---

icicle	icon	iconoclast	idea	ideal	idealistic	idiot	idiotic	idle	idolatry	idolize	ignorant	illiterate
īsikl	īkon	īkonəklast	īdēə	īdēəl	īdēəlistik	idēət	idēotik	īdl	idolətrē	idolīz	ignərənt	ilitərit

illumination		imbue		immobilize	
illumine		imitate		immoderate	
illusion		imitation		immodest	
illusionary		imitations		immodesty	
illusive		imitative		immoral	
illusory		imitator		immorality	
illustrate □		immaculate		immoralize	
illustrated □		immaterial ⊙		immortal	
illustrates □		immature		immortality	
illustrating □		immaturity		immortalize	
illustration □		immeasurable		immovable	
illustrations □		immeasurably		immune	
illustrative □		immediacy ⊙		immunity	
illustrator □		immediate ○		immunization	
illustrious		immediately ○		immunizations	
I'm ⊙		immemorial		immunize	
image		immense		immunology	
imagery		immensely		immutable	
images		immensity		impact	
imagination		immerse		impacts	
imaginative		immersion		impair	
imagine		immigrant		impaired	
imagined		immigrate		impairment	
imagining		immigrated		impairments	
imbalance		immigration		impairs	
imbecile		imminence		impale	
imbed		imminent		impart ⊙	
imbibe		immobile		imparted ⊙	
imbroglio		immobility		impartial	
imbrue		immobilization		impartiality	

imparts ⊙	imperialist	implication
impassable	imperil	implications
impasse	imperiled	implicit
impassion	imperious	implicitly
impassive	imperiously	implied
impassively	imperishable	implies
impatience	impersonal	implore
impatient	impersonalize	imploringly
impatiently	impersonally	imply
impeach	impersonate	impolite
impeccable	impersonation	impolitic
impeccably	impertinence	imponderable
impedance	impertinent	import
impede	impervious	importance ○
impeded	impetuous	important ○
impedes	impetus	importantly ⊙
impediment	impiety	importation
impel	impinge	imported
impelled	impious	importer
impeller	implacable	importers
impend	implant	importing
impending	implausibility	imports
impenetrable	implausible	importunate
impenetrate	implausibly	importunity
imperative	implement	impose
imperceptible	implementation	imposed
imperfect	implemented	imposes
imperfection	implementing	imposing
imperial	implements	imposition
imperialism	implicate	impositions

impossibility	impressive	impulse
impossible	imprint	impulses
impost	imprinted	impulsive
impotence	imprinting	impulsively
impotency	imprints	impulsivity
impotent	imprison	impunity
impound	imprisoned	impure
impounded	imprisonment	impurities
impounding	improbable ☉	impurity
impoundment	improbably ☉	imputation
impoverish	impromptu	impute
impoverished	improper	in ○
impracticable	improperly	inability
impractical	impropriety	inaccessibility
impracticality	improvable ☉	inaccessible
imprecate	improve ○	inaccuracies
imprecation	improved ☉	inaccuracy
imprecise	improvement ☉	inaccurate
imprecisely	improvements ☉	inaction
impregnable	improves ☉	inactivate ☉
impregnate	improving ☉	inactivation ☉
impregnation	improvisation	inactive ☉
impresario	improvise	inactively ☉
impress	improviser	inactivity ☉
impressed	imprudent	inadequacies
impresser	imprudently	inadequacy
impression	impudence	inadequate
impressionism	impudent	inadequately
impressionist	impudently	inadvertence ▫
impressions	impugn	inadvertent ▫

inadvertently ▫	incapable	incipience
inadvisable ⊙	incapacitant	incipiency
inalienability	incapacitate	incipient
inalienable	incapacitated	incise
inane	incapacity	incision
inanely	incarcerate	incisive
inanimate	incarceration	incisiveness
inapplicable	incarnate	incite
inappropriate	incarnation	incited
inapt	incautious	incitement
inaptly	incendiary	incivil
inaptitude	incense	inclement
inarticulate	incentive	inclination
inasmuch ⊙	incentives	inclinations
inattention ⊙	incept	incline
inattentive	inception	inclined
inaudible	incessant	includable
inaudibly	incessantly	include
inaugural	incest	included
inaugurate	inch	includes
inaugurated	inches	including
inaugurating	inching	inclusion
inauguration	incidence	inclusive
inboard	incident	inclusiveness
inborn	incidental	incoherence
inbound	incidentally	incoherent
inbreed	incidents	incoherently
incalculable	incinerate	income
incandescence	incinerator	incomes
incandescent	incinerators	incoming

incommode	incontestability	incredulous
incomparable	incontestable	incredulously
incomparably	inconvenience ☉	increment
incompatibility	inconvenienced ☉	incremental
incompatible	inconveniencing ☉	increments
incompetence	inconvenient ☉	incretion
incompetent	inconveniently ☉	incriminate
incompetently	inconvertible	incubate
incomplete	incorporate △	incubation
incompletely	incorporated △	incubator
incomprehensible	incorporates △	incubators
incomprehension	incorporating △	inculcate
inconceivable	incorporation △	inculcation
inconceivably	incorporations △	incumbent
inconclusive	incorporator △	incumbents
incongruity	incorporators △	incur
incongruous	incorrect	incurable
inconsequent	incorrectly	incurably
inconsequential	incorrupt	incurred
inconsiderable ☉	incorruptibility	incurring
inconsiderably ☉	incorruptible	incursion
inconsiderate ☉	incorruption	indebted
inconsistency	increase	indebtedness
inconsistent	increased	indecency
inconsistently	increases	indecent
inconsolable	increasing	indecently
inconspicuous	increasingly	indecipherable
inconspicuously	incredible	indecision
inconstancy	incredibly	indecisive
inconstant	incredulity	indecisively

indecisiveness	indexed	indirectness ☉
indecorum	indexes	indiscreet
indeed	indexing	indiscreetly
indefensible	indicate	indiscretion
indefinable	indicated	indiscriminate
indefinite	indicates	indiscriminately
indefinitely	indicating	indispensability
indelible	indication	indispensable
indelibly	indications	indispose
indelicacy	indicative	indisposition
indelicate	indicator	indisputable
indemnification	indicators	indisputably
indemnified	indicia	indissoluble
indemnify	indicium	indistinct ☉
indemnifying	indict	indistinction ☉
indemnity	indicted	indistinctly ☉
indent	indictment	indistinguishable ☉
indentation	indifference	indistinguishably ☉
indentations	indifferent	indite
indented	indigenous	indium
indention	indigent	individual ○
indentions	indigestible	individualism ○
indenture	indigestion	individualist ○
independence	indignant	individualistic ○
independent	indignation	individualists ○
independently	indignity	individuality ○
indescribable	indigo	individualization ○
indestructible	indirect ☉	individualize ○
indeterminate	indirection ☉	individualized ○
index	indirectly ☉	individualizing ☉

individually ⊙	industrialize ⊙	inertia
individuals ⊙	industrialized ⊙	inertial
indivisibility	industrially ⊙	inescapable
indivisible	industries ⊙	inevitability
indoctrinate	industrious ⊙	inevitable
indoctrinating	industriously ⊙	inevitably
indoctrination	industry ⊙	inexact
indolence	inebriate *v.; a., n.*	inexcusable
indolent	inedible	inexhaustible
indolently	ineffective ⊙	inexorable
indomitable	ineffectively ⊙	inexorably
indoor	ineffectiveness ⊙	inexpedient
indoors	ineffectual ⊙	inexpensive ⊙
indubitable	ineffectually ⊙	inexpensively ⊙
induce	inefficiencies	inexperience ⊙
inducement	inefficiency	inexperienced ⊙
inducements	inefficient	inexpert
induct	inelastic	inexplicable
inducted	inelegant	inexplicably
induction	ineligibility	inexpressible
inductive	ineligible	inexpressibly
indulge	inept	inextricable
indulgence	ineptitude	infallibility
indulgent	ineptly	infallible
indulging	inequalities ⊙	infamous
industrial ⊙	inequality ⊙	infamy
industrialism ⊙	inequitable	infancy
industrialist ⊙	inequities	infant
industrialists ⊙	inequity	infantile
industrialization ⊙	inert	infantry

indivisibility	indulge	inebriate	inebriate	inefficient	ineligibility	inequitable	inequity	infamy
indəvizəbɪlətē	indulj	inēbrēāt v.	inēbrēit a., n.	inəfishənt	ineləjəbilətē	inekwətəbl	inekwətē	infəmē

infantryman	infinite	influenza
infantrymen	infinitely	influx
infants	infinitesimal	inform ○
infatuate	infinitive	informal ○
infatuation	infinity	informality ○
infect	infirm	informally ○
infected	infirmary	informant ○
infection	infirmity	information ○
infections	inflame	informational ○
infectious	inflammation	informative ○
infer	inflammatory	informed ○
inference	inflatable	informer ○
inferences	inflate	informing ○
inferential	inflated	informingly ○
inferior	inflation	informs ○
inferiority	inflationary	infraction
infernal	inflect	infractions
infernally	inflection	infrared
inferno	inflexibility	infrasound
inferred	inflexible	infrequent
infertile	inflict	infrequently
infest	inflicted	infringe
infestation	infliction	infringement
infidel	inflow	infringements
infidelity	influence	infuriate
infield	influenced	infuriation
infielder	influences	infuse
infight	influencing	infused
infiltrate	influent	infusion
infiltration	influential	ingenious

ingeniously	inhibition	injunction
ingenuity	inhibitions	injunctive
ingenuous	inhibitor	injure
ingest	inhibitory	injured
ingestion	inhibits	injuries
ingratiate	inhomogeneity	injuring
ingratitude	inhomogeneous	injurious
ingredient	inhospitable	injury
ingredients	inhuman	injustice ⊙
ingress	inhumane	ink
inguinal	inhumanity	inked
inhabit	inimical	inking
inhabitant	iniquitous	inkling
inhabitants	iniquity	inks
inhabitation	initial	inlaid
inhalation	initialed	inland
inhale	initially	inlay
inhaler	initials	inlet
inharmonious	initiate	inlets
inharmony	initiated	inmate
inhaul	initiates	inmates
inhere	initiating	inn
inherence	initiation	innate
inherent	initiative	inner ⊙
inherently	initiator	innermost ⊙
inherit	initiators	innerspring ⊙
inheritance	inject	innervate
inherited	injected	innkeeper
inheritor	injection	innkeepers
inhibit	injects	innocence

innocent	inquiry	inserted
innocently	inquisition	inserting
innocuous	inquisitive	insertion
innovate	inquisitor	insertions
innovation	inroad	inserts
innovations	inroads	inset
innovative	inrush	inshore
inns	insane	inside
innuendo	insanely	insider
innumerable	insanity	insidious
inoculate	insatiable	insidiously
inoculating	inscribe	insight
inoculation	inscribed	insightful
inoffensive	inscript	insights
inoperable	inscription	insigne
inopportune	inscriptions	insignia
inordinate	inscrutability	insignificance ▢
inordinately	inscrutable	insignificant ▢
inorganic	insect	insignificantly ▢
inpatient	insecticide	insincere
input	insecticides	insincerely △
inputs	insects	insinuate
inquest	insecure	insinuated
inquire	insecurity	insinuation
inquired	insensibility	insipid
inquirer	insensible	insipidly
inquirers	insensitive	insist
inquires	inseparable	insisted
inquiries	insert	insistence
inquiring	insertable	insistent

insisting	installer	institutions
insists	installing	instruct ⊙
insofar ⊙	installment	instructed ⊙
insole	installments	instructing ⊙
insolence	instance	instruction ⊙
insolent	instances	instructional ⊙
insolently	instant	instructions ⊙
insolubility	instantaneous	instructive ⊙
insoluble	instantaneously	instructor ⊙
insomnia	instantly	instructors ⊙
inspect ⊙	instate ⊙	instructs ⊙
inspected ⊙	instated ⊙	instrument
inspecting ⊙	instead	instrumental
inspection ⊙	instigate	instrumentalist
inspections ⊙	instigated	instrumentalities
inspector ⊙	instigation	instrumentality
inspectorate ⊙	instigator	instrumentally
inspectors ⊙	instill	instrumentation
inspects ⊙	instillation	instrumentations
inspiration	instinct	instruments
inspirational	instinctive	insubordinate
inspire	instinctual	insubordination
inspired	institute	insubstantial
inspiring	instituted	insufferable
instability	institutes	insufferably
instable	instituting	insufficiency
install	institution	insufficient
installation	institutional	insufficiently
installations	institutionalization	insular
installed	institutionalize	insularity

insulate	intangible	intension
insulated	intangibles	intensional
insulating	integer	intensionally
insulation	integral	intensity
insulator	integrate _v.; a._	intensive
insulin	integrated	intensively
insult	integration	intent
insultingly	integrity	intention
insuperable	intellect	intentional
insuperably	intellectual	intentionally
insupportable	intellectually	intentions
insurability ⊙	intellectuals	intently
insurable ⊙	intelligence	intents
insurance ⊙	intelligent	inter
insurant ⊙	intelligently	interact
insure ⊙	intelligentsia	interacting
insured ⊙	intelligible	interaction
insureds ⊙	intemperance	interagency
insurer ⊙	intemperate	interbranch
insurers ⊙	intend	intercede
insures ⊙	intendant	interceded
insurge	intended	intercept
insurgence	intending	interceptor
insurgent	intends	intercession
insuring ⊙	intense	interchange ⊙
insurmountable	intensely	interchangeability ⊙
insurrect	intensification	interchangeable ⊙
insurrection	intensified	interchanged ⊙
intact	intensifier	interchanges ⊙
intake	intensify	interchanging ⊙

intercity	interfaith	intermarriage
interclass	interfere	intermarry
intercoastal	interfered	intermedia
intercollege	interference	intermediary
intercollegiate	interfering	intermediate
intercom	interferometer	intermediates
intercommunication	intergovernmental ⊙	interment
intercompany ⊙	intergroup	intermesh
interconnect	interim	interminable
interconnected	interior	intermission
interconnection	interiors	intermittence
interconnections	interject	intermittent
intercontinental	interlace	intermittently
intercorporate	interlacing	intermix
intercourse	interlay	intermodal
interdenominational	interlayer	intermountain
interdepartmental ⊙	interleaf	intern
interdependence	interleave	internal
interdependent	interleaved	internally
interdict	interlibrary	international
interdisciplinary	interline	internationalist
interest ○	interlineal	internationalize
interested ⊙	interlinear	internationally
interestedly ⊙	interlobular	internist
interesting ⊙	interlock	internists
interestingly ⊙	interlocker	internship
interests ⊙	interlockers	internships
interface	interlocutor	interoffice
interfacial	interlocutory	interpenetrate
interfacing	interlude	interpersonal

interplane	interruptible	interwoven
interplanetary	interrupting	intestate
interplant	interruption	intestinal
interplanted	interruptions	intestine
interplay	interscholastic	intima
interpolate	intersect	intimacy
interpolation	intersection	intimate *a., n.; v.*
interpose	intersections	intimately
interposition	intersensory	intimation
interpret	intersperse	intimidate
interpretable	interspersed	intimidating
interpretation	interstage	intimidation
interpretations	interstate ⊙	into
interpretative	interstellar	intolerable
interpreted	interstice	intolerance
interpreter	interstitial	intolerant
interpreting	intertwine	intonation
interpretive	interval	intone
interprets	intervals	intoxicant
interrelate	intervene	intoxicate
interrelated	intervening	intractable
interrelation	intervention	intradepartmental ⊙
interrelationship	intervertebral	intragroup
interrelationships	interview	intramural
interrogate	interviewed	intramurals
interrogation	interviewer	intransigence
interrogative	interviewers	intransigent
interrogator	interviewing	intrastate ⊙
interrupt	interviews	intravenous
interrupted	interweave	intrepid

interplanetary — intərplanəterē
interpolate — intérpəlāt
interpolation — intérpəlāshən
interposition — intərpəzishən
interpreter — intérprətər
interrogate — interəgāt
intimate — intəmit *a., n.*
intimate — intəmāt *v.*

intricate	intubated	inventories
intricately	intuit	inventors
intrigue	intuition	inventory
intrigued	intuitive	inverse
intriguing	intuitively	inversely
intriguingly	inundate	inversion
intrinsic	inundated	invert
intrinsical	inundation	inverted
intrinsically	inure	invest
introduce	invade	invested
introduced	invaded	investigate
introduces	invader	investigated
introducing	invaders	investigating
introduction	invalid	investigation
	a., n., v.; a.	
introductions	invalidate	investigations
introductory	invalided	investigative
introject	invaluable ⊙	investigator
introjection	invariable	investigators
introspect	invariably	investigatory
introspection	invariant	investing
introspective	invasion	investment
introversion	invasions	investments
introvert	inveigh	investor
introverted	invent	investors
intrude	invented	inveteracy
intruder	invention	inveterate
intruding	inventions	inviable
intrusion	inventive	invigorate
intrusive	inventor	invigoration
intubate	inventoried	invincibility

invincible	involves	ironers	
inviolability	involving	ironic	
inviolable	invulnerability	ironical	
inviolate	invulnerable	ironically	
invisibility	inward	ironing	
invisible	inwardly	irons	
invisibly	inwardness	ironside	
invitation ☉	iodate	ironwork ☉	
invitational ☉	iodic	ironworker ☉	
invitations ☉	iodide	irony	
invite ☉	iodinate	irradiate	
invited ☉	iodine	irradiation	
invitees ☉	iodize	irrational	
invites ☉	ion	irrationality	
inviting ☉	ionic	irrationally	
invitingly ☉	ionize	irreconcilable	
invocate	ionizing	irrecoverable	
invocation	ionosphere	irredeemable	
invoice	ionospheric	irredeemably	
invoiced	irate	irreducible	
invoices	ire	irregular ☉	
invoicing	iridic	irregularities ☉	
invoke	iridium	irregularity ☉	
involuntarily	iris	irregularly ☉	
involuntary	irk	irregulars ☉	
involute	irksome	irrelevance	
involution	iron	irrelevant	
involve	ironclad	irremediable	
involved	ironed	irremovable	
involvement	ironer	irreparable	

irreparably		irritate		issuance ⊙	
irreplaceable		irritating		issue ⊙	
irresistible		irritation		issued ⊙	
irresistibly		irrupt		issues ⊙	
irresolute		irruption		issuing ⊙	
irresolution		is ⊙		it ⊙	
irresolvable		island		italic	
irrespective ⊙		islander		italicize	
irresponsibility ⊙		islands		itch	
irresponsible ⊙		isle		itching	
irresponsibly ⊙		isles		item	
irresponsive ⊙		isn't ⊙		itemization	
irretraceable		isobutane		itemize	
irretrievable		isolate		itemized	
irreverence		isolated		itemizing	
irreverent		isolates		items	
irreversible		isolating		iterate	
irreversibly		isolation		iteration	
irrevocable		isolationism		itineracy	
irrevocably		isolationist		itinerant	
irrigate		isometrics		itineraries	
irrigating		isoprene		itinerary	
irrigation		isopropyl		its ⊙	
irrigations		isotone		it's ⊙	
irritability		isotonic		itself ⊙	
irritable		isotope		I've ⊙	
irritably		isotropic		ivory	
irritant		isotropy		ivy	

J

jab		jargon		jejunely	
jabberings		jargonize		jell	
jack		jarringly		jelled	
jacket		jars		jelly	
jacketing		jasmine		jellybean	
jackets		jasper		jellyroll	
jacks		jato		jenny	
jaculate		jaunt		jeopard	
jade		jauntier		jeopardize	
jag		jauntily		jeopardized	
jaggedly		jaunty		jeopardizing	
jaguar		javelin		jeopardy	
jail		jaw		jerk	
jailed		jawbone		jerkily	
jailer		jawless		jerkin	
jailhouse		jaws		jerkiness	
jam		jay		jerky	
jamboree		jazz		jersey	
jammed		jazzier		jerseys	
jangle		jazzy		jest	
jangly		jealous		jester	
janitor		jealously		jestingly	
janitorial		jealousy		jet	
jar		jean		jetboat	
		jeans		jetborne	
		jeep		jetliner	
		jeepload		jetport	
		jeer		jets	
		jeerer		jetsam	
		jejune		jetting	

jettison	jocosely	jolly
jetty	jocular	jolt
jewel	jocularly	jostle
jeweler	jocund	jostlement
jewelers	jocundity	jot
jewelry	jog	jounce
jewels	jogger	jouncy
jib	jogging	journal
jibe	joggle	journalism
jig	jogs	journalist
jigger	jogtrot	journalistic
jiggle	join	journalists
jigtime ⊙	joinder	journals
jingle	joined	journey
jingler	joiner	journeyman
jingling	joining	journeys
jingo	joinings	jovial
jingoism	joins	joviality
jinx	joint	jovially
jitter	jointless	jowl
jitters	jointly	jowliness
jittery	joints	joy
job	joist	joyful
jobber	joists	joyfully
jobbers	joke	joyless
jobbing	joker	joyous
jobholder	jokes	jubilance
jobs	jokingly	jubilant
jockey	jollier	jubilantly
jocose	jolliest	jubilation

J

---

jubilee	jumble	jurist
judge	jumbo	juror
judged	jump	jurors
judges	jumped	jury
judgeship	jumper	just ○
judging	jumpy	justice ⊙
judgment	junction	justices ⊙
judgments	juncture	justifiable ⊙
judicable	jungle	justifiably ⊙
judicial	jungly	justification ⊙
judiciary	junior	justifications ⊙
judicious	juniors	justified ⊙
jug	junk	justifies ⊙
juggle	junket	justify ⊙
juggler	junketeer	justifying ⊙
juice	junky	justly ⊙
juices	junta	justness ⊙
juiciest	juries	jut
juicy	jurisdiction	juvenile
juke	jurisdictional	juveniles
julep	jurisdictions	juxtapose
julienne	jurisprudence	juxtaposition

K

kainite	keep	ketone
kale	keeper	ketosis
kaleidoscope	keeping	kettle
kalium	keeps	kettledrum
kamacite	keepsake	key
kangaroo	keg	keyboard
kaolin	kegs	keyboards
kapok	kelep	keyed
²karat	keloid	keyhole
karate	kelp	keyman
karst	kelpie	keynote
karyoplasm	kemp	keynoter
karyosome	kempt	keypunch
katydid	kendo	keypunching
kava	kennel	keys
kayak	kennelman	keystone
kazoo	kennelmaster	keystroke
keel	kenning	keystrokes
keelboat	keno	keyway
keelless	kept	khaki
keen	keratin	kick
keener	keratinize	kickback
keenest	keratoid	kickbacks
keenly	kerchief	kicked
	kermes	kicker
	kernel	kickoff
	kerosene	kicks
	kersey	kid
	kestrel	kidded
	ketch	kidding

kidnap	kindnesses	klaxon
kidney	kindred	klister
kids	kinds	knack
kill	kinescope	knacker
killable	kinesiology	knapsack
killed	kinesthetic	knave
killer	kinesthetically	knead
killers	kinetic	kneaded
killing	king	knee
kills	kingcraft	kneebend
kiln	kingdom	kneecap
kilo	kingly	kneel
kilocycle	kingpin	kneepad
kilogram	kink	kneepan
kiloliter	kinker	knelt
kilometer	kinking	knew
kilovolt	kinky	knickers
kilowatt	kinship	knickknack
kilowatts	kinsman	knife
kilt	kipper	knight
kimono	kiss	knighthood
kin	kit	knightly
kind	kitchen	knit
kinder	kitchenette	knives
kindergarten	kitchenettes	knob
kindest	kitchens	knobs
kindle	kite	knock
kindliness	kits	knockabout ⊙
kindly	kitten	knockdown ⊙
kindness	kitty	knocked

kiln	kilocycle	kilogram	kiloliter	kilometer	kilowatt	kimono	kindergarten	kindliness	kinesthetic	klaxon
kiln	kiləsĭkl	kiləgram	kiləlētər	kiləmētər	kiləwot	kəmōnə	kindərgärtn	kĭndlēnis	kĭnəsthetik	klaksən

knocker	knotwork ⊙	knuckle
knocking	know	kola
knockout ⊙	knowing	kopeck
knockouts ⊙	knowingly	kosher
knocks	knowledge	krill
knoll	knowledgeability	krona
knot	knowledgeable	kroon
knothole	known	kulak
knotty	knows	

lab	lack	lags
label	lackadaisical	laid
labeled	lacked	lain
labeling	lackey	lair
labels	lacking	laity
labor	lacks	lake
laboratories	lacquer	lakefront
laboratory	lacrosse	lakes
laborer	lactate	lakeshore
laborers	lactation	lakeside
laborious	lacteal	lamb
laboriously	lactic	lambent
labors	lactose	lambs
labs	lacy	lame
labyrinth	lad	lamely
lace	ladder	lament
lacerate	ladders	lamentable
laceration	lade	lamentation
lacerations	laden	laminar
lacerator	ladies	laminate
laces	lading	laminated
lacework ⊙	ladle	laminating
laches	ladleful	lamination
lacily	lads	lamp
	lady	lamplight
	ladybird	lampoon
	ladylike	lamps
	lag	lance
	lager	lancer
	lagoon	land

landau	lantern	lash
landed	lap	lasher
landholder	lapel	lass
landing	lapidarian	lassie
landings	lapidary	lassitude
landlady	lapped	lasso
landlock	lapping	last
landlocked	lapse	lasted
landlord	lapsed	lasting
landlords	lapses	lastly
landmark	larcenist	lasts
landmarks	larceny	latch
landowner	larch	latchkey
landowners	lard	latchstring
landplane	larder	late
lands	large	latecomer
landscape	largely	lately
landscaped	larger	latency
landscaping	largest	latent
landslide	largo	later
lane	lariat	lateral
lanes	larine	lateralize
language	lark	laterally
languages	larkspur	latest
languid	laroid	latex
languish	larva	lathe
laning	larvae	lather
lank	larynx	lathes
lanky	lascivious	lathwork ⊙
lanolin	laser	latitude

latitudinal	lavatory	layman
latrine	lavender	laymen
latter	lavish	layoff
lattice	lavishly	layoffs
latticework ☉	lavishness	layout ☉
laud	law	layouts ☉
laudability	lawful	layover
laudable	lawfully	laziest
laudably	lawless	lazily
laudation	lawmaker	laziness
laudatory	lawmakers	lazy
lauded	lawman	leach
laugh	lawmen	leaching
laughingly	lawn	lead
laughter	lawns	leaden
launch	laws	leader
launched	lawsuit	leaderless
launches	lawsuits	leaders
launching	lawyer	leadership
launchings	lawyers	leading
launder	lax	leads
laundered	laxative	leaf
laundering	laxity	leafiest
laundries	laxness	leaflet
laundry	lay	leaflets
laundryman	layaway	leafy
laureate	layer	league
laurel	layers	leaguer
lava	layette	leagues
lavatorial	laying	leak

leakage	leathery	legally
leaked	leave	legate
leakproof	leaven	legatee
leaks	leaves	legation
leaky	leaving	legend
lean	lecher	legendary
leaner	lechery	leggings
leaning	lectern	leggy
leap	lecture	legibility
leaps	lecturer	legible
learn	lectures	legibly
learned	led	legion
learner	ledge	legislate □
learners	ledger	legislated □
learning	ledgers	legislating □
learnings	leer	legislation □
learns	leeward	legislations □
lease	leeway	legislative □
leased	left	legislator □
leasehold	leftist	legislators □
leaseholder	leftover	legislature □
leaseholders	leftovers	legislatures □
leases	leg	legitimacy
leash	legacy	legitimate _a.; v._
leasing	legal	legitimately
least	legalistic	legitimize
leather	legality	legs
leathercraft	legalization	legume
leathers	legalize	legumes
leatherwork ⊙	legalized	leguminous

leisure	leprosy	letters ⊙
leisureliness	lesion	letting
leisurely	lesions	lettuce
lemon	less	leukemia
lemonade	lessee	levant
lemons	lessees	levee
lemur	lessen	level
lend	lessened	leveled
lender	lessens	leveling
lenders	lesser	levels
lending	lesson	lever
length	lessons	leverage
lengthen	lessor	levers
lengthened	lessors	levied
lengthier	lest	levies
lengthiest	let	levitate
lengthily	lethal	levity
lengths	lethality	levy
lengthwise	lethargy	lewd
lengthy	lets	lewdly
lenience	let's	lexicon
leniency	letter ⊙	liabilities
lenient	lettered ⊙	liability
leniently	lettergram ⊙	liable
lens	letterhead ⊙	liaison
lenses	letterheads ⊙	liar
lent	lettering ⊙	libel
lentil	letterman ⊙	libelant
lentoid	lettermen ⊙	libelous
leper	letterpress ⊙	liberal

liberalism	lick	lighten
liberality	licked	lighter
liberalization	licking	lightest
liberalize	lid	lighthouse
liberalized	lids	lighting
liberally	lie	lightly
liberals	lien	lightness
liberate	liens	lightning
liberation	lies	lights
liberator	lieu	lightweight
libertarian	lieutenancy	lignite
libertine	lieutenant	lignites
liberty	life	likable
libido	lifeboat	like
librarian	lifeguard	liked
librarians	lifeless	likelihood
libraries	lifelike	likely
library	lifelong	liken
libretto	lifesaving	likeness
lice	lifetime ☉	likes
license	lifework ☉	likewise
licensed	lift	liking
licensee	lifted	lilac
licensees	lifting	lilt
licenses	lifts	liltingly
licensing	ligament	lily
licensure ☉	ligate	limb
lichen	ligation	limber
lichenoid	light	limbo
licit	lighted	limbs

lime	lineation	lintels
limed	linebacker	lion
limekiln	lined	lions
limelight	lineman	lip
limerick	linemen	lipoid
limestone	linen	lipoma
liminal	linens	lipstick
limit	lineout ☉	liquefaction
limitation	liner	liquefy
limitations	liners	liquid
limited	lines	liquidate
limiting	linesman	liquidated
limitless	linger	liquidating
limits	lingerie	liquidation
limousine	lingeringly	liquidations
limousines	lingo	liquidator
limp	linguist	liquidity
limpid	linguistic	liquids
limpidity	linguistics	liquor
limping	liniment	lira
limply	lining	lisle
limpness	link	lisp
linden	linkage	lissome
line	linked	list
lineage	linking	listed
lineal	links	listen
lineality	linoleum	listened
linear	linseed	listener
linearity	lint	listeners
linearly	lintel	listening

lister	liturgy	loanable
listing	livability	loaned
listings	livable	loaner
listless	live *a.; v.*	loaning
listlessly	lived *a.; v.*	loans
lists	livelier	loathe
lit	liveliest	loathsome
liter	livelihood	loaves
literacy	liveliness	lobar
literal	livelong	lobate
literally	lively	lobation
literalness	liver	lobbies
literary	livery	lobby
literate	lives *n.; v.*	lobbying
literature	livestock	lobbyist
lithe	livid	lobe
lithesome	lividly	loblolly
lithograph	living	lobster
lithographed	load	lobular
lithographer	loaded	lobule
lithographers	loader	local
lithographic	loading	locale
lithography	loads	localism
litigant	loaf	localities
litigate	loafer	locality
litigation	loafers	localization
litter	loafing	localize
little	loam	localized
littlest	loamy	locally
liturgical	loan	locals

locate	lofty	loner
located	log	lonesome
locater	logarithm	lonesomely
locating	loge	long
location	loges	longboat
locations	logger	longer
lock	logging	longest
locked	logic	longevity
locker	logical	longhand
lockers	logically	longhorn
locking	logistic	longing
lockout ☉	logistical	longingly
locks	logistics	longish
lockup	logo	longitude
locomotion	logotype	longitudinal
locomotive	logotypes	longitudinally
locomotives	logroll	longleaf
locomotor	logrolling	longs
locus	logs	longshore
locust	loin	longshoreman
locution	loincloth	longshoremen
lodge	loiter	look
lodged	loiterer	looked
lodges	loll	looking
lodging	lollipop	⁕ lookout ☉
lodgings	lone	looks
lodgment	lonelier	loom
loft	loneliest	loon
loftily	loneliness	loop
loftiness	lonely	looped

looper	lot	low
loophole	lotion	lower
loopholes	lots	lowered
loops	lottery	lowering
loose	loud	lowers
loosely	louder	lowest
loosen	loudest	lowland
looseness	loudly	lowliest
loosening	loudspeaker	lows
loosens	lounge	loyal
loot	lounges	loyalist
looting	loungewear	loyally
lop	louse	loyalty
lope	loused	lozenge
loper	lousiness	lube
lopsided	lousy	lubricant
lord	lout	lubricants
lordly	lovable	lubricate
lords	love	lubricated
lordship	loved	lubricating
lore	loveless	lubrication
lorry	loveliest	lubricity
lose	loveliness	lucid
loser	lovelorn	lucidity
losers	lovely	lucidly
loses	lover	luck
losing	lovers	luckily
loss	loves	lucky
losses	loving	lucrative
lost	lovingly	ludicrous

luff		lunar		luster	
lug		lunatic		lusterless	
luger		lunch		lustful	
luggage		luncheon		lustily	
lukewarm		luncheons		lustiness	
lull		lunches		lustrous	
lullaby		lunchroom		lusty	
lumbar		lung		luxuriance	
lumber		lunge		luxurious	
lumberman		lungs		luxury	
luminary		lurch		lyceum	
luminescence		lurcher		lying	
luminescent		lure		lymph	
luminosity		lures		lymphatic	
luminous		lurid		lynch	
lump		lurk		lyric	
lumped		luscious		lyrical	
lumpy		lush			
lunacy		lust			

M

machine	machined	machinery	machines	machining	machinist	machinists	mackerel	mackinaw	macrocommunication	macroeconomic ⊙	macroeconomics ⊙	macromolecular	macromolecule	macron	macronutrient	macronutrients	mad	madam	madden	made	madhouse	madly	madman

machine
machined
machinery
machines
machining
machinist
machinists
mackerel
mackinaw
macrocommunication
macroeconomic ⊙
macroeconomics ⊙
macromolecular
macromolecule
macron
macronutrient
macronutrients
mad
madam
madden
made
madhouse
madly
madman

madmen
madness
madrigal
maestro
magazine
magazines
maggot
magic
magical
magically
magician
magisterial
magistrate
magistrates
magnanimity
magnanimous
magnate
magnet
magnetic
magnetical
magnetically
magnetism
magnetize
magneto
magnetosphere
magnification
magnificence □
magnificent □
magnificently □
magnified

magnifies
magnify
magnifying
magnitude
magnum
magpie
mahogany
maid
maiden
maids
mail
mailability
mailable
mailbox
mailed
mailer
mailers
mailing
mailings
mailman
mailroom
mails
main
mainland
mainline
mainliner
mainly
mains
mainstay
mainstream

maintain	malediction	mamma
maintained	maleness	mammal
maintaining	males	mammalian
maintains	malevolence	mammalogy
maintenance	malevolent	mammoth
maize	malfeasance	man
majestic	malfeasant	mana
majestical	malformation ⊙	manage
majestically	malformations ⊙	manageable
majesty	malformed ⊙	managed
major	malfunction	management
majored	malfunctions	managements
majoring	malgovernment ⊙	manager
majority	malice	managerial
majors	malicious	managers
make	maliciously	manages
maker	malign	managing
makers	malignancies	mandarin
makes	malignancy	mandate
makeshift	malignant	mandatory
makeup	malinger	maneuver
making	malingerer	maneuverability
maladjusted ⊙	mall	maneuvered
maladjustment ⊙	malleability	maneuvering
malady	malleable	maneuvers
malaise	malnourished	mangle
malaria	malnutrition	manhood
malarial	malpractice	mania
male	malt	maniac
maledict	malty	maniacal

manic	mansion	marcasite
manifest	manslaughter	marcel
manifestation	mantel	march
manifestations	mantelet	marching
manifestly	mantelpiece	margarine
manifold	mantle	margin
manifolds	mantling	marginal
manikin	manual	marginality
manila	manually	marginally
manipulate	manuals	margins
manipulating	manufacture ☉	marijuana
manipulation	manufactured ☉	marina
manipulations	manufacturer ☉	marinas
manipulator	manufacturers ☉	marinate
mankind	manufactures ☉	marine
manlike	manufacturing ☉	mariner
manliness	manure	marines
manly	manurial	marionette
manned	manuscript	marital
manner	manuscripts	maritally
mannerism	many	maritime
mannerisms	map	mark
mannerly	maple	markdown ☉
manning	mapping	markdowns ☉
manometer	maps	marked
manometric	mar	markedly
manor	maraud	marker
manorial	marauder	markers
manpower	marble	market
manservant ☉	marbles	marketability

marketable	marshy	masseuse
marketed	mart	massive
marketing	martial	mast
marketings	martially	master
markets	martingale	mastered
marking	martini	masterful
markings	martyr	masterfully
marks	martyrdom	mastering
marksman	marvel	masterly
marksmanship	marvelous	mastermind
markup	marvelously	masterpiece
markups	mascara	masterpieces
marlin	masculine	masterplate
marmalade	masculinity	masters
maroon	mash	masterwork ☉
marooner	masher	mastery
marquee	mask	mastic
marquees	masking	masticate
marred	mason	mastication
marriage	masonic	mastiff
married	masonry	mastodon
marrow	masons	mastodonic
marrowbone	masque	mastoid
marrowy	masquerade	mastoids
marry	mass	mat
marsh	massacre	match
marshal	massage	matched
marshalcy	massed	matches
marshland	masses	matching
marshmallow	masseur	matchless

marksman	maroon	marquee	martingale	martyrdom	masculine	masonic	masquerade	massacre	masticate	mastodon
märksmən (man)	mərün	märkē	märtngāl	märtərdəm	maskülin	məsonik	maskərād	masəkər	mastəkāt	mastədon

mate		mats		mayonnaise	
material ○		matter		mayor	
materialism ○		matters		mayoral	
materialistic ○		mattress		mayors	
materialize ○		mattresses		mayorship	
materialized ○		maturate		maze	
materially ○		maturation		mazy	
materials ○		mature		me	
matériel		matured		mead	
maternal		matures		meadow	
maternally		maturing		meadows	
maternity		maturities		meager	
math □		maturity		meal	
mathematic □		maul		meals	
mathematical □		mauler		mealtime ○	
mathematically □		mausolean		mean	
mathematician □		mausoleum		meander	
mathematics □		maverick		meanderingly	
matinee		maw		meanest	
mating		mawkish		meaning	
matriarch		maxim		meaningful	
matriarchal		maximal		meaningfully	
matrices		maximization		meaningfulness	
matriculate		maximize		meaningless	
matriculation		maximizing		meanings	
matrimonial		maximum		meanness	
matrimony		may		means	
matrix		maybe ○		meant	
matron		mayflower		meantime ○	
matronly		mayhem		meanwhile ○	

measle	mediator	megalomania
measles	mediators	megaton
measurable	medicaid	megawatt
measurably	medical	megawatts
measure	medically	melancholia
measured	medicare	melancholy
measurement	medicate	melanoma
measurements	medication	melanomas
measures	medications	meld
measuring	medicenter	melee
meat	medicinal	meliorate
meats	medicine	melioration
meaty	medicines	mellow
mechanic	medieval	mellower
mechanical	medievally	melodial
mechanically	mediocre	melodic
mechanics	mediocrity	melodically
mechanism	meditate	melodious
mechanist	meditation	melodrama
mechanistic	meditative	melodramatic
mechanization	medium	melody
mechanize	mediumistic	melon
medal	medley	melt
medalist	meek	melting
medallion	meekest	member
meddle	meet	members
media	meeting	membership
median	meetings	memberships
mediate	meets	membrane
v.; a.	megacycle	memento
mediation		

memo	mentor	meridian
memoir	menu	meridional
memorabilia	menus	merit
memorable	mercantile	merited
memorandum	mercenary	meritorious
memorandums	mercerize	merits
memorial	mercerized	mermaid
memorialize	merchandise ○	merman
memorializing	merchandised ☉	merrier
memories	merchandiser ☉	merriest
memorization	merchandisers ☉	merriment
memorize	merchandising ☉	merry
memory	merchant	merrymaking
memos	merchantable	mesh
men	merchants	meshed
menace	merciful	meshwork ○
menacingly	mercifully	mesmerism
menagerie	merciless	mesmerize
mend	mercilessly	mess
mendacious	mercurial	message
mended	mercurialize	messages
mending	mercury	messenger
menfolk	mercy	messengers
mental	mere	messy
mentality	merely	met
mentally	merest	metabolic
mention	merge	metabolism
mentioned	merged	metabolite
mentioning	merger	metabolize
mentions	mergers	metal

memoir	memorial	memorialize	menace	menagerie	mercenary	merciless	merger	meridian	meritorious	metabolic
memwär	məmôrēəl	məmôrēəlīz	menis	mənajərē	mérsənerē	mérsilis	mérjər	məridēən	merətôrēəs	metəbolik

metallic	method	microcard
metallurgical	methodical	microchemical
metallurgist	methodically	microchemistry
metals	methodological	microcircuit
metalwork ⊙	methodology	microcircuitry
metalworker ⊙	methods	microcircuits
metalworkers ⊙	meticulous	microcommunication
metalworking ⊙	meticulously	microcopy
metamorphic	métier	microcosm
metamorphose	metric	microcosmical
metamorphosis	metrical	microcrystal
metaphor	metrically	microcrystals
metaphoric	metricate	microdot
metaphorical	metrication	microecology
metaphysic	metro	microeconomic ⊙
metaphysical	metrology	microeconomics ⊙
metaphysics	metronome	microelectronics
mete	metropolis	microfiche
meteor	metropolitan	microfilm
meteoric	metroport	microfilmed
meteorite	metroports	microfilming
meteoritic	mettle	microfossil
meteorological	mettlesome	microgroove
meteorology	mew	micrometeor
meter	mezzanine	micrometeorite
metered	mica	micrometer
metering	mice	micromotion
meters	micro	micron
methadone	microbe	microphone
methane	microbiology	microphones

microscope	midweek	militarily
microscopic	midwestern	militarism
microscopical	midwife	militarist
microscopically	midwinter	militarize
microscopy	midwives	military
microsecond	midyear	militate
microstate ⊙	mien	militia
microteach	might	milk
microteaching	mightier	milking
microwatt	mightiest	milkman
microwave	mightily	milky
mid	mighty	mill
midcontinent	migrant	millennial
midday	migrate	millennium
middle	migration	miller
middleman	migratory	millers
middlemen	mild	milligram
middling	milder	milligrams
middlings	mildest	milliliter
midfield	mildew	millimeter
midland	mildly	millinery
midlands	mildness	milling
midline	mile	million
midnight	mileage	millionaire
midpoint	miler	millions
midseason	miles	millionth
midsemester	milestone	millrace
midst	milestones	mills
midsummer	militant	millstone
midway	militantly	millwork ⊙

mimeograph	mingle	mint
mimeographed	mini	minter
mimeographing	miniature	mints
mimesis	miniatures	minuet
mimetic	miniaturization	minus
mimetically	miniaturize	minute
mimic	miniaturized	*n.; a.*
minar	minibus	minuteman
minaret	minimal	minutemen
mince	minimally	minutes
mincing	minimize	minutia
mind	minimized	minutiae
minded	minimizes	miracle
minder	minimizing	miracles
mindful	minimum	miraculous
minding	mining	miraculously
mindless	miniskirt	mirage
minds	ministate ⊙	mire
mine	minister	miriness
mined	ministerial	mirror
miner	ministers	mirrors
mineral	ministration	mirth
mineralogical	ministry	mirthless
mineralogist	mink	misalign
mineralogy	minor	misalignment
minerals	minorities	misanthrope
miners	minority	misanthropic
mines	minors	misapplication
minesweeper	minstrel	misapply
minesweepers	minstrelsy	misapprehend
		misapprehension

misbehave	misdirection ☉	misinterpretation
misbehavior	misemploy ☉	misinterpreted
misbrand	misemployment ☉	misinterpreter
miscalculate	miser	misjudge
miscalculated	miserable	mislabel
miscalculation	miserably	mislabeled
miscall	miserly	mislaid
miscarriage	misery	mislay
miscarry	misevaluation ☉	mislead
miscellanea	misfile	misleading
miscellaneous	misfiled	misled
miscellany	misfire	mislike
mischance	misfit	mismanage
mischief	misform ☉	mismanaging
mischievous	misfortune	mismatch
misconceive	misgive	mismatched
misconception	misgivings	mismate
misconceptions	misgovern ☉	misname
misconduct	misgovernment ☉	misnamed
misconstruction ☉	misguide	misnomer
misconstrue	misguided	misplace
miscount ☉	mishandle	misplaced
miscreant	mishandled	misplacement
miscreate	mishandling	misprint
miscue	mishap	mispronounce
misdeed	mishaps	mispronunciation
misdemean	misinform ☉	misquotation
misdemeanor	misinformation ☉	misquote
misdirect ☉	misinformer ☉	misread
misdirecting ☉	misinterpret	misreading

misrepresent ☉		mistakes		mixtures	
misrepresentation ☉		mister △		moan	
misrepresented ☉		mistier		mob	
misrepresents ☉		mistiness		mobile	
misroute		mistletoe		mobility	
misrouted		mistook		mobilization	
misrule		mistreat		mobilize	
miss		mistreatment		mobilizing	
missed		mistress		moccasin	
misses		mistrial		mock	
misshape		mistrust		mockery	
misshapen		misty		mockingly	
missile		misunderstand ☉		modal	
missilery		misunderstanding ☉		modality	
missiles		misunderstandings ☉		mode	
missing		misunderstood		model	
mission		misuse		modeling	
missionaries		misused		models	
missionary		mite		moderate	
missions		miter		*v.; a., n.*	
missive		mitered		moderated	
misspell		mitigate		moderately	
misspelled		mitigation		moderating	
misstate ☉		mitigative		moderation	
misstatement ☉		mitten		moderator	
misstep		mix		modern	
mist		mixed		modernism	
mistake		mixer		modernist	
mistaken		mixing		modernistic	
mistakenly		mixture		modernity	
				modernization	

---

misroute	miss	missile	misspell	misstep	mistake	mistiness	mistletoe	mistrust	misty	mix	moderate	moderate
misrüt	mis	misl	misspel	misstep	mistāk	mistēnis	misltō	mistrust	mistē	miks	modərāt *v.*	modərit *a., n.*

modernizations	molded	moneys
modernize	molding	monies
modernized	molds	monitor
modernizing	mole	monitored
modes	molecular	monk
modest	molecule	monkey
modestly	molecules	monochrome
modesty	molehill	monochromic
modicum	moleskin	monocle
modification	molest	monocular
modifications	mollification	monogamous
modified	mollify	monogamy
modifier	mollusk	monogram
modify	mollycoddle	monogrammed
modifying	molt	monograph
modish	molten	monolith
modular	moly	monolithic
modulate	mom	monolithically
modulation	moment	monologue
module	momentarily	monomer
moire	momentary	monomers
moist	momentous	monopolist
moisten	moments	monopolistic
moistener	momentum	monopolization
moisteners	monarch	monopolize
moisture	monastery	monopolizing
molar	monastic	monopoly
molars	monaural	monorail
molasses	monetary	monosyllable
mold	money	monotone

modular	modulate	module	molasses	molecular	molecule	momentum	monastery	monogram	monograph	monopolistic
mojúlər	mojúlāt	mojúl	məlasiz	məlekū́lər	moləkū́l	mōmentəm	monəsterē	monəgram	monəgraf	mənopəlistik

monotonous	moral	morsel
monotony	morale	mort
monsoon	moralist	mortal
monster	moralistic	mortality
monstrosity	morality	mortar
monstrous	moralize	mortars
montage	morally	mortgage ⊙
monte	morass	mortgaged ⊙
month	morassy	mortgagee ⊙
monthly	moratorium	mortgagees ⊙
months	moratory	mortgages ⊙
monument	morbid	mortgagor ⊙
monumental	morbidly	mortgagors ⊙
monumentally	more ⊙	mortician
monuments	morel	mortuary
mood	moreover ⊙	mosaic
moodily	mores	mosque
moody	morgue	mosquito
moon	morning	mosquitoes
mooncraft	mornings	moss
moonlight	moron	mossy
moonlit	moronic	most
moonman	morose	mostly
moonward	morosely	motel
moor	morphine	motels
mooring	morphologic	moth
moot	morphological	mother
mop	morphology	motherhood
mopping	morphophoneme	mother-in-law ⊙
mops	morphophonemic	motherland

motherly	motors	movement
mothers	mottle	movements
mothproof	mottler	mover
mothproofed	motto	movers
moths	mound	moves
motif	mount	movie
motion	mountain	movies
motionless	mountaineer	moving
motions	mountainous	movingly
motivate	mountainously	mow v.; n.
motivated	mountains	mowed
motivates	mountainside	mower
motivating	mounted	mowers
motivation	mounting	mowing
motivational	mountings	much
motive	mounts	muck
motives	mourn	mucker
motley	mourner	mucosa
motor	mournful	mud
motorcycle	mournfully	muddle
motorcycles	mourning	muddy
motorcyclist	mouse	mudflat
motorcyclists	mouth	mudflow
motoring	mouthful	mudguard
motorist	mouthpiece	muff
motorists	mouths	muffin
motorize	mouthwash	muffle
motorized	movable	muffler
motorman	move	mug
motormen	moved	mugger

muggy	multiwall	muscleman
mulch	mum	musclemen
mulching	mumble	muscles
mule	mumbled	muscular
mules	mumbling	muse
mull	mummification	musette
multicolor	mummify	museum
multicolored	mumps	museums
multidisciplinary	munch	mushroom
multifaceted	mundane	music
multifamily	municipal	musical
multiform ☉	municipalities	musicale
multigrade	municipality	musicality
multilateral	municipally	musically
multilevel	munition	musician
multimedia	mural	musicians
multimillionaire	muralist	musicianship
multiple	murals	musicologist
multiples	murder	musket
multiplication	murderer	muslin
multiplicity	murderers	muss
multiplied	murderous	must ○
multiplier	muriate	mustache
multiplies	muriatic	mustang
multiply	murk	mustard
multipurpose	murky	muster
multistate ☉	murmur	mustiness
multitude	murmuringly	mustn't
multitudinous	murmurs	musty
multiversity	muscle	mutant

mule	multicolored	multitude	multitudinous	mummify	mural	muscular	muse	music	musical	musicale	mutant
mūl	multikulərd	multətüd	multətüdənəs	muməfī	mūrəl	muskūlər	mūz	mūzik	mūzəkl	mūzəkal	mūtnt

mutate	mutualism	mysteriously
mutation	mutually	mystery
mutational	muzzle	mystic
mute	muzzleloader	mystical
muted	muzzleloading	mystically
mutely	my	mysticism
mutilate	mycologist	mystification
mutilated	mycology	mystified
mutilation	mycosis	mystify
mutineer	myna	mystifying
mutiny	mynas	mystique
mutism	myopia	myth
mutter	myopic	mythic
mutterer	myriad	mythologic
mutteringly	myself	mythological
mutton	mysteries	mythology
mutual	mysterious	myths

nab	narcotic	nationals
nag	narrate	nationhood
nail	narration	nations
nailing	narrative	nationwide
nails	narrator	native
naive	narrow	natron
naively	narrower	nattily
naivete	narrowing	natty
naked	narrowly	natural
nakedly	narrowness	naturalism
nakedness	nasal	naturalist
name	nasalize	naturalistic
named	nascency	naturalization
nameless	nascent	naturalize
namely	nastier	naturalized
nameplate	nastiest	naturally
nameplates	nastily	naturalness
names	nasty	nature
namesake	natal	natured
nankeen	natatorial	natures
nap	natatorium	naught
napkin	nation	naughtier
napkins	national	naughty
narcosis	nationalism	nausea
	nationalist	nautic
	nationalistic	nautical
	nationality	naval
	nationalization	navel
	nationalize	navigable
	nationally	navigate

navigation	necklaces	negligible
navigator	neckline	negotiable
navy	necks	negotiate □
neap	necktie	negotiated □
near	neckties	negotiates □
nearby ☉	necrology	negotiating □
nearer	necromancy	negotiation □
nearest	necrose	negotiations □
nearing	necrosis	negotiator □
nearly	necrotic	neighbor
nearness	nectar	neighborhood
nears	need	neighborhoods
neat	needed	neighboring
neatest	needing	neighborly
neatly	needle	neighbors
neatness	needles	neither
nebula	needless	nemesis
nebular	needlessly	neologism
nebulous	needs	neologize
necessaries ☉	needy	neology
necessarily ☉	negate	neon
necessary ☉	negation	neoplasm
necessitate	negative	neoplastic
necessitated	negatively	neoplasty
necessitates	negativism	neoprene
necessitating	neglect	neorealism
necessities	neglected	neorealistic
necessity	neglecting	nephew
neck	negligence	nepotism
necklace	negligent	nerve

N

nerveless	neurotic	newspaperman ☉
nerves	neuter	newspapermen ☉
nervous	neutral	newspapers ☉
nervously	neutralism	newsprint
nervousness	neutralist	newsreel
nest	neutrality	newsroom
nesting	neutralization	newsstand ☉
nestle	neutralize	newsstands ☉
nestlings	neutron	newsweekly
net	neutrophil	newsworthy ☉
nether	never	next ○
nets	nevermore ☉	nibble
netted	nevertheless ☉	nice
nettle	new	nicely
network ☉	newborn	nicer
networks ☉	newcomer	nicest
neural	newcomers	nicety
neuralgia	newer	niche
neurasthenia	newest	nick
neurasthenic	newly	nickel
neuritis	newness	nickname
neurological	news	nicotine
neurologist	newsboy	niece
neurology	newscast	night
neuron	newscasts	nightclub
neuronal	newsletter ☉	nightfall
neuropsychiatric ☐	newsletters ☉	nightingale
neuroses	newsman	nightly
neurosis	newsmen	nightmare
neurosurgery	newspaper ○	nightmares

nether	neural	neuralgia	neurasthenia	neurasthenic	neuritis	neurologist	neurology	neutrality	news	niche
nethər	nùrəl	nùraljə	nùrəsthēnēə	nùrəsthenik	nùrītis	nùroləjist	nùroləjē	nütralətē	nüz	nich

nightmarish	nodes	nonassessable
nights	nodular	nonavailability
nightshirt	nodulate	noncancelable
nighttime ☉	nodule	noncandidate
nihilist	noel	noncash
nihilistic	nog	noncertified ☉
nil	noise	nonchalance
ninth	noiseless	nonchalant
nip	noisemaker	noncommercial
nipper	noisier	noncommissioned
nipple	noisily	noncommunist
nirvana	noisy	noncompetitive
nitrate	nomad	noncompliance
nitration	nomadic	nonconfining
nitric	nomenclature	nonconformist ☉
nitrogen	nominal	nonconsecutive
no	nominalism	nonconstructive ☉
nob	nominally	noncontributory ☉
nobility	nominate	noncorresponding ☉
noble	nominated	noncredit
nobleman	nominating	noncritical
nobler	nomination	nondirectional ☉
noblest	nominations	nondisabling ☉
nobody	nominee	nondrinking
nocturnal	nominees	nondrying
nocturnally	nonabsorbent	nonduplicate
nocturne	nonadult	nondurable
nod	nonagricultural ☉	none
nodal	nonalcoholic	nonelectric
node	nonaligned	nonelectrical

nonessential	nonpolitical	nonspecialists ⊙
nonetheless ⊙	nonproductive ⊙	nonspecific ⊙
nonexclusive	nonprofessional	nonstandard ⊙
nonexistent	nonprofit	nonstop
nonexplosive	nonproliferation	nonstriking
nonfarm	nonpublished ⊙	nonsubscriber
nonfederal	nonquantitative ⊙	nonsubscribers
nonfinancial	nonreader	nonsurgical
nonforfeiture	nonreceipt	nonsystematic
nonfreezing	nonrecurring	nontable
nongiver	nonrefundable	nontaxable
nongivers	nonrenewal	nonteaching
nongraded	nonresident	nontechnical
nonhazardous	nonresidential	nonthesis
nonimmigrant	nonresidents	nontoxic
noninterference	nonresponsive ⊙	nontransferable
nonledger	nonreturnable ⊙	nonunion
nonlinear	nonrotating	nonuse
nonlisted	nonroutine	nonuser
nonliterary	nonrubber	nonusers
nonlocal	nonscheduled ▢	noodle
nonmachine	nonsense	noodling
nonmagnetic	nonsensical	nook
nonmedicare	nonsigner	noon
nonmember	nonsigners	noontime ⊙
nonmembers	nonskid	noose
nonmerit	nonsmoker	nor
nonmetered	nonsmokers	norm
nonpartisan ⊙	nonsocial	normal
nonpayment	nonspecialist ⊙	normalcy

normalize	notch	novelist
normally	note	novels
normative	notebook	novelties
north	notebooks	novelty
northbound	noted	novice
northeast	notes	novitiate
northeasterly	noteworthy ⊙	now
northeastern	nothing ⊙	nowadays
northerly	notice ⊙	nowhere ⊙
northern	noticeable ⊙	noxious
northward	noticeably ⊙	nozzle
northwest	noticed ⊙	nozzles
northwestern	notices	nuance
nose	noticing ⊙	nuances
nosebleed	notification	nub
nostalgia	notifications	nubbin
nostalgic	notified	nuclear
nostalgically	notifies	nucleate
nostril	notify	nuclei
nostrum	notifying	nucleus
not ○	noting	nuclide
notable	notion	nude
notably	notoriety	nudge
notaries	notorious	nudism
notarization	notoriously	nudist
notarize	notwithstanding ⊙	nudity
notarized	noun	nugget
notary	nourish	nuisance
notation	nourishment	null
notations	novel	nullifier

nullify	numerical	nutrients
nullity	numerically	nutriment
numb	numerological	nutrition
number ○	numerology	nutritional
numbered ☉	numerous	nutritionist
numbering ☉	nun	nutritious
numberless ☉	nurse	nutritive
numbers ☉	nursery	nuts
numbingly	nurses	nutshell
numbness	nursing	nuzzle
numeral	nurture	nyctalopia
numerals	nut	nyctalopic
numerate	nutcracker	nylon
numerator	nutmeg	nylons
numeric	nutrient	

oak

oaken

oaks

oakwood

oar

oasis

oat

oath

oaths

oatmeal

oats

obedience

obedient

obelisk

obese

obesity

obey

obeying

obituary

object

objected

objection

objectionable

objections

objective

objectively

objectiveness

objectives

objectivity

objector

objects

oblate

oblation

obligate

obligated

obligates

obligation

obligational

obligations

oblige

obliged

obliger

obligingly

oblique

obliquely

obliterate

obliterated

obliteration

obliviate

oblivion

oblivious

oblong

obnoxious

oboe

obscene

obscenity

obscure

obscurely

obscurity

obsequious

observable ⊙

observance ⊙

observant ⊙

observation ⊙

observational ⊙

observations ⊙

observatory ⊙

observe ⊙

observed ⊙

observer ⊙

observes ⊙

observing ⊙

obsess

obsession

obsessive

obsidian

obsolescence

obsolescent

obsolete

obstacle

obstacles

obstetric

obstetrics

obstinacy

obstinate	occupation	odds
obstruct	occupational	odeum
obstructed	occupations	odious
obstruction	occupied	odor
obstructionist	occupies	odorless
obtain	occupy	odors
obtainable	occupying	of ○
obtained	occur	off
obtaining	occurred	offend
obtains	occurrence	offended
obtrude	occurrences	offender
obtrusion	occurring	offenders
obverse	occurs	offending
obviate	ocean	offense
obviation	oceanaut	offenses
obvious	oceanfront	offensive
obviously	oceanic	offensively
occasion	oceanography	offer
occasional	ocher	offered
occasionally	octagon	offerer
occasioned	octagonal	offerers
occasions	octane	offering
occidental	octave	offerings
occipital	octillion	offers
occlude	octopus	offhand
occlusion	ocular	office
occult	oculist	officeholder
occultism	odd	officer
occupancy	oddity	officers
occupant	oddly	offices

official		olden		on	
officialdom		older		once ⊙	
officially		oldest		oncoming	
officials		oldster		one ⊙	
officiate		oleander		oneness ⊙	
officious		oleandomycin		onerous	
offish		oleaster		ones ⊙	
offset		oleate		oneself ⊙	
offsetting		oleo		onetime ⊙	
offshore		oligopoly		ongoing ⊙	
offspring		olivary		onion	
often		olive		onions	
oftener		olives		onlooker	
oftentimes ⊙		olympic		only	
ogive		ombudsman		onrush	
ogle		omega		onset	
ohm		omelet		onside	
oil		omen		onslaught	
oilcloth		ominous		onsweep	
oiler		ominously		onto	
oiliness		omission		ontogeny	
oils		omissions		ontological	
oilseed		omit		ontology	
oilskin		omits		onus	
oilstone		omitted		onward	
oily		omitting		onyx	
ointment		omnibus		oolite	
ointments		omniform ⊙		ooze	
okay △		omnipotence		opacity	
old		omnipresent ⊙		opal	

opalesce	operators	opprobrium
opalescence	operetta	opsin
opalescent	ophthalmology	opt
opalize	opiate	optic
opaque	opine	optical
open	opinion	optically
opened	opinional	optician
opener	opinions	opticist
openers	opiology	optimal
opening	opium	optimism
openings	opossum	optimist
openly	opponent	optimistic
openness	opponents	optimistically
opens	opportune	optimization
openwork ☉	opportunism	optimize
opera	opportunist	optimum
operable	opportunistic	option
operand	opportunities ☉	optional
operant	opportunity ☉	options
operate	opposable	optometry
operated	oppose	optophone
operates	opposed	opulence
operatic	opposing	opulent
operating	opposite	opus
operation	opposition	or
operational	oppositions	oracle
operationally	oppress	oracular
operations	oppression	oral
operative	oppressive	orally
operator	oppressor	orange

orangeade	orderings ⊙	orgiastic
oranges	orderliness ⊙	orgy
orangewood	orderly ⊙	oriel
orate	orders ⊙	orient
oration	ordinal	oriental
orator	ordinance	orientate
oratorial	ordinances	orientating
oratorical	ordinarily	orientation
oratorio	ordinary	oriented
oratory	ordinate	orienting
orb	ordnance	orifice
orbit	ore	orifices
orbital	orebody	origin
orbited	organ	original
orbiter	organdy	originality
orbits	organic	originally
orchard	organism	originals
orchesis	organisms	originate
orchestra	organist	originated
orchestral	organization ⊙	originates
orchestras	organizational ⊙	originating
orchestrate	organizationally ⊙	origination
orchestration	organizations ⊙	originator
orchid	organize ⊙	oriole
orchidology	organized ⊙	orlop
ordain	organizer ⊙	ornament
ordeal	organizers ⊙	ornamental
order ⊙	organizes ⊙	ornamentalism
ordered ⊙	organizing ⊙	ornamentation
ordering ⊙	organs	ornate

ornately		ossify		outburst ⊙	
ornithology		ostensible		outbursts ⊙	
orphan		ostensibly		outcast ⊙	
orphanage		ostentatious		outcasts ⊙	
orphans		osteopath		outclass ⊙	
orthicon		osteopathic		outcome ⊙	
ortho		osteopathy		outcomes ⊙	
orthodontic		ostracism		outcrop ⊙	
orthodontist		ostracize		outcropping ⊙	
orthodontists		other		outcry ⊙	
orthodox		others		outdate ⊙	
orthodoxy		otherwise		outdated ⊙	
orthograph		otter		outdid ⊙	
orthographic		ought		outdistance ⊙	
orthography		ounce		outdo ⊙	
²orthopaedic		ounces		outdoor ⊙	
¹orthopedic		our ⊙		outdoors ⊙	
orthopedics		ours ⊙		outdoorsman ⊙	
oscillate		ourself ⊙		outdoorsmen ⊙	
oscillating		ourselves ⊙		outer ⊙	
oscillation		oust		outerwear ⊙	
oscillations		ouster		outface ⊙	
oscillator		out ⊙		outfield ⊙	
osmic		outage ⊙		outfielder ⊙	
osmose		outages ⊙		outfit ⊙	
osmosis		outback ⊙		outfits ⊙	
osmotic		outbid ⊙		outflow ⊙	
ossein		outboard ⊙		outfox ⊙	
osseous		outbound ⊙		outgo ⊙	
ossification		outbreak ⊙		outgoing ⊙	

outgrow ☉	outmost ☉	outsiders ☉
outgrowth ☉	outnumber ☉	outsize ☉
outguess ☉	outnumbered ☉	outskirt ☉
outhouse ☉	outpace ☉	outskirts ☉
outing ☉	outpatient ☉	outsmart ☉
outings ☉	outpayment ☉	outsold ☉
outland ☉	outplay ☉	outspeak ☉
outlander ☉	outpost ☉	outspoken ☉
outlandish ☉	outpour ☉	outspokenly ☉
outlast ☉	outpull ☉	outspread ☉
outlaw ☉	output ☉	outstand ☉
outlawed ☉	outputs ☉	outstanding ☉
outlawry ☉	outrage ☉	outstandingly ☉
outlay ☉	outrageous ☉	outstate ☉
outlays ☉	outran ☉	outstrip ☉
outlet ☉	outrank ☉	outtalk ☉
outlets ☉	outranked ☉	outvote ☉
outlie ☉	outreach ☉	outwalk ☉
outline ☉	outrig ☉	outward ☉
outlined ☉	outrigger ☉	outwardly ☉
outlines ☉	outright ☉	outwear ☉
outlining ☉	outrode ☉	outweigh ☉
outlive ☉	outrun ☉	outweighed ☉
outlived ☉	outs ☉	outwit ☉
outlook ☉	outsail ☉	outwitting ☉
outlying ☉	outscore ☉	outwork ☉
outmaneuver ☉	outsell ☉	outworn ☉
outmatch ☉	outset ☉	oval
outmode ☉	outside ☉	ovally
outmoded ☉	outsider ☉	ovate

ovation	overconfidence	overfamiliar
oven	overconfident	overfamiliarity
ovens	overcook	overfill
over	overcool	overflow
overachieve	overcount ⊙	overflowed
overachiever	overcrowd	overflowing
overactive ⊙	overcrowded	overfull
overage n.; a.	overcrowding	overgraze
overages	overcurrent	overgrow
overall	overdevelop ⊙	overgrown
overbalance	overdo	overhand
overbalanced	overdone	overhang
overbalances	overdraft	overhanging
overbear	overdrafts	overhaul
overbid	overdraw	overhauled
overblown	overdrawn	overhauls
overboard	overdrive	overhead
overbuild	overdue	overhear
overburden	overeat	overheard
overcame	overemphasis	overheat
overcast	overemphasize	overheated
overcharge	overestimate v.; n.	overheating
overcharged	overestimated	overjoy
overcharges	overestimation	overjoyed
overcoat	overexcite	overkill
overcome	overexpend	overland
overcomes	overexpenditure	overlap
overcoming	overexpose	overlapping
overcompensate	overextend	overlay
overcompensation	overfall	overline

overload

overloaded

overlong

overlook

overlooked

overlooking

overlooks

overlord

overly

overnight

overnighter

overpack

overpaid

overpass

overpay

overpayment

overpayments

overplay

overpopulate

overpopulation

overpower

overpowering

overpressure

overprice

overpriced

overprint

overprinting

overproduce

overprotect

overprotection

overqualified

overran

overrate

overreach

overreact

overridden

override

overriding

overrule

overruled

overrun

overrunning

overs

oversave

overseas

oversee

oversell

overselling

overshadow

overshadowed

overshoe

overshot

oversight

oversimplification

oversimplified

oversimplify

oversize

oversoft

overspecialization ⊙

overspend

overstate ⊙

overstatement ⊙

overstep

overstock

overstocked

overstocks

oversubscribe

oversubscribed

oversupply

overt

overtake

overtaken

overtax

overthrow

overthrown

overtime ⊙

overtly

overtone

overtones

overtook

overture

overturn

overuse

overvalue ⊙

overview

overweight

overwhelm

overwhelmed

overwhelming

overwhelmingly

overwork ⊙		ownership		oxidation	
overworked ⊙		ownerships		oxide	
owe		owning		oxidize	
owed		owns		oxidizer	
owes		ox		oxidizes	
owing		oxalate		oxygen	
owl		oxalic		oyster	
own		oxen		oysters	
owned		oxford		ozone	
owner		oxfords			
owners		oxidate			

P

pace	padded	painters
pacemaker	padding	painting
pacer	paddle	paintings
pacesetter	paddler	paints
pacific	paddles	pair
pacifier	paddock	pairings
pacifism	padlock	pairs
pacifist	padlocks	pajama
pacify	pads	pajamas
pack	pagan	palace
package	paganism	palatability
packaged	page	palatable
packager	pageant	palate
packages	pageantry	pale
packaging	pages	paleness
packed	pagoda	palest
packer	paid	palisade
packers	pail	pall
packet	pails	palladium
packets	pain	pallet
packing	painful	palletization
packs	painfully	palletize
pact	painless	palletized
pad	painlessly	pallets
	pains	palliate
	painstaking	palliative
	painstakingly	pallid
	paint	pallor
	painted	palm
	painter	palmetto

P

---

pact	paddock	pagoda	pajama	pajamas	palace	palatable	palate	pall	palladium	pallet	palliate	palliative
pakt	padək	pəgōdə	pəjämə	pəjäməz	palis	palətəbl	palit	pôl	pəlādēəm	palit	palēāt	palēātiv

palpability	pantograph	paragraphing
palpable	pantomime	paragraphs
palpably	pantomimic	parakeet
palsy	pantry	parallel
pamper	pants	parallelism
pamphlet	panty	parallels
pamphlets	papal	paralysis
pan	paper	paralyze
panacea	paperback	paramagnetic
pancake	paperboard	paramedic
pancakes	papers	paramedical
panda	paperweight	parameter
pander	paperwork ⊙	parameters
pane	papery	parametric
panel	paprika	paramount
paneling	par	paranoia
panelist	parable	paranoid
panelists	parabola	parapet
panels	parachute	paraphernalia
pang	parade	paraphrase
panic	paradigm	paraplegia
panicky	paradise	paraplegic
panned	paradox	paraprofessional
panning	paradoxical	paraprofessionals
panorama	paradoxically	parapsychology
panoramic	paradrop	parasite
pans	paraffin	parasitic
pansy	paraglider	parasol
pant	paragon	parasympathetic
panther	paragraph	paratroop

paratrooper	parking	parted ⊙
parboil	parkland	partial
parcel	parks	partially
parcels	parkway	participant ⊙
parch	parlance	participants ⊙
parchment	parlay	participate ⊙
pardon	parley	participated ⊙
pardonable	parliament	participates ⊙
pare	parliamentarian	participating ⊙
parenchyma	parliamentary	participation ⊙
parent	parlor	particle ⊙
parentage	parlors	particles ⊙
parental	parochial	particular ○
parentheses	parochialize	particularity ⊙
parenthesis	parody	particularize ⊙
parenthetical	parole	particularly ⊙
parenthetically	parolee	particulars ⊙
parenthood	parquet	particulate ⊙
parents	parrot	parties ⊙
parfait	parrotlike	parting ⊙
pariah	parry	partings ⊙
pari-mutuel	parsimonious	partisan ⊙
parings	parsimony	partisanship ⊙
parish	parsley	partition ⊙
parishioner	parson	partitioned ⊙
parity	parsonage	partitions ⊙
park	parsons	partly ⊙
parka	part ○	partner ⊙
parked	partake ⊙	partners ⊙
parker	partaker ⊙	partnership ⊙

partnerships ⊙	passports	patented
partook ⊙	past	patentee
parts ⊙	paste	patents
party ⊙	pasted	pater
parvenu	pastel	paternal
paschal	pastern	paternalism
pasha	pasteurization	paternalistic
pass	pasteurize	paternally
passable	pasteurizing	path
passage	pastime ⊙	pathetic
passageway	pastimes ⊙	pathogenic
passageways	pasting	pathologic
passbook	pastor	pathological
passbooks	pastoral	pathologist
passed	pastoralize	pathologists
passenger	pastorate	pathology
passengers	pastries	pathos
passer	pastry	paths
passers	pasture	pathway
passes	pastured	pathways
passing	pastures	patience
passion	pasty	patient
passionate	pat	patiently
passionately	patch	patients
passive	patched	patina
passively	patches	patio
passiveness	patching	patriarch
passkey	patchwork ⊙	patriarchal
passout ⊙	pate	patriarchy
passport	patent	patrician

patrimonial		paving	peacock
patrimony		paw	peak
patriot		pawn	peaks
patriotic		pawnshop	peal
patriotically		pay	peanut
patriotism		payable	peanuts
patrol		paycheck	pear
patrolled		payday	pearl
patrolman		payee	pearlite
patrolmen		payees	pearly
patrols		payer	pears
patron		paying	peasant
patronage		payload	peat
patronize		payloads	pebble
patrons		paymaster	pecan
patter		payment	pecans
pattern		payments	peck
patterned		payoff	pecked
patterns		payroll	pectoral
patting		payrolls	peculate
patty		pays	peculiar
paucity		pea	peculiarity
paunch		peace	peculiarly
paunchy		peaceable	pecuniary
pause		peaceful	pedagogical
pauses		peacefully	pedagogue
pave		peacemaking	pedal
paved		peacetime ⊙	pedant
pavement		peach	pedantic
pavilion		peaches	peddle

peddler		penalty		pensioner	
pedestal		penance		pensions	
pedestrian		pencil		pensive	
pediatric		penciled		pentagon	
pediatrician		pencils		penthouse	
pediatrics		pend		penult	
pedicure		pendant		penultimate	
pedigree		pendants		penurious	
peek		pendency		penury	
peel		pending		peon	
peeling		pendulum		peonies	
peep		penetrant		peony	
peer		penetrate		people	
peerless		penetrated		peoples	
peers		penetrating		pep	
peg		penetration		pepper	
pekoe		penguin		peppermint	
pelf		penicillin		peppery	
pellet		peninsula		per	
pelt		penitent		per annum	
peltry		penitentiaries		per capita	
pelts		penitentiary		perceive	
pelvic		penman		perceived	
pelvis		pennant		percent	
pembina		penned		percentage	
pen		pennies		percentages	
penal		penniless		percentagewise	
penalize		penny		percentile	
penalized		pens		percept	
penalties		pension		perceptible	

perception	perforations	periodicals
perceptive	perforator	periodicity
perceptual	perforce	periods
perch	perform ⊙	peripheral
percipient	performance ⊙	peripherally
percolate	performances ⊙	periphery
percolator	performed ⊙	periscope
percuss	performer ⊙	perish
percussion	performers ⊙	perishability
percussive	performing ⊙	perishable
per diem	performs ⊙	perishables
perempt	perfume	peristylar
peremptory	perfumery	peristyle
perennial	perfunctorily	perjury
perennially	perfunctory	perk
perfect	perfuse	perky
v.; a., n.	perfusive	permanence
perfected	perhaps	permanent
perfectibility	pericardial	permanently
perfecting	pericarditis	permeability
perfection	perigee	permeable
perfectionist	peril	permeate
perfectly	perilous	permissibility
perfervid	perilously	permissible
perfervor	perils	permission
perfidious	perimeter	permissions
perfidy	period	permissive
perforate	periodic	permissiveness
perforated	periodical	permit
perforating	periodically	permits
perforation		

permitted	persist	pertain
permittee	persistence	pertaining
permittees	persistency	pertains
permitting	persistent	pertinence
permutation	persistently	pertinent
permute	persists	perturb
pernicious	person	perturbation
peroxide	personable	perusal
perpendicular	personage	peruse
perpendicularly	personal	perused
perpetrate	personalities	perusing
perpetration	personality	pervade
perpetrator	personalize	pervasive
perpetual	personalized	pervasively
perpetually	personally	perverse
perpetuate	personification	perversely
perpetuation	personify	perversion
perpetuity	personnel	perversity
perplex	persons	pervert
perplexed	perspective	peso
perplexing	perspectives	pessimism
perplexity	perspiration	pessimist
per se	perspire	pessimistic
persecute	persuade	pest
persecuted	persuaded	pester
persecution	persuader	pesticide
perseverance	persuasion	pesticides
persevere	persuasive	pestilence
persiflage	persuasively	pestilent
persimmon	pert	pestle

pests	pharmacy	phonemic
pet	pharmic	phonetic
petal	phase	phonic
petite	phasedown ⊙	phoning
petition	phases	phonograph
petitioned	pheasant	phonologic
petitioner	phenol	phonology
petitions	phenolic	phony
petrify	phenomena	phosphate
petrochemical	phenomenal	phosphates
petrochemicals	phenomenon	phosphide
petrol	phenothiazine	phosphor
petroleum	philanthropic	phosphoric
petroleums	philanthropist	phosphorous
pets	philanthropy	photo
pettiness	philatelist	photocathode
petty	philately	photocell
petulance	philharmonic	photochemical
petulant	philological	photocopier
pew	philologist	photocopies
pewter	philology	photocopy
phalange	philosopher	photoelectron
phalanx	philosophic	photoelectronic
phantom	philosophical	photoengrave
pharmaceutic	philosophically	photoengraver
pharmaceutical	philosophize	photoengravers
pharmacist	philosophy	photogenic
pharmacological	phone	photograph
pharmacology	phoned	photographed
pharmacopoeia	phoneme	photographer

photographers	physicians	pickle
photographic	physicist	picks
photographically	physics	pickup
photographing	physiogonomy	pickups
photographs	physiographic	picnic
photography	physiologic	picnicker
photolithograph	physiological	picnicking
photolithographer	physiologically	picnics
photon	physiologist	pictorial
photoprint	physiologists	pictorially
photoproduct ⊙	physiology	picture
photos	physiotherapist	pictured
photostat	physiotherapy	pictures
photostated	physique	picturesque
photostatic	pi	picturing
photostats	pianist	piddle
phototype	pianistic	pie
phrase	pianists	piece
phrased	piano	piecemeal
phraseology	pianos	pieces
phrases	piazza	piecework ⊙
phrasing	pica	pier
phrasings	picayune	pierce
phrenic	pick	pierced
phrenology	pickax	piers
physic	picked	piety
physical	picker	piezoelectric
physically	picket	pig
physicals	picketing	pigeon
physician	picking	pigeonhole

pigeonholed	pinafore	pip
piggyback	pincer	pipe
pigment	pinch	piped
pigmented	pine	pipeline
pigments	pineapple	pipelines
pigskin	pines	piper
pigtail	ping	pipes
pike	pinhead	pipette
pile	pinhole	piping
piled	pinion	piquancy
piles	pinions	piquant
pilfer	pink	pique
pilferage	pinnacle	piqued
pilferer	pinned	piracy
pilferers	pinnings	pirate
pilfering	pinochle	pirates
pilgrim	pinpoint	pirating
pilgrimage	pinpointing	pirouette
piling	pins	pistachio
pill	pinsetter	pistol
pillage	pinspot	pistols
pillar	pinspotter	piston
pillory	pint	pistons
pillow	pinto	pit
pillows	pints	pitch
pills	pioneer	pitcher
pilot	pioneered	pitchers
pilots	pioneers	pitchfork
pimple	pious	pitching
pin	piously	piteous

pitfall	placing	planisphere
pitfalls	plagiarism	plank
pith	plagiarize	planking
pithy	plague	planks
pitiable	plagued	planned
pitiful	plaid	planner
pitifully	plain	planners
pitiless	plainer	planning
pitilessly	plainest	plans
pits	plainly	plant
pituitary	plains	plantain
pity	plaint	plantation
pityingly	plaintiff	plantations
pivot	plaintiffs	planted
pivotal	plaintive	planter
pixy	plan	planters
pizza	planar	planting
pizzas	planarian	plantings
placability	plane	plants
placable	planeload	plaque
placard	planer	plaques
placards	planers	plasma
placate	planes	plaster
place	planet	plasterboard
placed	planetarium	plastered
placement	planetary	plasterer
placements	planetoid	plasterwork ⊙
placer	planets	plastic
places	planform ⊙	plasticity
placid	planing	plasticize

plasticized	players	pleases ⊙	
plastics	playful	pleasing ⊙	
plat	playgoer ⊙	pleasingly ⊙	
plate	playground ⊙	pleasurable	
plateau	playgrounds ⊙	pleasure	
plateaus	playhouse	pleasures	
plated	playing	pleat	
platen	playmate	plebeian	
plates	playroom	pledge	
platform ⊙	playrooms	pledged	
platforms ⊙	plays	pledger	
plating	plaything ⊙	pledges	
platinoid	playtime ⊙	pledging	
platinum	playwright	plenarily	
platitude	playwriting	plenary	
platitudinize	plaza	plenipotentiary	
platoon	plazas	plenitude	
platted	plea	plentiful	
platter	plead	plenty	
platters	pleader	plenum	
platting	pleading	pleura	
plaudit	pleadings	pliability	
plausibility	pleads	pliable	
plausible	pleas	pliancy	
play	pleasant	pliant	
playable	pleasanter	plier	
playback	pleasantly	pliers	
playboy	pleasantness	plight	
played	please ○	plod	
player	pleased ⊙	plot	

plots		pluralistic		pointed	
plotted		plurality		pointedly	
plotter		plus		pointer	
plow		plush		pointers	
plowing		plutocrat		pointing	
plowman		plutocratically		pointless	
plowshare		ply		points	
pluck		plywood		poise	
plug		pneumatic		poison	
plugged		pneumonia		poisoning	
plugging		poach		poisonous	
plugs		pocket		poke	
plum		pocketbook		poker	
plumage		pocketbooks		polar	
plumb		pocketful		polarity	
plumber		pockets		polarization	
plumbers		pod		polarize	
plumbing		podger		pole	
plume		podium		polecat	
plummet		poem		polemic	
plump		poems		polemical	
plumpness		poet		polemics	
plunder		poetic		poles	
plunderer		poetical		police	
plunge		poetically		policeman	
plunger		poetry		policemen	
plunges		poignancy		policies	
plunk		poignant		policy	
plural		poinsettia		policyholder	
pluralism		point		policyholders	

plume   pneumatic   pneumonia   podium   poet   poetic   poignancy   poinsettia   polarization   polemic   polemical   police
plüm   nümatik   nümōnyə   pōdēəm   pōit   pōetik   poinənsē   poinsetēə   pōlərəzāshən   pəlemik   pəleməkl   pəlēs

policymaker	pollution	pompano
polio	polo	pompon
poliomyelitis	polonaise	pompous
polish	poltroon	pond
polished	polyacrylate	ponder
polishes	polyacrylates	pondering
polishing	polybutadiene	ponderous
polite	polychrome	pons
politely	polyclinic	pontiff
politeness	polycrystalline	pontifical
politic	polyester	pontificate
political	polyesters	pontoon
politically	polyethylene	pony
politician	polyethylenes	poodle
politicians	polymer	pool
politics	polymeric	pools
polka	polymerization	poor
poll	polymerize	poorer
pollack	polymers	poorest
polled	polynomial	poorly
pollen	polyphosphate	pop
pollinate	polypropylene	popcorn
polling	polystyrene	pope
polls	polystyrenes	poplar
pollster	polytechnic	poplin
pollutant	polytype	popover
pollutants	polyurethane	popovers
pollute	pomology	popped
polluted	pomp	poppies
polluting	pompadour	poppy

pops	portage	positivist
populace	portal	posse
popular	portend	possess
popularity	portent	possesses
popularize	portentous	possessing
popularly	porter	possession
populate	porterhouse	possessions
populated	portfolio	possessive
population	portfolios	possessives
populations	porthole	possessor
populous	portico	possibilities
porcelain	portion	possibility
porcelainize	portions	possible
porch	portly	possibly
porches	portrait	possum
porcupine	portray	post
pore	portrayal	postage
pores	portrayed	postal
porgy	portraying	postals
pork	ports	postcard
pornographer	posada	postcards
pornographic	pose	postdate
pornography	posed	postdated
porosity	position	posted
porous	positioned	poster
porpoise	positioning	posterior
porridge	positions	posterity
port	positive	posters
portable	positively	postgraduate ⊙
portables	positivism	posthaste

posting	potency	powdery
postman	potent	power
postmark	potential	powered
postmarked	potentiality	powerful
postmaster	potentially	powerfully
postmasters	potentials	powering
postmen	pothole	powerless
post-mortem	potion	powers
postoperative	potluck	powwow
postpaid	potpourri	practicability
postpartum ☉	potted	practicable
postplane	potter	practical
postpone	potters	practicalities
postponed	pottery	practicality
postponement	pouch	practically
postponing	poult	practice
posts	poultice	practiced
postscript	poultry	practices
postscripts	pound	practicing
postulate	pounding	practitioner
posture	pounds	practitioners
postwar	pour	pragmatic
posy	poured	pragmatism
pot	pourer	prairie
potash	pouring	praise
potassium	pourings	praised
potato	pout	praiseworthy ☉
potatoes	poverty	praline
potboil	powder	pram
potboiler	powdered	prance

prank	precede	preconception
pray	preceded	precondition ⊙
prayer	precedence	precontract ⊙
prayerful	precedent	precook
prayerfully	precedents	precool
prayers	precedes	precut
prays	preceding	predate
preach	precept	predator
preacher	preceptor	predatory
preachers	precinct	predawn
preaching	precincts	predecease
preaddressed	precious	predecessor
preadmission	precipice	predecessors
preamble	precipitate	predefine
preapplication	precipitated	predefined
prearrange	precipitates	predeliver ⊙
prearranged	precipitation	predeliveries ⊙
preassemble	précis	predelivery ⊙
preassembled	precise	predestine
preauthorize	precisely	predetermine
preauthorized	preciseness	predetermined
precamp	precision	predicament
precancel	preclude	predicate _v.; a., n._
precanceled	precluded	predicated
precarious	precludes	predicator
precariously	precluding	predict
precast	precocious	predictability
precaution	precociously	predictable
precautionary	precocity	predictably
precautions	preconceive	predicted

predicting	preexisting	preholiday
prediction	prefab	preholidays
predictions	prefabricate	prejudge
predictive	prefabricated	prejudged
predicts	preface	prejudice
predigest	prefatory	prejudicial
predilection	prefect	prejudicing
predispose	prefecture	prelate
predisposition	prefer	prelatic
prednisone	preferable	prelight
predominance	preferably	preliminary
predominant	preference	prelude
predominantly	preferences	premarital
predominate	preferential	premature
predominates	preferentially	prematurely
predomination	preferment	premedical
preelect ⊙	preferred	premier
preelection ⊙	prefers	première
preeminence	prefigure ⊙	premise n.; v.
preeminent	prefile	premises n.; v.
preemploy ⊙	prefiled	premium
preemployment ⊙	prefinance	premiums
preempt	prefinancing	premix
preemptive	prefit	premolar
preen	prefix	premonish
preenroll	prefixes	premonition
preenrollment	pregnancy	premonitory
preentrance	pregnant	prenatal
preexist	prehearing	prenotion
preexistence	prehistoric	prenursing

prednisone	preeminent	preempt	preexist	prefect	prefecture	preference	premature	premise	premise
prednəsōn	priemənənt	priempt	prēegzist	prēfekt	prēfekchər	prefərəns	prēməchŭr	premis *n.*	primīz *v.*

preoccupation	prepositional	presence
preoccupied	preposterous	present ⊙
preoccupy	prepped	presentable ⊙
preopening	preprint	presentation ⊙
preoperative	preprinted	presentational ⊙
preorder ⊙	preprints	presentations ⊙
prep	preprofessional	presented ⊙
prepack	prepublication ⊙	presenter ⊙
prepackaged	prepublish ⊙	presenting ⊙
prepaid	prequalification	presently ⊙
preparation	prequalified	presentment ⊙
preparations	prequalify	presents ⊙
preparative	prequalifying	preservation ⊙
preparatory	preregistration	preservations ⊙
prepare	prerelease	preservative ⊙
prepared	prerequisite	preserve ⊙
preparedness	prerequisites	preserved ⊙
preparer	prerogative	preserver ⊙
preparers	prerule	preservers ⊙
prepares	preruled	preserves ⊙
preparing	presage *n., v.*	preserving ⊙
prepay	preschool	preside
prepaying	prescribe	presidency
prepayment	prescribed	president
prepayments	prescribes	presidential
preplan	prescribing	presidents
preplanning	prescription	presiding
preponderance	prescriptions	preslung
preponderantly	prescriptive	press
preposition	preseason	pressboard

pressed	pretends	preview
presser	pretense	previewing
presses	pretension	previews
pressing	pretentious	previous
pressings	preterminal	previously
pressroom	pretest	prevision
pressure	pretested	prevocational
pressured	pretext	prewar
pressures	pretimed ⊙	prewire
pressurization	pretranscription	prewired
pressurize	pretreat	prey
pressurizing	pretrial	price
prestige	prettier	priced
presto	pretties	priceless
prestress	prettiest	pricer
prestressed	prettily	pricers
presumable	pretty	prices
presumably	pretzel	pricing
presume	prevail	prick
presumed	prevailed	prickly
presuming	prevailing	pride
presummer	prevails	prideful
presumption	prevalence	prides
presumptive	prevalent	priest
presumptuous	prevent	priestly
presuppose	prevented	prim
presupposes	preventing	primacy
presupposition	prevention	primal
pretend	preventive	primarily
pretender	prevents	primary

primate	priority	probity
prime	prism	problem ○
primed	prison	problematic ⊙
primer	prisoner	problematical ○
primeval	prisoners	problems ⊙
priming	prisons	procedural
primitive	pristine	procedure
primitivism	privacy	procedures
primly	private	proceed
primrose	privately	proceeded
prince	privation	proceeding
princess	privet	proceedings
principal	privilege	proceeds
principally	privileged	process
principals	privileges	processed
principalship	privy	processes
principle	prize	processing
principles	prized	procession
print	prizes	processional
printable	pro	processor
printed	probabilistic ⊙	processors
printer	probability ⊙	proclaim
printers	probable ○	proclaimed
printing	probably ⊙	proclamation
printings	probate	proclivity
printout ⊙	probation	procrastinate
prints	probationary	procrastination
printworks ⊙	probe	procreate
prior	probes	procreation
priorities	probings	procreative

proctor	profess	profuse
proctoscope	professedly	profusely
proctoscopic	profession	profusion
procure	professional	progeny
procured	professionalism	prognoses
procurement	professionalize	prognosis
procurements	professionally	program
procurer	professionals	programmed
procures	professions	programmer
procuring	professor	programmers
prod	professors	programming
prodigal	professorship	programs
prodigally	proffer	progress
prodigious	proficiency	progressed
prodigy	proficient	progresses
produce	proficiently	progressing
produced	profile	progression
producer	profiles	progressive
producers	profit	progressively
produces	profitability	progressivism
producing	profitable	prohibit
product ○	profitably	prohibited
production ⊙	profited	prohibition
productions ⊙	profiting	prohibitive
productive ⊙	profits	prohibitory
productively ⊙	pro forma ⊙	prohibits
productivity ⊙	profound ⊙	project
products ⊙	profoundly ⊙	projected
profane	profoundness ⊙	projectile
profanity	profundity	projecting

projection	promotable	pronouncements
projections	promote	pronunciation
projective	promoted	proof
projector	promoter	proofer
projectors	promotes	proofers
projects	promoting	proofing
prolapse	promotion	proofread
prolapsed	promotional	proofreader
proletariat	promotionally	proofreading
proliferate	promotions	proofs
proliferation	prompt ☉	prop
prolific	prompted ☉	propaganda
prolix	prompting ☉	propagandist
prolixity	promptings ☉	propagandistic
prologue	promptitude ☉	propagate
prolong	promptly ☉	propagated
prolongate	promptness ☉	propagation
prolongation	prompts ☉	propane
prolonged	promulgate	propel
prolusion	promulgated	propellant
promenade	promulgation	propelled
prominence	pronate	propeller
prominent	prone	proper
prominently	proneness	properly
promise	prong	properties
promised	prongs	property
promises	pronoun	prophecy
promising	pronounce	prophesy
promissory	pronounced	prophet
promotability	pronouncement	prophetic

prophetically	propulsive	protect
propitiate	propylene	protected
propitious	pro rata	protecting
propone	prorate	protection
proponent	prorated	protections
proponents	prorating	protective
proportion	proration	protectively
proportional	pros	protector
proportionality	proscribe	protectorate
proportionally	proscription	protects
proportionate a.; v.	prose	protégé
proportionately	prosecute	protein
proportioned	prosecuted	proteins
proportions	prosecuting	protest
proposal	prosecution	protested
proposals	prosecutor	protester
propose	prospect □	protests
proposed	prospective □	protocol
proposes	prospects □	proton
proposing	prospectus □	protoplasm
proposition	prosper	prototype
propositions	prosperity	protract
[1]proprietary	prosperous	protraction
proprietor	prostate	protractor
proprietors	prosthesis	protrude
proprietorship	prostrate	protrusion
[2]proprietory	prostration	protuberance
propriety	prosy	protuberant
props	protagonist	proud
propulsion	protease	prouder

proudest		provoke		psyche	
proudly		provoked		psychiatric □	
provable		provoker		psychiatrist	
prove		provoking		psychiatry	
proved		provost		psychic	
proven		prow		psychical	
proverb		prowess		psychically	
proverbial		prowl		psychoanalysis	
proves		prowler		psychoanalytic	
provide ○		proxies		psychologic	
provided ⊙		proximal		psychological	
providence		proximate		psychologically	
provident		proximity		psychologist	
providential		proximo		psychologists	
provides ⊙		proxy		psychology	
providing ⊙		prude		psychopath	
province		prudence		psychopathic	
provincial		prudent		psychotherapy	
provincialism		prudential		psychotic	
proving		prudentially		pub	
provision		prudently		public ○	
provisional		prudery		publication ⊙	
provisionally		prune		publications ⊙	
provisioning		prurience		publicist	
provisions		prurient		publicity	
proviso		pry		publicize	
provisory		prying		publicized	
provocation		psalm		publicizing	
provocative		pseudo		publicly ○	
provocatively		pseudonym		publics ⊙	

publish ⊙		pulping		puncture	
publishable ⊙		pulpit		punctures	
published ⊙		pulpiteer		pundit	
publisher ⊙		pulsate		pung	
publishers ⊙		pulsation		pungent	
publishes ⊙		pulsator		punish	
publishing ⊙		pulsatory		punishable	
puck		pulse		punished	
pucker		pulsed		punishes	
puckish		pulses		punishment	
pudding		pulverization		punitive	
puddings		pulverize		punk	
puddle		pumice		punt	
puddler		pummel		puny	
puff		pump		pup	
puffiness		pumped		pupil	
puffy		pumping		pupils	
pull		pumpkin		puppet	
pulled		pumps		puppeteer	
pullet		pun		puppetry	
pulley		punch		puppy	
pulleys		punched		purchase	
pulling		puncher		purchased	
pullings		punches		purchaser	
pullman		punching		purchasers	
pullout ⊙		punctual		purchases	
pullover		punctuality		purchasing	
pulls		punctually		pure	
pulmonary		punctuate		purely	
pulp		punctuation		purest	

purgation	pursuant	putter
purgative	pursue	putters
purgatory	pursued	putting
purge	pursuer	putty
purification	pursues	puzzle
purify	pursuing	puzzled
purism	pursuit	puzzlement
purist	pursuits	puzzler
puritan	purvey	puzzles
puritanical	purveyor	pylon
purity	purview	pyorrhea
purl	pus	pyramid
purloin	push	pyramidal
purple	pushed	pyramided
purport	pusher	pyre
purportedly	pushes	pyrene
purports	pushing	pyres
purpose	pushup	pyrite
purposeful	pussy	pyrolysis
purposefully	pustulant	pyrometer
purposely	pustular	pyrometers
purposes	put	pyrostat
purposive	putative	pyrotechnic
purr	putrid	pyrotechnics
purse	puts	python
pursual	putt	
pursuance	puttee	

Q

qua		quaker		quarterfinal	
quack		qualification		quarterly	
quackery		qualifications		quartermaster	
quad		qualified		quarters	
quadrangle		qualifier		quartet	
quadrant		qualify		quartile	
quadratic		qualifying		quarto	
quadrennial		qualitative ⊙		quarts	
quadrennially		qualitatively ⊙		quartz	
quadric		qualities ⊙		quash	
quadrille		quality ○		quasi	
quadrillion		qualm		quatrain	
quadriplegic		quandary		quaver	
quadriplegics		quantify		quaveringly	
quadruplane		quantitative ⊙		quay	
quadruple		quantitatively ⊙		queen	
quadruplicate		quantities ⊙		queenly	
quads		quantity ○		queenship	
quag		quantize		queer	
quagmire		quantum		quell	
quail		quarantine		quench	
quaint		quark		quenchless	
quaintly		quarrel		queries	
quake		quarreler		querulous	
		quarrelsome		querulously	
		quarrier		query	
		quarry		querying	
		quart		quest	
		quarter		question ○	
		quarterback		questionable ⊙	

questionably ☉	quietly	quit
questioned ☉	quietness	quitclaim
questioner ☉	quill	quite
questioners ☉	quillwork ☉	quits
questioning ☉	quilt	quitter
questioningly ☉	quilter	quiver
questionnaire ☉	quince	quixotic
questionnaires ☉	quinine	quiz
questions ☉	quinoid	quizzical
queue	quint	quoin
quibble	quintal	quoit
quick	quintessence	quoits
quicken	quintessential	quorum
quicker	quintet	quota
quickest	quintillion	quotable
quickly	quintuple	quotas
quickness	quintuplet	quotation
quicksilver	quinze	quotations
quickstep	quip	quote
quiescence	quipster	quoted
quiescent	quire	quotient
quiet	quirk	quotients
quieter	quirky	quoting
quietist	quirt	

R

rabbi		rackety		radiographs	
rabbinical		racks		radiography	
rabbit		racy		radiology	
rabbitry		radar		radiophare	
rabbits		radars		radiophone	
rabble		radarscope		radiophony	
rabid		radiac		radiophoto	
rabidly		radial		radios	
raccoon		radially		radioscope	
race		radiance		radiosensitive	
racer		radiant		radiotelegram	
races		radiate		radiotelephone	
raceway		radiating		radiotelephones	
raceways		radiation		radiotelephony	
racial		radiator		radiotherapist	
racially		radical		radiotherapy	
racing		radicalism		radish	
racings		radically		radium	
racism		radii		radiumize	
racist		radio		radius	
rack		radioactive ☉		radix	
racket		radioactivity ☉		radome	
racketeer		radiobiology		radon	
racketeers		radiocarbon		raffle	
		radiocast		raft	
		radiochemistry		rafter	
		radiogram		rafters	
		radiograph		raftsman	
		radiographer		rag	
		radiographic		rage	

ragged	rainy	rampart ☉
raggedness	raise	ramps
raggy	raised	ramrod
raging	raiser	ramshackle
rags	raisers	ran
ragtime ☉	raises	ranch
ragweed	raisin	rancher
raid	raising	ranchers
rail	raisins	ranches
railhead	rajah	rancho
railings	rake	rancid
raillery	raking	rancidity
railman	rakish	rancor
railroad	rallied	rancorous
railroader	rallies	random
railroading	rally	randomization
railroads	rallying	randomize
rails	ram	randomly
railway	ramble	rang
railworker ☉	rambler	range
raiment	ramblings	ranged
rain	ramification	rangeland
rainbow	ramifications	rangelands
raincoat	ramiform ☉	ranger
rained	ramify	rangers
rainfall	ramjet	ranges
raining	rammer	ranging
rainless	ramp	rangy
rains	rampage	rank
rainstorm	rampant	ranked

rankest	rareness	rational
ranking	rarer	rationale
rankle	rarest	rationalism
ranks	rarity	rationalist
ransack	rascal	rationalistic
ransom	rascally	rationality
rant	rash	rationalization
rantingly	rashness	rationalize
rants	rasp	rationally
rap	raspberry	rationing
rape	rasper	ratios
rapeseed	rat	ratline
rapid	rata	ratoon
rapidity	ratability	rattan
rapidly	ratable	ratteen
rapids	ratchet	rattle
rapier	rate	rattlebox
rapierlike	rated	rattlebrain
rapine	rater	rattlehead
rappee	rates	rattler
rappel	rather	rattleroot
rapping	rathskeller	rattlesnake
rapport	ratification	rattly
rapt	ratified	ratty
raptly	ratify	raucous
raptorial	rating	raucously
rapture	ratings	ravage
rare	ratio	rave
rarefy	ratiocinate	ravel
rarely	ration	raven

ravenous		reactant		reaffirm	
ravine		reacted		reaffirmation	
ravioli		reaction		reaffirmed	
ravish		reactionary		reaffirming	
ravishment		reactions		reagent	
raw		reactivate ☉		real	
rawer		reactivation ☉		realign	
rawhead		reactive ☉		realism	
rawhide		reactivity ☉		realist	
rawin		reactor		realistic	
rawinsonde		reactors		realistically	
rawness		reacts		realities	
ray		read		reality	
rayon		readability		realization	
rays		readable		realize	
raze		reader		realized	
razon		readers		realizing	
razor		readily		reallocate	
razorback		readiness		reallocation	
razorbill		reading		really	
razorstrop		readings		realm	
re		readjust ☉		realtor	
reach		readjustable ☉		realtors	
reached		readjusting ☉		realty	
reaches		readjustment ☉		ream	
reaching		readmitted		reamer	
reacquaint		readopt		reaming	
reacquainted		readout ☉		reams	
react		reads		reanalyze	
reactance		ready		reanalyzed	

reap		reassembly		rebound	
reaped		reassert		rebounded	
reaper		reassertion		rebroadcast	
reaping		reasserts		rebuff	
reappear		reassess		rebuild	
reappearance		reassessment		rebuilding	
reapplication		reassign		rebuilt	
reapply		reassignment		rebuke	
reappoint		reassociate ⊙		rebut	
reappointment		reassociation ⊙		rebuttal	
reapportion		reassume		rebutted	
reapportionment		reassurance ⊙		rebutting	
reappraisal		reassure ⊙		recalcitrant	
reappraise		reassured ⊙		recalcitrate	
rear		reassuring ⊙		recalculate	
reared		reassuringly ⊙		recalculation	
reargue		reattain		recall	
rearm		reawake		recalled	
rearmament		reawaken		recalling	
rearmost		rebate		recant	
rearrange		rebel v.; a., n.		recantation	
rearrangement		rebellion		recap	
rearward		rebellious		recapitalization	
reason		rebelliously		recapitalize	
reasonable		rebels v.; n.		recapitulate	
reasonableness		rebid		recapitulation	
reasonably		rebill		recapped	
reasoning		rebind		recapping	
reasons		rebirth		recapture	
reassemble		reborn		recarry	

recede		recharging		recline	
receded		recharter		reclining	
receipt		recheck		reclothe	
receipted		rechecked		recluse	
receipting		rechecking		reclusion	
receipts		recipe		recognition ▢	
receivable ⊙		recipes		recognizable ▢	
receivables ⊙		recipient		recognizably ▢	
receival ⊙		recipients		recognizance ▢	
receive ○		reciprocal		recognize ▢	
received ⊙		reciprocate		recognized ▢	
receiver ⊙		reciprocating		recognizes ▢	
receivers ⊙		reciprocity		recognizing ▢	
receivership ⊙		recital		recoil	
receives ⊙		recitation		recoilless	
receiving ⊙		recitations		recoin	
recent		recite		recollect	
recently		reckless		recollection	
receptacle		recklessly		recombination	
receptacles		recklessness		recombine	
reception		reckon		recommence	
receptionist		reckoner		recommencement	
receptions		reckonings		recommend	
receptive		reclaim		recommendation	
recertified ⊙		reclaimed		recommendations	
recertify ⊙		reclamation		recommended	
recess		reclassification		recommending	
recession		reclassifications		recommends	
recessive		reclassified		recommit	
recharge		reclassify		recommittal	

recompense	recontrol ⊙	recreation
recompose	reconvene	recreational
recompress	reconvened	recreationally
recompression	reconvening	recriminate
recomputation	reconversion	recrimination
recompute	reconvert	recruit
reconcile	recopy	recruited
reconciled	record ⊙	recruiter
reconciliation	recordable ⊙	recruiters
recondition ⊙	recorded ⊙	recruiting
reconditioned ⊙	recorder ⊙	recruitment
reconditioner ⊙	recorders ⊙	recruits
reconditioning ⊙	recordholder ⊙	rectal
reconnaissance	recording ⊙	rectangle
reconnect	recordings ⊙	rectangular
reconnection	records ⊙	rectifier
reconnoiter	recount	rectifiers
reconsider ⊙	recounted ⊙	rectify
reconsideration ⊙	recounting ⊙	rectifying
reconsiderations ⊙	recounts ⊙	rectilinear
reconsidered ⊙	recoup	rectilinearly
reconsign	recourse	rectitude
reconsignment	recover	rector
reconstitute	recoverable	rectorial
reconstitution	recovered	rectory
reconstruct ⊙	recoveries	rectum
reconstructed ⊙	recovering	recumbency
reconstruction ⊙	recovers	recumbent
reconstructive ⊙	recovery	recuperate
reconstructor ⊙	recreate	recuperating

recuperative	redemption	redoubt	
recur	redemptions	redout ⊙	
recurred	redemptive	redraft	
recurrence	redeposit	redraw	
recurrent	redepositing	redress	
recurrently	redeposition	reduce	
recurring	redesign	reduced	
recycle	redesigned	reducer	
recycled	redesigning	reduces	
recycling	redevelop ⊙	reducing	
red	redeveloper ⊙	reduction	
redbird	redevelopment ⊙	reductions	
redbud	redhead	redundancy	
redcap	redirect ⊙	redundant	
redcoat	redirecting ⊙	redwood	
redden	rediscount ⊙	redwoods	
redder	rediscounted ⊙	reed	
reddish	rediscover	reedbuck	
redeal	rediscovery	reeducate ⊙	
redecorate	rediscuss ⊙	reeducation ⊙	
redecoration	redistribute ⊙	reedy	
rededicate	redistributed ⊙	reef	
rededication	redistribution ⊙	reefer	
redeem	redistrict	reek	
redeemability	redness	reeky	
redeemable	redo	reel	
redeemed	redoing	reelect ⊙	
redefine	redolence	reelected ⊙	
redefined	redolent	reelection ⊙	
redefinition	redouble	reeler	

reeling		referent		reflectors	
reels		referral		reflects	
reembark		referrals		reflex	
reemerge		referred		reflexes	
reemphasize		referring		reflexibility	
reemploy ☉		refers		refloat	
reemployment ☉		refigure ☉		reflux	
reenact		refigured ☉		refold	
reenlist		refill		reforest	
reenter		refilled		reforestation	
reentrance		refills		reform ☉	
reentry		refinance		reformation ☉	
reequip ☉		refinancing		reformatories ☉	
reequipment ☉		refine		reformatory ☉	
reestablish ☉		refined		reformed ☉	
reestablished ☉		refinement		reformer ☉	
reestablishment ☉		refineries		reformers ☉	
reevaluate ☉		refiner		reforming ☉	
reevaluation ☉		refiners		reforms ☉	
reexamination		refinery		reformulate ☉	
reexamine		refining		reformulation ☉	
reexamined		refinish		refract	
refer		refinished		refractive	
referee		refinishing		refractory	
refereed		reflect		refrain	
reference		reflected		refrained	
referenced		reflecting		refraining	
references		reflection		refresh	
referencing		reflective		refreshed	
referendum		reflector		refresher	

refreshing	regain	registered
refreshingly	regained	registering
refreshment	regaining	registers
refreshments	regal	registrant
refrigerate	regale	registrants
refrigerated	regalia	registrar
refrigerating	regard ⊙	registrars
refrigeration	regardable ⊙	registration
refrigerator	regarded ⊙	registrations
refrigerators	regardful ⊙	registry
refuel	regarding ⊙	reglet
refueler	regardless ⊙	regress
refuge	regards ⊙	regressing
refugee	regatta	regression
refund	regency	regressive
refundable	regeneracy	regret
refunded	regenerate	regretful
refunding	regenerator	regretfully
refunds	regent	regrets
refurbish	regents	regrettable
refurbished	regime	regrettably
refusal	regimen	regretted
refusals	regiment	regretting
refuse	regimental	reground ⊙
refused	region	regroup
refuses	regional	regrouping
refusing	regionalism	regular ⊙
refutation	regionally	regularity ⊙
refute	regions	regularization ⊙
refuted	register	regularize ⊙

regularly ⊙	reigning	reinterpret
regulars ⊙	reimbursable	reintroduce
regulate	reimburse	reintroduction
regulated	reimbursed	reinvest
regulates	reimbursement	reinvested
regulating	reimbursing	reinvestigate
regulation	rein	reinvestigation
regulations	reincarnate	reinvestment
regulative	reincarnation	reinvoice
regulator	reindeer	reissue ⊙
regulators	reinforce	reissued ⊙
regulatory	reinforced	reissues ⊙
rehabilitate	reinforcement	reiterate
rehabilitating	reinforcements	reiterated
rehabilitation	reinforcing	reject
rehandle	reins	rejected
rehandling	reinsert	rejecting
rehang	reinstall	rejection
reharmonize	reinstate ⊙	rejections
rehash	reinstated ⊙	rejects
rehear	reinstatement ⊙	rejoice
rehearsal	reinstating ⊙	rejoicing
rehearsals	reinstruct ⊙	rejoin
rehearse	reinstruction ⊙	rejoinder
reheat	reinsurance ⊙	rejuvenate
reheater	reinsurances ⊙	rejuvenation
reheel	reinsure ⊙	rekindle
rehire	reinsured ⊙	relapse
rehiring	reinsurer ⊙	relate
reign	reinsurers ⊙	related

relatedness	relent	relinquished
relates	relentless	relinquishment
relating	relentlessly	relish
relation	relentlessness	relishable
relations	relet	relisten
relationship	relevance	relitigate
relationships	relevancy	relitigated
relative	relevant	relive
relatively	reliability	reload
relatives	reliable	reloader
relativism	reliably	reloading
relativist	reliance	reloan
relativistic	reliant	relocate
relativity	relic	relocated
relax	relied	relocating
relaxation	relief	relocation
relaxed	relieve	reluctance
relaxing	relieved	reluctant
relay	relieves	reluctantly
relayed	relieving	relume
relayer	relight	rely
relaying	relights	relying
relays	religion	remade
relearn	religionist	remain
releasable	religions	remainder
release	religious	remained
released	religiously	remaining
releases	reline	remains
releasing	relined	remake
relegate	relinquish	reman

remand	reminiscence	removal	
remandment	reminiscent	remove	
remanufacture ⊙	remiss	removed	
remanufactured ⊙	remissible	remover	
remanufacturer ⊙	remission	removers	
remark	remit	removes	
remarkable	remittal	removing	
remarkably	remittance	remunerate	
remarked	remittances	remuneration	
remarks	remitted	remunerative	
remarque	remitting	remunerator	
remarried	remnant	renaissance	
remarry	remnants	rename	
remedial	remodel	renamed	
remedied	remodeled	renascent	
remedies	remodeling	rend	
remedy	remold	render	
remember	remonetize	rendered	
remembered	remonstrance	rendering	
remembering	remonstrate	renders	
remembers	remorse	rendezvous	
remembrance	remorseful	rendition	
remind	remorsefully	rendrock	
reminded	remorseless	renegade	
reminder	remote	renege	
reminders	remotely	renegotiate ⊡	
remindful	remoteness	renegotiated ⊡	
reminding	remotest	renegotiation ⊡	
reminds	remount	renew	
reminisce	removable	renewable	

renewal		reoccur		repairman
renewals		reoccurrence		repairmen
renewed		reopen		repairs
renewing		reopened		reparation
renews		reopener		repartee
renominate		reopening		repass
renomination		reorder ☉		repast
renounce		reordered ☉		repave
renounced		reordering ☉		repaving
renounces		reorders ☉		repay
renovate		reorganization ☉		repayable
renovated		reorganizational ☉		repaying
renovating		reorganize ☉		repayment
renovation		reorganized ☉		repayments
renovations		reorganizing ☉		repeal
renown		reorient		repealed
renowned		reorientation		repealing
rent		rep		repeat
rental		repack		repeated
rentals		repackaged		repeatedly
rented		repacked		repeater
renter		repacking		repeating
renters		repaid		repeats
renting		repaint		repel
rents		repainted		repellence
renumber ☉		repainting		repellent
renunciate		repair		repent
renunciation		repairable		repentance
renunciatory		repaired		repentant
reoccupy		repairing		repercussion

repercussions	replicas	represent ⊙
repertoire	replicate *v.; a.*	representable ⊙
repertoires	replication	representation ⊙
repertory	replied	representational ⊙
repetition	replier	representationally ⊙
repetitions	replies	representations ⊙
repetitious	reply	representative ⊙
repetitive	replying	representatives ⊙
rephrase	report ⊙	represented ⊙
repine	reportable ⊙	representing ⊙
repiningly	reportage ⊙	represents ⊙
replace	reported ⊙	repress
replaceable	reportedly ⊙	repression
replaced	reporter ⊙	repressive
replacement	reporters ⊙	repressor
replacements	reporting ⊙	repressure
replaces	reportorial ⊙	repressuring
replacing	reports ⊙	reprieval
replan	reposal	reprieve
replant	repose	reprimand
replantable	reposit	reprimander
replanting	reposition	reprimandingly
replay	repository	reprint
replead	repossess	reprinted
replenish	repossessed	reprinting
replenisher	repossession	reprints
replenishment	reprehend	reprisal
replete	reprehensible	reprise
repletion	reprehension	reproach
replica	reprehensive	reproachable

reproachful	repulsive	reran
reproachless	repurchase	reread
reprobate	repurchased	rereading
reproduce	reputable	reroute
reproduced	reputation	rerouting
reproducible	reputations	rerun
reproducing	repute	resalable
reproduction ⊙	reputedly	resale
reproductions ⊙	request ⊙	reschedule ▢
reproductive ⊙	requested ⊙	rescheduled ▢
reprogram	requester	rescind
reprogramming	requesting ⊙	rescindable
reproof	requestion ⊙	rescission
reproval	requests ⊙	rescore
reprove	require ⊙	rescreen
reprovingly	required ⊙	rescue
reptile	requirement ⊙	rescuer
reptilelike	requirements ⊙	reseal
republic ⊙	requires ⊙	research
republican ⊙	requiring ⊙	researchable
republicanism ⊙	requisite	researched
republication ⊙	requisites	researcher
republish ⊙	requisition	researchers
repudiate	requisitioned	researches
repudiation	requisitioning	researching
repugn	requisitions	reseat
repugnance	requital	resect
repugnant	requite	resection
repulse	requote	reseed
repulsion	requoted	reseeded

reseeding	reshipped ⊙	resinate	
resell	reshipping ⊙	resinlike	
reseller	reshuffle	resins	
resemblance	reshufflement	resist	
resemble	reside	resistance	
resembles	resided	resistant	
resent	residence	resisted	
resentful	residences	resistible	
resentfully	residency	resisting	
resentment	resident	resistive	
reservation ⊙	residential	resistless	
reservationist ⊙	residentially	resistor	
reservations ⊙	residents	resistors	
reserve ⊙	resides	resists	
reserved ⊙	residing	resize	
reservedly ⊙	residual	resizing	
reserves ⊙	residuary	reslant	
reserving	residue	resold	
reservist ⊙	residues	resole	
reservists ⊙	resign	resolicitation	
reservoir ⊙	resignation	resolute	
reservoirs ⊙	resignations	resolutely	
reset	resigned	resolution	
resettable	resignedly	resolutions	
resettle	resigns	resolvable	
resettlement	resile	resolve	
reshape	resilience	resolved	
reshaper	resiliency	resolvent	
reship ⊙	resilient	resolves	
reshipment ⊙	resin	resolving	

resent	resettlement	reshape	reside	residence	residency	residential	residue	resignation	resin	resolute
rizent	rĕsetlmənt	rēshāp	rizīd	rezədəns	rezədənsē	rezədenshəl	rezədü	rezignāshən	rezn	rezəlüt

resonance	respite	restaurateur
resonant	resplend	restful
resonate	resplendence	restfully
resort	resplendent	resting
resorting	respond	restitute
resound	responded	restitution
resounding	respondent	restive
resoundingly	respondents	restively
resource	responding	restless
resourceful	responds	restlessly
resourcefully	response ⊙	restlessness
resourcefulness	responses ⊙	restock
resources	responsibilities ⊙	restocking
respect ⊙	responsibility ⊙	restorable
respectability ⊙	responsible ⊙	restoration
respectable ⊙	responsibly ⊙	restorative
respectably ⊙	responsive ⊙	restore
respected ⊙	responsively ⊙	restored
respecter ⊙	responsiveness ⊙	restorer
respectful ⊙	responsivity ⊙	restoring
respectfully ⊙	respray	restrain
respecting ⊙	rest	restrained
respective ⊙	restaff	restrainer
respectively ⊙	restart	restraint
respects ⊙	restate ⊙	restraints
respell	restatement ⊙	restrict
respiration	restates ⊙	restricted
respirator	restating ⊙	restricting
respiratory	restaurant	restriction
respire	restaurants	restrictions

restrictive	resurgence	retene	
restricts	resurgent	retention	
restrike	resurrect	retentive	
restring	resurrectionist	retentiveness	
restructure	resurrective	retest	
rests	resurvey	rethink ⊙	
restudy	resuscitate	reticence	
restyle	resuscitation	reticent	
resubject	resuscitator	reticle	
resubmit	retail	reticular	
resubmitted	retailed	reticulate	
resubmitting	retailer	reticulation	
result ○	retailers	retiform ⊙	
resultant ⊙	retailing	retina	
resultants ⊙	retails	retinal	
resulted ⊙	retain	retinue	
resultful ⊙	retained	retire	
resulting ⊙	retainer	retired	
resultless ⊙	retaining	retiree	
results ⊙	retake	retirees	
resume	retaker	retirement	
résumé	retaliate	retiring	
resumed	retaliation	retold	
resumes	retaliatory	retool	
resuming	retard	retort	
resumption	retardation	retouch	
resupply	retarded	retrace	
resurface	retarding	retraceable	
resurfacing	retell	retracement	
resurge	retellable	retracements	

retract	returnable ⊙	revegetate
retractile	returned ⊙	revegetation
retractive	returnee ⊙	reveille
retrain	returning ⊙	revel
retraining	returns ⊙	revelation
retransform ⊙	retype	reveler
retranslate	retyping	revelings
retread	reunification	revelry
retreat	reunify	revenge
retreatal	reunion	revenger
retreats	reunionist	revenue
retrench	reunions	revenues
retrial	reunite	reverberate
retribution	reunitedly	reverberation
retributive	reupholster	reverberator
retrieval	reusable	revere
retrieve	reuse	reverence
retrieved	reused	reverend
retriever	reusing	reverent
retrieving	revaluate ⊙	reverently
retroactive ⊙	revaluated ⊙	reverie
retroactively ⊙	revaluation ⊙	reversal
retroactivity ⊙	revalue ⊙	reversals
retrocede	revamp	reverse
retrograde	revarnishing	reversed
retrogress	reveal	reverses
retrogressive	revealed	reversibility
retrospect	revealing	reversible
retrospective	revealingly	reversing
return ⊙	reveals	reversion

revert	revokes	rewrites	
revertible	revoking	rewriting	
revet	revolt	rewritten	
revetment	revoltingly	rhapsodize	
review	revolution	rhapsody	
reviewed	revolutionary	rheology	
reviewer	revolutionist	rhetoric	
reviewing	revolutionize	rhetorical	
reviews	revolutions	rhetorician	
revile	revolve	rheumatic	
revilement	revolver	rheumatism	
reviler	revolves	rheumatoid	
revise	revolving	rhinestone	
revised	revote	rhinoceros	
revising	revue	rhinology	
revision	reward	rhodium	
revisionist	rewarded	rhyme	
revisions	rewarding	rhythm	
revisit	rewards	rhythmic	
revitalize	rewind	rhythmical	
revival	rewinding	rib	
revivalism	rewire	ribald	
revivalist	rewired	ribbon	
revive	reword	ribbons	
revived	reworded	ribs	
revivifier	rework ⊙	rice	
revivify	reworked ⊙	rich	
revocable	reworking ⊙	richer	
revocation	rewound	richest	
revoke	rewrite	richly	

richness	rig	rings
rick	rigger	ringside
rickets	rigging	ringsider
rickety	right	rink
rickrack	righteous	rinse
ricks	righteousness	riot
ricochet	rightful	rioter
rid	rightfully	riots
riddance	rightist	rip
ridden	rightly	riparian
riddle	rightness	ripe
riddlingly	rights	ripen
ride	rigid	ripener
rider	rigidity	ripped
riderless	rigidly	ripping
riders	rigor	ripple
rides	rigorous	riprap
ridge	rigorously	rise
ridgeway	rigors	risen
ridicule	rigs	rises
ridiculous	rile	rising
ridiculously	rill	risk
riding	rim	risking
ridings	rimless	risks
rife	rimrock	risky
riffle	rind	rite
rifle	ring	ritual
rifleman	ringer	ritualize
riflemen	ringleader	rival
rift	ringlet	rivalry

riven		rob		rogue	
river		robbed		roguish	
riverbank		robber		roil	
riverboat		robbery		roily	
rivers		robe		roister	
riverside		robin		role	
rivet		robot		roles	
riveter		robotism		roll	
rivulet		robust		rollaway	
roach		robustly		rollback	
road		robustness		rolled	
roadability		rock		roller	
roadbed		rocker		rollers	
roadblock		rocket		rollick	
roadbuilder		rocketry		rolling	
roadhouse		rocketsonde		rolls	
roads		rockiness		romance	
roadside		rocks		romancer	
roadster		rockwork ☉		romantic	
roadway		rocky		romanticism	
roadways		rococo		romanticize	
roadwork ☉		rod		romp	
roadworthy ☉		rode		romper	
roam		rodent		roof	
roamer		rodeo		roofer	
roar		rods		roofing	
roaringly		roe		roofs	
roast		roentgen		rooftop	
roasted		roentgenize		rooftree	
roaster		roentgenology		room	

rivet	rivulet	roadability	roadway	robot	robust	rocket	rocky	rococo	roentgen	roister	romantic	roofer
rivit	rivūlit	rōdəbilətē	rōdwā	rōbət	rōbust	rokit	rokē	rōkōkō	rentgən	roistər	rōmantik	rüfər

roomer		rotary		roughneck	
roomful		rotate		roughness	
rooming		rotated		roulade	
roommate		rotater		roulette	
rooms		rotates		round	
roomy		rotating		roundabout ⊙	
roost		rotation		roundhouse	
rooster		rotational		rounding	
root		rotationally		roundly	
rooter		rotations		roundness	
rootless		rote		rounds	
roots		rotogravure		roundup	
rope		rotor		rouse	
roper		rotors		rousingly	
ropes		rotten		roustabout ⊙	
ropework ⊙		rotting		route	
rosary		rotund		routed	
rose		rotunda		routeman	
rosebud		rotundity		routes	
rosebush		rouge		routine	
roselle		rough		routinely	
roses		roughcast		routines	
rosette		roughed		routing	
rosily		roughen		rove	
rosin		roughened		rover	
roster		roughening		row	
				_n., v.; n., v._	
rosters		rougher		rowboat	
rostrum		roughest		rowboats	
rosy		roughing		rowdy	
rot		roughly		rowdyism	

rows *n., v.; n., v.*		rudimentary		rump	
royal		rudiments		rumple	
royalist		rue		rumpus	
royally		rueful		run	
royalties		ruefully		runabout ☉	
royalty		ruefulness		runabouts ☉	
rub		ruffian		runaway	
rubbed		ruffle		rundown ☉	
rubber		rug		rung	
rubberize		rugged		runner	
rubberized		ruggedly		runners	
rubbery		ruggedness		running	
rubbing		rugs		runout ☉	
rubbish		ruin		runs	
rubble		ruined		runt	
rubdown ☉		ruinous		runway	
rubicund		rule		runways	
rubies		ruled		rupee	
rubric		ruler		rupture	
ruby		rules		rural	
ruckus		ruling		ruralize	
rudd		rulings		rurally	
rudder		rum		ruse	
rudderless		rumble		ruses	
ruddiness		ruminant		rush	
ruddy		ruminate		rushed	
rude		rummage		rushing	
rudely		rumor		rust	
rudeness		rumored		rustic	
rudiment		rumors		rusting	

rustle		rut		ruthlessness	
rustler		rutabaga		rye	
rustproof		ruthless			
rusty		ruthlessly			

S

sabbatical	sacrum	sagging
saber	sad	sags
saberlike	sadden	said
sable	sadder	sail
sabotage	saddest	sailboat
saboteur	saddle	sailed
sachem	saddlebag	sailing
sachet	saddlery	sailings
sack	saddles	sailor
sacker	saddlesore	sailorly
sackful	sadism	sails
sacks	sadist	saint
sacral	sadistic	sainthood
sacrament	sadly	saintliness
sacre	sadness	saintly
sacred	safari	saints
sacredness	safe	sake
sacrifice	safeguard	salability
sacrificed	safeguarded	[1]salable
sacrifices	safeguarding	salacious
sacrificial	safeguards	salad
sacrificing	safekeeping	salads
sacrilege	safely	salamander
sacrosanct	safer	salami
	safest	salaried
	safety	salaries
	saffron	salary
	sag	sale
	saga	[2]saleable
	sage	sales

salesclerk	salts	sanctimonious
saleslady	salty	sanction
salesman	salubrious	sanctuary
salesmanship	salutary	sand
salesmen	salutation	sandal
salespeople	salutations	sandals
salesperson	salute	sandalwood
salesroom	salvage	sandblast
saleswoman	salvageable	sandbox
saleswomen	salvaged	sanded
salework ☉	salvaging	sander
salience	salvation	sanders
salient	salve	sandlot
saline	salves	sandman
salinity	salvo	sandpaper
saliva	salvor	sands
salivary	samara	sandstone
salivate	same	sandstorm
sallow	sameness	sandwich
sally	samp	sandy
salmon	sampan	sane
salmonella	sample	sanely
salon	sampler	saner
salons	samples	sanest
saloon	sampling	sanforize[1]
salsify	samplings	sanforized
salsilla	samurai	sang
salt	sanative	sanguinary
saltcellar	sanatorium	sanguine
salter	sanctify	sanify

salience	saliva	salmonella	salon	salsilla	salute	samara	sampan	samurai	sanatorium	sanforize
sālēəns	səlīvə	salmənelə	səlon	salsilə	səlüt	samərə	sampan	samürī	sanətôrēəm	sanfərīz

sanitarian	sarsaparilla	saturate
sanitarium	sartorial	saturated
sanitary	sash	saturation
sanitation	sassafras	saturnine
sanitize	sassy	satyr
sanitizer	sat	sauce
sanitizers	satchel	saucepan
sanity	sate	saucer
sank	satellite	saucerful
sans	satellites	saucerize
sant	satiate	sauces
sap	satiety	saucy
sapid	satin	sauerkraut
sapient	satire	saunter
sapling	satiric	saunteringly
saplings	satirical	sausage
sapor	satirically	sauté
sapper	satirist	sauterne
sappy	satirize	sautoir
sapwood	satisfaction ☉	savable
sarcasm	satisfactions ☉	savage
sarcastic	satisfactorily ☉	savagely
sarcastically	satisfactoriness ☉	savagery
sarcocarp	satisfactory ☉	savant
sarcology	satisfied ☉	save
sardine	satisfies ☉	saved
sardonic	satisfy ○	saver
sari	satisfying ☉	savers
sarong	satisfyingly ☉	saves
saros	satrap	saving

savings		scalene	scarcities
savior		scaler	scarcity
savor		scales	scare
savorless		scallion	scarecrow
savory		scallop	scared
savoy		scalp	scaremonger
saw		scalpel	scares
sawdust		scaly	scarf
sawhorse		scamp	[1]scarfs
sawing		scamper	scarify
sawman		scan	scarless
sawmill		scandal	scarlet
saws		scandalization	scarp
sawtimber		scandalize	scarring
sawyer		scandalous	scars
sax		scandia	[2]scarves
saxhorn		scanned	scary
saxophone		scanner	scat
say		scanning	scathe
saying		scans	scatheless
sayings		scant	scathingly
says		scantily	scatter
scab		scanty	scatteration
scabbard		scapegoat	scatterbrain
scaffold		scapement	scattered
scaffoldings		scapula	scattergun
scalage		scapular	scattering
scalar		scar	scattershot
scald		scarce	scavenge
scale		scarcely	scavenger

scenario	scholarships	scissorlike	
scenarist	scholastic	scissors	
scene	scholastically	sclerose	
scenery	school	sclerosis	
scenes	schoolbook	scoff	
scenic	schoolboy	scoffingly	
scenography	schoolgirl	scold	
scent	schoolhouse	scoldings	
schedule □	schooling	scone	
scheduled □	schoolmate	scoop	
scheduler □	schoolroom	scoopful	
schedules □	schools	scoot	
scheduling □	schoolwork ⊙	scooter	
schema	schooner	scope	
schemata	sciatic	scopola	
schematic	sciatica	scorch	
schematically	science	scorcher	
schematize	sciences	score	
scheme	scientific	scoreboard	
schemer	scientifically	scorecard	
schilling	scientist	scored	
schism	scientists	scorekeeper	
schist	scintilla	scoreless	
schizoid	scintillant	scores	
schizophrenia	scintillate	scoring	
schizophrenic	scintillation	scorn	
scholar	scintillator	scornful	
scholarly	scion	scornfully	
scholars	scission	scornfulness	
scholarship	scissor	scotch	

scoundrel	scrapping	scribe
scoundrelism	scrappy	scrim
scoundrelly	scraps	scrimmage
scour	scratch	scrimp
scourer	scratched	scrimpy
scourfish	scratches	scrip
scourge	scratching	script
scourger	scratchy	scripts
scourway	scrawl	scriptural
scout	scrawly	scripture
scoutcraft	scrawny	scrod
scouts	scream	scroll
scow	screamer	scrolls
scowl	screams	scrollwork ☉
scrabble	scree	scrounge
scrabbly	screech	scrub
scrag	screechingly	scrubber
scraggly	screechy	scrubbing
scraggy	screen	scrubby
scramble	screened	scrubs
scrambler	screening	scruff
scrambly	screenings	scrunch
scramjet	screenplay	scruple
scrap	screens	scrupulous
scrapbook	screw	scrupulously
scrape	screwdriver	scrutable
scraped	screws	scrutinize
scraper	screwworm	scrutiny
scrapings	scribble	scuba
scrapped	scribbler	scud

scuff	seamanship	seaweed
scuffle	seamed	seaworthiness ☉
scull	seamen	seaworthy ☉
sculpt	seamer	secant
sculptor	seamless	secede
sculptural	seams	seceder
sculpture	seaplane	secession
sculptured	seaport	secessional
scum	sear	secessionist
scurrility	search	seclude
scurrilous	searched	secluded
scurry	searching	seclusion
scurvy	searchingly	second
scuttle	searchlight	secondarily
sea	sears	secondary
seabed	seas	seconded
seaboard	seashore	secondly
seacoast	seasick	seconds
seacopter	seaside	secrecy
seafarer	season	secret
seafood	seasonable	secretarial ☉
seafoods	seasonal	secretariat ☉
seagoing ☉	seasonally	secretaries ☉
seal	seasoned	secretary ☉
sealant	seasons	secrete
sealed	seat	secretion
sealing	seated	secretive
seals	seating	secretly
seam	seats	secrets
seaman	seaway	sect

sectarian	sedimentary	seemly
sectarianism	sedimentation	seems
section	sedition	seen
sectional	seditious	seep
sectionalize	seduce	seepage
sectionalizing	seducee	seer
sectionals	seducer	seersucker
sectioned	seductive	sees
sectioning	sedulous	seesaw
sections	sedulously	seethe
sector	see	seethingly
sectors	seed	segment
secular	seedbed	segmental
secularism	seeded	segments
secularist	seeding	segregate
secularize	seedless	segregated
secure	seedlings	segregationist
secured	seeds	seine
securely	seedtime ☉	seism
securing	seedy	seismic
securities	seeing	seismograph
security	seek	seismological
sedan	seeker	seismology
sedate	seeking	seize
sedately	seekingly	seized
sedative	seeks	seizing
sedentary	seem	seizure
sedge	seemed	seldom
sedgeland	seeming	select
sediment	seemingly	selected

selecting	self-destruction	self-pacing
selection	self-determination	self-pity
selections	self-direction ⊙	self-praise
selective	self-discipline	self-rating
selectively	self-educated ⊙	self-realization
selectivity	self-employed ⊙	self-regard ⊙
selectman	self-esteem	self-reliance
selector	self-evaluating ⊙	self-reliant
selectors	self-evaluation ⊙	self-respect ⊙
selects	self-evident	self-restraint
self	self-examination	selfsame
self-activity ⊙	self-explanatory	self-satisfaction ⊙
self-addressed	self-government ⊙	self-satisfied ⊙
self-adjustment ⊙	self-guidance	self-service ⊙
self-administered ⊙	self-help	self-study
self-appraisal	self-image	self-styled
self-censorship	self-importance ⊙	self-sufficient
self-centered	self-imposed	self-supporting
self-command	self-improvement ⊙	self-sustaining
self-concern	self-indulgence	self-taught
self-confidence	self-insurance ⊙	self-unloading
self-confident	self-interest ⊙	self-will ⊙
self-conscious	selfish	self-worth ⊙
self-contained ⊙	self-loading	sell
self-content	self-made	seller
self-control ⊙	self-mastery	sellers
self-criticism	self-motivated	selling
self-deceit	self-motivation	sellout ⊙
self-defense	self-opinion	sells
self-denial	self-organized ⊙	selves

semantic		senatorial		sensitive
semantically		senators		sensitively
semblance		send ○		sensitivities
semester		sender ⊙		sensitivity
semesters		senders ⊙		sensitize
semiannual		sending ⊙		sensor
semiannually		sends ⊙		sensory
semicolon		senescence		sensual
semiconductor		senile		sensuality
semiconductors		senior		sensuous
semifinal		seniority		sent
semifinished		seniors		sentence
semimonthly		senna		sentences
seminal		señor		sentience
seminar		señora		sentient
seminars		sensate		sentiment
seminary		sensation		sentimental
semiperishable		sensational		sentimentalist
semiprivate		sensationalism		sentimentality
semipublic ⊙		sensationally		sentimentalize
semiretired		sensations		sentiments
semiretirement		sense		sentinel
semiskilled		sensed		sentinels
semitrailer		senseless		sentry
semitrailers		senselessly		separable
semitropical		senses		separate v.; a., n.
semiweekly		sensibility		separated
sen		sensible		separately
senate		sensibly		separates v.; n.
senator		sensing		separating

separation	serge	serviceman ⊙
separations	sergeant	servicemen ⊙
separatist	serial	services ⊙
separator	serialize	servicing ⊙
sepia	serially	servile ⊙
sepias	series	serving ⊙
septa	serious	servings ⊙
septic	seriously	servitor ⊙
septum	seriousness	servitude ⊙
sequel	sermon	servo ⊙
sequence	sermonize	servocontrol ⊙
sequences	sermons	servosystem ⊙
sequencing	serological	sesame
sequent	serology	session
sequential	serpent	sessions
sequentially	serpentine	set
sequester	serrate	setback
sequestrate	serration	setbacks
sequestration	serum	setout ⊙
sequin	servant ⊙	sets
sequins	servants ⊙	setter
sera	serve ⊙	setters
seraph	served ⊙	setting
serenade	server ⊙	settings
serendipity	serves ⊙	settle
serene	service ⊙	settled
serenely	serviceability ⊙	settlement
serenity	serviceable ⊙	settlements
serf	serviceably ⊙	settler
serfdom	serviced ⊙	settlers

settling	shadow	shape
setup	shadows	shaped
seventh	shadowy	shapeless
sever	shady	shapelessness
several	shaft	shapely
severalfold	shafting	shapes
severally	shafts	shaping
severance	shag	share
severe	shaggy	shared
severed	shake	shareholder
severely	shaken	shareholders
severity	shaker	shareowner
sew	shakers	shareowners
sewage	shakes	shares
sewed	shakily	sharing
sewer	shaky	shark
sewerage	shall ○	sharks
sewers	shallow	sharp
sewing	shallower	sharpen
sewn	shallowness	sharpened
sex	sham	sharpener
sextet	shamble	sharpeners
sexton	shame	sharpening
shabbily	shamed	sharpens
shabby	shamefacedly	sharper
shack	shameful	sharpest
shackle	shampoo	sharply
shade	shamrock	sharpness
shaded	shank	shatter
shades	shanty	shatteringly

shave	shellac	shingle
shaven	shells	shingles
shaver	shelter	shining
shaving	sheltered	shiny
shavings	shelve	ship ☉
shawl	shelves	shipboard ☉
shay	shelving	shipbuilder ☉
she	shepherd	shipbuilding ☉
sheaf	sherbet	shipload ☉
shear	sheriff	shipman ☉
shears	she's ☉	shipmaster ☉
sheath	shield	shipmate ☉
sheathing	shielded	shipmates ☉
shed	shielding	shipment ☉
she'd ☉	shift	shipments ☉
shedding	shifted	shipowner ☉
sheds	shifting	shipped ☉
sheen	shiftless	shipper ☉
sheep	shifts	shippers ☉
sheepshead	shifty	shipping ☉
sheepskin	shilling	shippings ☉
sheer	shillings	ships ☉
sheet	shim	shipshape ☉
sheeting	shimmer	shipside ☉
sheets	shimming	shipworm ☉
sheetwork ☉	shimmy	shipwreck ☉
sheik	shin	shipwrecked ☉
shelf	shinbone	shipwright ☉
shell	shine	shipyard ☉
she'll ☉	shined	shipyards ☉

shawl	shay	shear	sheen	sheep	sheer	sheik	shellac	shelve	sherbet	sheriff	shilling	shin	shine	shingle
shôl	shā	shēr	shēn	shēp	shēr	shēk	shəlak	shelv	shérbət	sherif	shiling	shin	shīn	shinggl

shire		shoplifters		shorthorn ☉	
shirk		shoplifting		shortie ☉	
shirt		shopped		shortish ☉	
shirts		shopper		shortleaf ☉	
shiver		shoppers		shortly ☉	
shoal		shopping		shortness ☉	
shock		shops		shorts ☉	
shockingly		shopwork ☉		shortstop ☉	
shod		shopworn		shot	
shoddy		shore		shotgun	
shoe		shoreline		shotguns	
shoehorn		shores		shots	
shoelace		shoreside		should	
shoeless		shorn		shoulder	
shoemaker		short ○		shouldered	
shoes		shortage ☉		shoulders	
shoeshine		shortages ☉		shouldn't	
shoestring		shortbread ☉		shout	
shone		shortcake ☉		shouting	
shook		shortcoming ☉		shouts	
shooks		shortcomings ☉		shove	
shoot		shorten ☉		shovel	
shooter		shortened ☉		shoveler	
shooting		shortening ☉		shovelful	
shootings		shorter ☉		shovelhead	
shoots		shortest ☉		show	
shop		shortfall ☉		showboat	
shopkeeper		shorthair ☉		showcase	
shoplift		shorthand ☉		showdown ☉	
shoplifter		shorthanded ☉		showed	

shower n.; n., v.		shrimp		shutter	
showers n.; n., v.		shrimpy		shutterless	
showing		shrine		shutting	
showings		shrink		shuttle	
showman		shrinkable		shuttlecock	
showmanship		shrinkage		shy	
shown		shrinker		shyer	
showplace		shrinking		shyest	
showroom		shrivel		shyly	
showrooms		shroff		shyster	
shows		shroud		sibilance	
showy		shroudless		sibilant	
shrank		shrub		sibling	
shrapnel		shrubbery		sic	
shred		shrubby		sick	
shredded		shrubs		sicken	
shredder		shrug		sickened	
shredders		shrunk		sicker	
shredding		shrunken		sickish	
shreds		shuck		sickle	
shrew		shudder		sickly	
shrewd		shuddery		sickness	
shrewdest		shuffle		sicknesses	
shrewdly		shuffleboard		side	
shrewish		shuffling		sidearm	
shriek		shun		sideboard	
shrill		shunless		sideburns	
shriller		shunner		sided	
shrillness		shunt		sidelight	
shrilly		shut		sideline	

sidelong	sightworthy ☉	silent
sidepiece	sigma	silently
sides	sign	silhouette
sidewalk	signal	silhouettes
sidewalks	signaling	silica
sideway	signalize	silicate
sideways	signals	silicon
sidewise	signature	silicone
siding	signatures	silicosis
sidle	signboard	silk
siege	signed	silken
sierra	signer	silkily
siesta	signers	silkiness
sieve	significance □	silkworm
sieving	significancy □	silky
sift	significant □	sill
sifted	significantly □	silliest
sifting	signification □	sills
sifts	signified	silly
sigh	signifies	silo
sighingly	signify	silt
sight	signifying	silver
sighted	signing	silvering
sightless	signor	silverware
sightline	signora	silvery
sightliness	signpost	silviculture
sights	signs	similar
sightsee	silage	similarities
sightseeing	silence	similarity
sightseer	silencer	similarly

simile	sinew	sinuous
similitude	sinewy	sinuously
simmer	sinful	sinus
simmers	sinfully	sip
simple	sinfulness	siphon
simpler	sing	sir
simplest	singe	sire
simpleton	singer	siren
simplicity	singers	sires
simplification	singing	sirloin
simplified	single	sister
simplifies	singled	sister-in-law ⊙
simplify	singleness	sisters
simplifying	singles	sit
simplistic	singleton	site
simply	singly	sites
simulate	sings	sits
simulated	singsong	sitter
simulation	singular	sitting
simulator	singularity	sittings
simulcast	singularly	situate ⊙
simultaneous	sinister	situated ⊙
simultaneously	sink	situating ⊙
sin	sinkhole	situation ⊙
since	sinking	situational ⊙
sincere	sinless	situations ⊙
sincerely △	sinlessly	situs
sincerest	sinner	sixth
sincerity	sins	¹sizable
sine	sinter	size

[2]sizeable	skids	skirt
sized	skier	skirtlike
sizes	skiers	skirts
sizing	skiff	skit
sizzle	skiing	skits
sizzling	skill	skitter
skate	skilled	skittle
skater	skillet	skulk
skein	skillful	skull
skeletal	skillfully	skullcap
skeleton	skillfulness	skullfish
skeletons	skills	skunk
skeptic	skim	skunks
skeptical	skimming	sky
skeptically	skimp	skycap
skepticism	skimpy	skycaps
sketch	skin	skyjack
sketchbook	skinless	skyjacker
sketched	skinned	skylark
sketches	skinner	skylight
sketchiest	skinnier	skyline
sketchiness	skinniness	skyliner
sketchy	skinny	skyport
skew	skip	skyrocket
skewer	skipped	skyrocketing
skewness	skipper	skyrockets
ski	skips	skyscraper
skiagram	skirl	skyway
skiagraph	skirmish	slab
skid	skirmisher	slabs

slack	slaughter	sleepy
slacken	slaughtered	sleet
slackens	slaughterhouse	sleeve
slackened	slaughterman	sleeveless
slacker	slave	sleeves
slacks	slavery	sleigh
slag	slavish	sleight
slain	slavishness	slender
slake	slay	slenderer
slakeless	slayer	slenderize
slam	slayings	slept
slander	sleave	sleuth
slanderer	sleazily	sleuthing
slanderous	sleazy	slew
slang	sled	slice
slangy	sledge	sliceable
slant	sledlike	slicer
slanted	sleek	slick
slantwise	sleekest	slicker
slap	sleep	slid
slappy	sleeper	slide
slapstick	sleepier	slider
slash	sleepily	slides
slasher	sleeping	sliding
slat	sleepless	slight
slate	sleeplessly	slighted
slated	sleeplessness	slighter
slater	sleepwalk	slightest
slats	sleepwalker	slightly
slattern	sleepwear	slim

slime	slogan	slowly
slimly	sloganeer	slowness
slimmer	sloop	slowpoke
slimy	slop	slowup
sling	slope	sloyd
slingshot	slopes	slub
slingstone	sloppily	sludge
slink	sloppiness	sludger
slinky	sloppy	sludges
slip	slopwork ☉	slug
slipcover	slosh	slugger
slipcovers	sloshing	slugging
slipover	slot	sluggish
slippage	sloth	sluice
slipped	slothful	sluiceway
slipper	slothound	sluicy
slipperiness	slotted	slum
slippers	slouch	slumber
slippery	slouching	slumberland
slipping	slouchy	slumberless
slips	slough	slumlord
slit	*n.; n., v.*	
slither	sloven	slummer
slitter	slovenliness	slump
slitting	slovenly	slung
sliver	slow	slunk
slob	slowdown ☉	slur
slobber	slowed	slush
sloe	slower	sly
slog	slowest	slyly
	slowgoing ☉	slyness

smack	smirch	smotheration
small	smirk	smotheringly
smallage	smirky	smudge
smaller	smite	smudges
smallest	smith	smudgy
smallholder	smithwork ⊙	smug
smallmouth	smitten	smuggle
smallness	smock	smuggler
smallpox	smocks	smugly
smart	smog	smut
smarter	smoke	snack
smartest	smokehouse	snacks
smartly	smokeless	snaffle
smartness	smokepot	snag
smash	smoker	snagging
smashed	smokers	snail
smatter	smokes	snailery
smatteringly	smokiness	snake
smatterings	smoking	snakebite
smear	smoky	snakeroot
smearing	smolder	snakeweed
smears	smolderingly	snakewood
smell	smolt	snap
smelly	smooth	snapdragon
smelt	smoothbore	snapped
smelter	smoother	snapper
smile	smoothest	snappily
smiley	smoothly	snapping
smiling	smoothness	snappy
smilingly	smother	snaps

snapshot	snob	snowsuit
snare	snobbery	snowy
snarl	snobbish	snub
snarly	snood	snuff
snatch	snooker	snuffer
snatchily	snoop	snug
snatchy	snoopy	snugger
sneak	snoot	snuggle
sneaked	snooze	snugly
sneaker	snore	so
sneaky	snorer	soak
sneer	snoring	soaked
sneeringly	snorkel	soap
sneeze	snort	soaproot
sneezed	snout	soaps
sneezy	snow	soapsuds
snick	snowball	soapy
snicker	snowdrift	soar
snide	snowed	soared
sniff	snowfall	soaring
sniffle	snowfield	sob
sniffy	snowflake	sobbingly
snifter	snowman	sobeit ⊙
snip	snowmobile	sober
snipe	snowmobiles	sobering
sniper	snowpack	soberly
snippy	snowplow	sobriety
snips	snowshoe	sobriquet
snivel	snowslide	soccer
snivelings	snowstorm	sociability

social		softballs		soleiform ☉	
socialism		soften		soleil	
socialist		softened		solely	
socialistic		softener		solemn	
socialization		softeners		solemnity	
socialize		softens		solemnly	
socialized		softer		soleness	
socially		softly		solenoid	
societal		software		soleplate	
societies		softwood		soleprint	
society		soggy		soles	
socioeconomic ☉		soil		solicit	
socioeconomically ☉		soilage		solicitation	
sociological		soiled		solicitations	
sociologically		soils		solicited	
sociologist		soiree		soliciting	
sociology		sojourn		solicitor	
sock		sojourner		solicitors	
socket		sol		solicitous	
sockets		solace		solicitude	
socks		solacement		solid	
sod		solar		solidarity	
soda		solarium		solidity	
sodden		solarize		solidly	
sodding		sold		solids	
sodium		solder		soliloquize	
sofa		soldier		soliloquy	
sofas		soldiers		solitaire	
soft		sole		solitaires	
softball		soled		solitary	

solitude	sometimes ⊙	soothsayer
solo	somewhat ⊙	sootiness
soloist	somewhere ⊙	sooty
soloists	somnolence	sop
solubility	somnolent	sophist
soluble	son	sophisticate
solute	sonar	sophisticated
solution	sonata	sophistication
solutions	song	sophomore
solvable	songbook	sophomoric
solve	songbooks	soppy
solved	songfest	soprano
solvency	songs	sorb
solvent	songster	sorbent
solvents	sonic	sorcerer
solver	son-in-law ⊙	sorcery
solves	sonnet	sordid
solving	sonny	sore
soma	sonorant	sorehead
somatic	sonority	sorely
somber	sonorous	soreness
some	sons	sorghum
somebody	soon	sorghums
someday	sooner	sororities
somehow ⊙	soonest	sorority
someone ⊙	soot	sorrel
someplace	soothe	sorrier
somersault	soothing	sorriest
something ⊙	soothingly	sorrow
sometime ⊙	soothsay	sorrowful

sorry		sources		spaced	
sort		sourdough		spaceman	
sorted		sourly		spaceport	
sorter		sousaphone		spacer	
sortie		souse		spacers	
sorting		south		spaces	
sorts		southbound		spaceship ⊙	
sot		southeast		spacewalk	
sou		southeastern		spaceworthy ⊙	
soufflé		southerly		spacing	
sought		southern		spacious	
soul		southland		spaciousness	
soulful		southward		spade	
soulfully		southwest		spadework ⊙	
soulless		southwestern		spaghetti	
soullessly		souvenir		span	
souls		sovereign		spandrel	
sound		sovereignty		spangle	
sounded		soviet		spangled	
sounder		sow v.; n.		spaniel	
soundest		sower		spank	
sounding		sown		spanner	
soundly		sox		spare	
soundness		soy		spared	
soundproof		soybean		sparingly	
sounds		soybeans		spark	
soup		spa		sparked	
soupy		space		sparkle	
sour		spaceborne		sparkler	
source		spacecraft		sparkling	

sparks	speciality ⊙	speckle
sparky	specialization ⊙	speckled
sparrow	specializations ⊙	specs
sparse	specialize ⊙	spectacle
sparsely	specialized ⊙	spectacular
spasm	specializes ⊙	spectacularly
spasms	specializing ⊙	spectaculars
spastic	specially ⊙	spectate
spat	specials ⊙	spectator
spate	specialties ⊙	specter
spatial	specialty ⊙	spectra
spatially	speciate	spectral
spatter	specie	spectrally
spatterwork ⊙	species	spectrograph
spatula	specific ○	spectrometer
spavin	specifical ⊙	spectroscope
spawn	specifically ⊙	spectroscopy
speak	specification ⊙	spectrum
speaker	specifications ⊙	specular
speakers	specificity ⊙	speculate
speakership	specifics ⊙	speculation
speaking	specified ⊙	speculative
speaks	specifier ⊙	speculatively
spear	specifies ⊙	speculator
spearhead	specify ○	speculators
spearheading	specifying ⊙	sped
special ○	specimen	speech
specialist ⊙	specimens	speeches
specialists ⊙	specious	speechless
specialities ⊙	speck	speechlessly

speechlessness	spice	spirit
speed	spicery	spirited
speedboat	spicy	spirits
speedier	spider	spiritual
speedily	spidery	spiritualist
speeding	spigot	spirituality
speedometer	spike	spiritually
speeds	spiker	spirituel
speedway	spikes	spit
speedy	spile	spite
speleology	spill	spiteful
spell	spillage	spitfire
spellbound	spilled	spittle
spelled	spiller	splash
spelling	spills	splashdown
spellings	spillway	splashing
spells	spin	splashy
spend	spinach	splat
spendable	spinal	splatter
spending	spindle	splay
spends	spine	splayfoot
spent	spineless	spleen
sperm	spinner	spleenless
spew	spinneret	splendid
spewings	spinners	splendidly
spews	spinning	splendor
sphere	spinster	splenetic
spherical	spiral	splice
spherically	spirally	splicer
sphinx	spire	splicers

spline	spontaneous	spots
splinter	spontaneously	spotted
splintery	spoof	spotty
splints	spook	spouse
split	spooky	spout
splits	spool	spouts
splitting	spools	sprain
splotch	spoon	sprang
splotchy	spoonful	sprat
splurge	spoons	sprawl
splutter	spoor	sprawled
spoil	sporadic	spray
spoilage	spore	sprayed
spoiled	sport	sprayer
spoiler	sportiest	spraying
spoiling	sporting	sprays
spoke	sports	spread
spoken	sportsman	spreader
spokesman	sportsmanlike	spreading
spokesmen	sportsmanship	spreads
spoliate	sportsmen	spree
spondee	sportswear	sprig
sponge	sportswriter	sprightly
spongy	sporty	spring
sponsor	spot	springboard
sponsored	spotless	springer
sponsoring	spotlessly	springs
sponsors	spotlight	springtime ☉
sponsorship	spotlighting	sprinkle
spontaneity	spotlights	sprinkler

spondee	spontaneity	spoof	spook	sporadic	sport	sporty	spot	spouse	sprain	sprang	sprat	sprawl	spray
spondē	spontənēətē	spüf	spük	spəradik	spôrt	spôrtē	spot	spous	sprān	sprang	sprat	sprôl	sprā

sprinklers	squall	squirm
sprint	squalor	squirmy
sprinter	squander	squirrel
sprite	square	squirrelfish
sprocket	squarely	squirrels
sprockets	squares	squirt
sprout	squash	stab
spruce	squat	stabbed
sprue	squatter	stability
sprung	squaw	stabilization
spry	squawk	stabilize
spume	squeak	stabilized
spun	squeaky	stabilizer
spunk	squeal	stable
spur	squealer	staccato
spurious	squeamish	stack
spurn	squeamishness	stacked
spurt	squeegee	stacking
sputnik	squeeze	stackstand ⊙
sputter	squeezes	stade
sputum	squeezing	stadium
spy	squelch	staff
spyglass	squib	staffed
spyplane	squid	staffing
squabble	squiggle	staffman
squad	squill	staffmen
squadron	squint	staffs
squadronal	squire	stag
squalene	squirearchy	stage
squalid	squires	stagecoach

staged	stalky	standings ⊙
stager	stall	standpipe ⊙
stages	stallion	standpoint ⊙
stageworthy ⊙	stalwart	standpoints ⊙
stagger	stalwarts	stands ⊙
staggeringly	stamen	standstill ⊙
stagnant	stamina	stank
stagnate	staminal	stanza
stagnation	staminate	staple
staid	stammer	stapled
stain	stamp	stapler
stained	stamped	staplers
stainless	stampede	staples
stains	stamper	stapling
stair	stamping	star
staircase	stampings	starboard ⊙
stairs	stamps	starch
stairway	stance	starchy
stairways	¹stanch	stardom
stairwell ⊙	¹stanchest	stare
stake	stand ○	staring
staked	standard ⊙	stark
stakeout ⊙	standardization ⊙	starkly
stakes	standardize ⊙	starlet
staking	standardized ⊙	starlight
stalag	standardizing ⊙	starlike
stale	standards ⊙	starling
stalemate	standaway ⊙	starlings
stalk	standfast ⊙	starred
stalker	standing ⊙	starry

stars		statesmanly ⊙		²staunchest	
start		statesmanship ⊙		stave	
started		statesmen ⊙		stay	
starter		static		stayed	
starters		stating ⊙		staying	
starting		station		stays	
startle		stationary		stead	
startled		stationed		steadfast	
startling		stationer		steadfastly	
startlingly		stationers		steadier	
starts		stationery		steadiest	
starvation		stations		steadily	
starve		statism ⊙		steadiness	
stash		statist ⊙		steady	
stasis		statistical		steak	
state ⊙		statistically		steal	
statecraft ⊙		statistician		stealing	
stated ⊙		statisticians		stealth	
statehood ⊙		statistics		stealthier	
statehouse ⊙		stator ⊙		stealthily	
stateliness ⊙		statuary		steam	
stately ⊙		statue		steamboat	
statement ⊙		statues		steamed	
statements ⊙		stature		steamer	
stateroom ⊙		status ⊙		steamers	
staterooms ⊙		status quo ⊙		steaminess	
states ⊙		statute		steamship ⊙	
stateside ⊙		statutes		steamy	
statesman ⊙		statutory		steed	
statesmanlike ⊙		²staunch		steel	

steelhead	stenographic	sterol
steelmaker	stenography	stet
steelwork ⊙	step	stethoscope
steelworker ⊙	stepchild	stevedore
steep	stepdaughter	stevedoring
steeper	stepladder	stew
steepest	stepless	steward
steeple	stepmother	stewardess
steeplechase	steppe	stewardesses
steeplejack	stepped	stewards
steeply	stepping	stewardship
steer	steps	stick
steering	stepson	sticker
steers	stepwise	stickers
steeve	stereo	sticking
stein	stereophonic	stickle
stele	stereophony	stickler
stellar	stereotype	stickpin
stem	stereotypy	sticks
stemmery	sterile	stickseed
stemple	sterility	sticky
stems	sterilization	stiff
stench	sterilize	stiffen
stencil	sterilizes	stiffener
stenciled	sterilizing	stiffeners
stenciling	sterling	stiffer
stencils	stern	stiffly
steno	sternal	stiffness
stenographer	sterner	stifle
stenographers	sternly	stifler

stein	stele	stellar	stemmery	stench	stencil	steno	stenographer	stereophonic	stereotypy	sterol	steward
stīn	stēlē	stelər	stemərē	stench	stensl	stenō	stənogrəfər	sterēəfonik	sterēətīpē	sterōl	stüərd

stigma	stipends	stockpile
stigmata	stipple	stockpiled
stigmatize	stipulate	stockpiles
stile	stipulated	stockpiling
stiles	stipulates	stockroom
still	stipulating	stocks
stillborn	stipulation	stockyard
stillness	stipulations	stogie
stills	stir	stoic
stilt	stirringly	stoicism
stimulant	stirrup	stoke
stimulate	stitch	stoker
stimulated	stitched	STOL
stimulates	stitches	stole
stimulating	stitching	stolen
stimulation	stitchwork ⊙	stolid
stimulator	stock	stolidly
stimulators	stockade	stomach
stimuli	stockage	stomp
stimulus	stockboy	stone
sting	stockbroker	stonecutter
stinger	stocked	stonemason
stingy	stocker	stones
stink	stockholder	stoneware
stinkpot	stockholders	stonework ⊙
stinkweed	stockily	stoneworks ⊙
stint	stocking	stonily
stints	stockings	stony
stipe	stockman	stood
stipend	stockmen	stool

stools		story		strand	
stoop		storyboard		strange	
stop		storyboards		strangely	
stopgap		storyteller		strangeness	
stopover		stoup		stranger	
stopovers		stout		strangest	
stoppage		stoutly		strangle	
stopped		stove		strangulate	
stopper		stovemaker		strangulating	
stoppers		stover		strangulation	
stopping		stow		strap	
stops		stowage		strapping	
storage		straddle		straps	
storages		strafe		strata	
store		straggle		stratagem	
stored		straight		stratal	
storefront		straightaway		strategic	
storehouse		straightedge		strategical	
storekeeper		straighten		strategically	
storekeepers		straightened		strategy	
storeroom		straightening		stratification	
storerooms		straighter		stratify	
stores		straightforward		stratosphere	
storewide		straightway		stratum	
stories		strain		straw	
storing		strained		strawberry	
stork		strainer		strawflower	
storm		strainers		stray	
storms		straining		streak	
stormy		strait		streaks	

streaky	strew	strip
stream	strewn	stripe
streamer	striate	striped
streamers	strick	stripes
streamline	stricken	striping
streamlined	strict	stripped
streamliner	stricter	stripping
streamliners	strictest	strips
streams	strictly	strive
street	stricture	striven
streetcar	stride	strives
streets	strident	striving
strength	strides	strivings
strengthen	strife	strode
strengthened	strike	stroke
strengthening	strikebreaker	strokes
strengthens	strikeout ⊙	stroking
strengths	striker	stroll
strenuous	striking	stroller
strenuously	strikingly	strong
streptomycin	string	stronger
stress	stringcourse	strongest
stressed	stringencies	stronghold
stresses	stringency	strongly
stressful	stringent	strop
stressing	stringently	stropper
stretch	stringer	strove
stretched	stringers	struck
stretcher	strings	structural
stretchers	stringy	structurally

structure	studiously	sturdy
structured	study	sturgeon
structures	studying	stutter
structuring	stuff	stuttered
struggle	stuffer	stuttering
struggling	stuffers	stutters
strum	stuffy	sty
strummer	stultify	style
strung	stumble	stylebook
strut	stumbly	styled
struts	stump	styleless
strychnine	stumpland	styles
stub	stumpy	styling
stubble	stun	stylish
stubborn	stung	stylist
stubbornly	stunk	stylistic
stubbornness	stunned	stylization
stubby	stunning	stylize
stubs	stunningly	styloid
stucco	stunt	stymie
stuck	stupefier	stymied
stud	stupefy	styptic
studding	stupendous	styrene
student	stupid	suasion
students	stupidest	suave
studied	stupidity	suavity
studies	stupidly	sub
studio	stupor	subagent
studios	sturdier	subagents
studious	sturdiness	subaltern

subarctic	subject	submit
subassemblies	subjected	submittal
subassembly	subjecting	submitted
subcenter	subjective	submitting
subcentral	subjectively	subnormal
subcommittee ☉	subjectivist	suborder ☉
subcommittees ☉	subjectivity	subordinal
subconscious	subjects	subordinate v.; a., n.
subconsciously	subjoin	subordinated
subcontinent	subjugate	subordinates v.; n.
subcontract ☉	subjugation	suborn
subcontracting ☉	sublease	subornation
subcontractor ☉	sublessee	subparagraph
subcontractors ☉	sublessor	subpoena
subcontracts ☉	sublet	subpoena duces tecum
subculture	sublevel	subprofessional
subdepartment ☉	sublimate	subrogation
subdepot	sublime	subroutine
subdivide	sublimest	subscribe
subdividing	subliminal	subscribed
subdivision	sublinear	subscriber
subdivisions	submachine	subscribers
subdue	submarginal	subscribes
subfloor	submarine	subscribing
subflooring	submarines	subscript
subfoundation ☉	submerge	subscription
subgrade	submerged	subscriptions
subgroup	submersion	subscripts
subhead	submission	subsection
subheading	submissive	subsequent

---

subhead	sublessee	subliminal	sublinear	submarine	subordinate	subordinate	suborn	subpoena duces tecum
subhed	sublesē	sublimənl	sublinēər	submərēn	səbôrdənāt *v.*	səbôrdənit *a.*, *n.*	səbôrn	səpēnə düsēz tēkum

subsequently	substantiate	subtlety
subserve ⊙	substantiated	subtly
subservience ⊙	substantiates	subtotal
subserviency ⊙	substantiating	subtract
subservient ⊙	substantiation	subtracted
subserviently ⊙	substantive	subtraction
subset	substantively	subtracts
subside	substation	subtreasurer
subsidiaries	substations	subtropical
subsidiary	substitute	subtype
subsidies	substituted	suburb
subsiding	substitutes	suburban
subsidize	substituting	suburbanite
subsidized	substitution	suburbanize
subsidy	substitutions	suburbia
subsist	substrata	suburbs
subsistence	substrate	subversion
subsistent	substratum	subversive
subsoil	substructure	subvert
subsolar	subsume	subvertible
subsonic	subsurface	subway
subspace	subsystem	subzero
subspecialties ⊙	subtenant	succeed
subspecialty ⊙	subtend	succeeded
subspecies	subterfuge	succeeding
substance	subterrane	succeeds
substances	subterranean	success ○
substandard ⊙	subtitle	successes ⊙
substantial	subtle	successful ⊙
substantially	subtler	successfully ⊙

successfulness ⊙	sufferers	suicidal
succession ⊙	suffering	suicide
successional ⊙	sufferings	suicides
successive ⊙	suffers	suing
successively ⊙	suffice	suit
successor ⊙	sufficiency	suitability
successors ⊙	sufficient	suitable
succinct	sufficiently	suitably
succinctly	suffix	suitcase
succor	suffixes	suite
succulence	suffocate	suited
succulent	suffocating	suites
succumb	suffocation	suiting
such	suffrage	suitor
suck	suffuse	suits
sucker	suffusion	sulfa
suckers	sugar	sulfate
suction	sugarless	sulfide
sudden	suggest ⊙	[1]sulfite
suddenly	suggested ⊙	sulfur
suddenness	suggester ⊙	sulfuric
suds	suggestibility ⊙	sulk
sue	suggestible ⊙	sulkier
suede	suggesting ⊙	sulky
suedes	suggestion ⊙	sullen
sues	suggestions ⊙	sullenly
suffer	suggestive ⊙	sully
sufferance	suggestively ⊙	[2]sulphite
suffered	suggestiveness ⊙	sultan
sufferer	suggests ⊙	sultry

succinct	succor	succulent	succomb	sue	suede	sufferance	suffice	suffuse	sugar	suicide	suite	sulfa	sully
səksingkt	sukər	sukūlənt	səkum	sū	swād	sufərəns	səfīs	səfūz	shúgər	süəsīd	swēt	sulfə	sulē

sum		sunbathing		supercharge	
sumac		sunbonnet		supercharger	
summaries		sunburn		supercilious	
summarily		sunburnt		supercritical	
summarization		sundae		superego	
summarize		sunder		superficial	
summarized		sundial		superficiality	
summarizes		sundown ⊙		superficially	
summarizing		sundry		superfine	
summary		sunfast		superfluous	
summate		sunfish		superfuel	
summation		sung		superhighway	
summer		sunk		superhuman	
summerlike		sunken		superimpose	
summers		sunless		superimposed	
summertime ⊙		sunlight		superimposing	
summery		sunny		superintend	
summing		sunrise		superintendency	
summit		sunroom		superintendent	
summitry		sunset		superintendents	
summon		sunshade		superior	
summoned		sunshine		superiority	
summoning		sunshiny		superiors	
summons		sunspot		superjet	
sump		sunstroke		superlative	
sumptuous		suntan		superlinear	
sumptuously		sup		superliner	
sums		super		superlunar	
sun		superb		superlunary	
sunbathe		superbly		supermarket	

supermarkets	supervising	supporters
supernational	supervision	supporting
supernatural	supervisor	supportive
supernaturalism	supervisors	supports
supernormal	supervisory	suppose
superplastic	supine	supposed
superpose	supinely	supposedly
superposed	supper	supposition
superposition	supplant	suppositories
superpower	supplanted	suppository
supersalesman	supple	suppress
superscribe	supplement	suppression
superscribed	supplemental	suppressions
superscript	supplementary	supra
superscripts	supplementation	supranational
supersede	supplemented	supranationalism
superseded	supplementing	supremacy
supersedes	supplements	supreme
supersensitive	suppleness	supremely
supersonic	supplicate	surcharge
superstar	supplication	surcharges
superstition	supplied	sure ○
superstitious	supplier	surely ○
superstructure	suppliers	sureness ○
supertanker	supplies	surest ○
supertankers	supply	sureties ○
supervene	supplying	surety ○
supervise	support	surf
supervised	supported	surface
supervises	supporter	surfaced

surfaces	surrealist	survivor
surfacing	surrealistic	survivors
surfeit	surrender	survivorship
surfing	surrendered	susceptibility
surge	surrendering	susceptible
surgeon	surrenders	suspect v.; n.
surgeons	surreptitious	suspected
surgery	surreptitiously	suspecting
surgical	surrey	suspects v.; n.
surging	surrogate	suspend
surliness	surround	suspended
surly	surrounding	suspending
surmise	surroundings	suspense
surmised	surrounds	suspension
surmount	surtax	suspicion
surmounted	surtout	suspicious
surname	surveillance	suspiciously
surpass	surveillant	suspire
surpassed	survey	sustain
surpasses	surveyed	sustainable
surplice	surveyor	sustained
surplus	surveyors	sustaining
surpluses	surveyorship	sustenance
surprise	surveys	sutler
surprised	survivability	suture
surprises	survival	sutured
surprising	survive	sutures
surprisingly	survived	suturing
surreal	survives	svelte
surrealism	surviving	swab

---

surfeit   surgery   surliness   surly   surrogate   surveillance   survival   suspect   suspect   svelte
sérfit   sérjərē   sérlēnis   sérlē   sérəgāt   sərvāləns   sərvīvl   səspekt v.   suspekt n.   svelt

swaddle		swearing		swelter	
swag		sweat		swept	
swagger		sweatband		swerve	
swale		sweater		swift	
swallow		sweaters		swifter	
swallower		sweating		swiftly	
swallowtail		sweaty		swiftness	
swam		sweep		swig	
swamp		sweeper		swim	
swamped		sweepers		swimmer	
swampland		sweeping		swimming	
swamps		sweepingly		swimsuit	
swampy		sweepings		swindle	
swan		sweeps		swindler	
swank		sweepstake		swine	
swankier		sweet		swing	
swanky		sweeten		swinger	
swap		sweetener		swings	
swarm		sweeteners		swipe	
swart		sweeter		swirl	
swarthiness		sweetest		swirly	
swarthy		sweetheart		swish	
swash		sweetish		switch	
swashbuckle		sweetly		switchblade	
swat		sweetness		switchboard	
swatch		sweets		switchboards	
swatches		sweetwood		switched	
swath		swell		switcher	
sway		swelling		switches	
swear		swellings		switching	

switchman	symbolist	syndicated
switchmen	symbolize	syndication
swivel	symbols	syndrome
swollen	symmetric	synergism
swoon	symmetrical	synergistic
swoop	symmetrically	synod
sword	symmetry	synonymous
swordfish	sympathetic	synopsis
swordplay	sympathetically	syntactic
swore	sympathize	syntactical
sworn	sympathy	syntax
swung	symphonic	synthesis
sycamore	symphony	synthesize
sycophant	²symposia	synthetic
sycophantic	symposium	synthetics
²syllabi	¹symposiums	syringe
syllabicate	symptom	syringes
syllabication	symptomatic	syrup
syllabification	symptoms	syrupy
syllabify	synagogue	system
syllable	synagogues	systematic
syllables	synapse	systematically
syllabus	synchronism	systematization
¹syllabuses	synchronization	systematize
symbol	synchronize	systematology
symbolic	synchronous	systemic
symbolical	syndic	systems
symbolically	syndical	
symbolism	syndicate v.; n.	

T

tab	tabulate	taffeta
tabbed	tabulates	taffy
tabby	tabulating	tag
tabernacle	tabulation	tagged
tabescence	tabulations	tags
tabla	tabulator	tail
table	tachometer	tailback
tableau	tachygraph	tailboard
tableaux	tacit	tailed
tablecloth	tacitly	tailgate
tabled	taciturn	tailgunner
table d'hôte	tack	tailor
tableland	tacked	tailored
tables	tackle	tailoring
tablespoon	tackled	tailpiece
tablet	tackling	tailstock
tabletop	tact	tailwalk
tabletops	tactful	taint
tablets	tactfully	take
tableware	tactfulness	takedown ⊙
tabloid	tactic	taken
taboo	tactical	takeout ⊙
tabs	tactically	taker
tabular	tactics	takers
	tactile	takes
	tactless	taking
	tactlessness	talc
	tactual	talcum
	tactually	tale
	tadpole	talent

talented	tammy	tanks
talents	tamp	tankship ⊙
talisman	tamper	tanner
talk	tamping	tannery
talkative	tampon	tannin
talked	tan	tansy
talker	tanbark	tantalate
talking	tandem	tantalite
talks	tang	tantalization
talky	tangency	tantalize
tall	tangent	tantalizer
taller	tangential	tantalizingly
tallest	tangerine	tantamount
tallow	tangibility	tantrum
tallowwood	tangible	tantrums
tallowy	tangibly	tap
tally	tangle	tape
tallyman	tangleberry	taped
talon	tangled	tapeless
talons	tanglefoot	taper
tam	tango	taperecord ⊙
tamale	tangram	tapered
tamarack	tangy	tapes
tamarin	tania	tapestry
tamarind	tank	tapeworm
tambo	tankage	taphouse
tambourine	tankard	taping
tame	tanker	tapings
tamely	tankers	tapioca
tamer	tankful	tapped

tappet	tartarize	tauten
tapping	tartrate	tautological
tappoon	tarvia	tautologize
taproot	tarweed	tautology
tar	task	tavern
tarantism	taskmaster	tavernkeeper
tarantist	tasks	tawdriness
tarantula	taskwork ⊙	tawdry
tarbush	tassel	tawny
tardily	tastable	tax
tardiness	taste	taxability
tardy	tasteful	taxable
tare	tastefully	taxation
target	tasteless	taxed
tariff	tastes	taxeme
tariffs	tasting	taxes
tarlatan	tasty	taxi
tarnish	tat	taxicab
tarnishable	tatter	taxidermal
taro	tattery	taxidermy
tarpaulin	tattle	taxied
tarpon	tattler	taxiing
tarrer	tattoo	taxing
tarry	tattooer	taxiplane
tarsal	tattooing	taxiway
tarsia	taught	taxiways
tart	taunt	taxman
tartan	tauntingly	taxonomy
tartar	taurine	taxpayer
tartaric	taut	taxpayers

taxpaying	tearing	tediously
tea	tearless	tedium
teacart	tearoom	tee
teach	tears *n.; n., v.*	teem
teachability	teary	teemed
teachable	tease	teen
teacher	teasing	teens
teachers	teaspoon	teeter
teaches	teaspoonful	teeth
teaching	teatowel	teetotal
teachings	tech	teetotaler
teacup	technic	teetotum
teahouse	technical	telautogram
teakettle	technicalities	telecast
teakwood	technicality	telecaster
teal	technically	telecommunication
tealess	technician	telecommunications
team	technicians	telecon
teamed	technique	teleconference
teaming	techniques	telecontrol ⊙
teammate ⊙	technocracy	telecourse
teams	technocratic	telegram
teamster	technologic	telegrams
teamwork ⊙	technological	telegraph
teaplanter	technologically	telegrapher
teapot	technologies	telegraphic
tear *n.; n., v.*	technologist	telegraphone
teardrop	technologists	telegraphones
tearful	technology	telegraphy
tearfully	tedious	telelecture

telelectures	teller	temporarily
telemeter	tellers	temporary
telemetering	telling	temporize
telemetry	tellingly	temporizer
teleological	tells	tempt
teleology	telltale	temptation
telepathic	telluride	temptations
telepathically	tellurion	tempted
telepathy	tellurium	tempter
telephone	tellurize	tempting
telephoned	telpher	temptingly
telephones	temerity	tenable
telephoning	temper	tenacious
telephoto	temperament	tenaciously
teleplay	temperamental	tenacity
teleprompter[1] ⊙	temperance	tenancy
teleran	temperate	tenant
telerecord ⊙	temperately	tenants
telescope	temperature	tenantship
telescopic	temperatures	tend
telescoping	tempered	tended
telethon	tempers	tendencies
telethons	tempest	tendency
teletype	template	tender
teletypesetter	templates	tendered
teletypewriter	temple	tenderfoot
televise	temples	tenderloin
television	tempo	tenderly
televisions	temporal	tenderness
tell	temporally	tenders

---

telemeter	teleology	teleran	telescope	teletype	telluride	tellurium	temerity	tenacious
telemətər	telēoləjē	telərən	teləskōp	telətīp	telūrīd	telūrēəm	təmerətē	tináshəs

tending		tepid		terrific	
tendon		term		terrified	
tendril		termed		terrify	
tends		terminable		territorial	
tenebrous		terminably		territories	
tenement		terminal		territory	
tenet		terminals		terror	
tenfold		terminate		terrorism	
tennis		terminated		terrorize	
tenor		terminates		terry	
tenpenny		termination		terse	
tenpin		terminations		tersely	
tense		terminology		tertial	
tensely		terminus		tertian	
tensile		termite		test	
tension		termites		testament	
tensional		terms		testaments	
tensionless		tern		testator	
tent		ternary		testatrix	
tentacle		terrace		tested	
tentative		terrain		tester	
tentatively		terrarium		testicle	
tenth		terrazzo		testified	
tenting		terrella		testify	
tents		terrene		testifying	
tenuous		terrestrial		testimonial	
tenure		terrible		testimonials	
tenurial		terribly		testimonies	
tepary		terrier		testimony	
tepee		terriers		testing	

testings		thankful ⊙	then ⊙
tests		thankfully ⊙	thence ⊙
tetanus		thankfulness ⊙	thenceforth ⊙
tether		thanking ⊙	thenceforward ⊙
tetherball		thankless ⊙	theocracy
tetra		thanks ⊙	theodicy
tetrabasic		thanksgiving ⊙	theologian
tetrachloride		that ⊙	theologic
tetrad		thatch	theological
tetragon		that's ⊙	theology
tetragonal		thaw	theorem
tetralogy		the ⊙	theoretic
text		theater	theoretical
textbook		theaters	theoretically
textbooks		theatrical	theories
textile		theatrically	theorist
textiles		thee	theorize
texts		theft	theory
textual		thefts	therapeutic
textually		their ⊙	therapist
texture		theirs ⊙	therapists
textured		theism	therapy
textures		theist	there ⊙
texturing		theistic	thereabouts ⊙
texturize		them ⊙	thereafter ⊙
thalassian		thematic	thereamong ⊙
than ⊙		thematical	thereat ⊙
thane		theme	thereby ⊙
thank ⊙		themes	therefor ⊙
thanked ⊙		themselves ⊙	therefore ⊙

therefrom ☉		thermos[1]		thimble	
therein ☉		thermostat		thin	
thereinafter ☉		thermostats		thing ☉	
thereinbefore ☉		thesaurus		things ☉	
thereinto ☉		these		think ☉	
thereof ☉		theses		thinkable ☉	
thereon ☉		thesis		thinker ☉	
there's ☉		thespian		thinkers ☉	
thereto ☉		they		thinking ☉	
theretofore ☉		they'll ☉		thinkingly ☉	
thereunder ☉		they're ☉		thinks ☉	
thereupon ☉		they've ☉		thinly	
therewith ☉		thick		thinner	
therm		thicken		thinness	
thermal		thickener		thinning	
thermalize		thicker		third	
thermally		thickest		thirst	
thermic		thicket		thirsty	
thermite		thickly		this	
thermochemistry		thickness		thistle	
thermocouple		thicknesses		thistly	
thermocouples		thickskin		thither	
thermodynamic		thief		thole	
thermodynamically		thieve		tholepin	
thermoelectric		thievery		tholos	
thermometer		thieves		thong	
thermometers		thievish		thorax	
thermometry		thigh		thoric	
thermonuclear		thighbone		thorite	
thermoplastic		thighboot		thorn	

[1]Cap trademark

thermal	thermoelectric	thermonuclear	thermostat	theses	thesis	thespian	thievery	thong	thorax
thérmǝl	thérmōïlektrik	thérmōnüklēǝr	thérmǝstat	thēsēz	thēsis	thespēǝn	thēvǝrē	thông	thôraks

thornbush		threadbare		thriving	
thornier		threading		throat	
thornless		threads		throatily	
thorny		threat		throatlatch	
thorough		threaten		throaty	
thoroughbred		threatened		throb	
thoroughfare		threatening		throbbing	
thoroughgoing ⊙		threateningly		throe	
thoroughly		threatens		thrombosis	
thoroughness		threats		throne	
thoroughpin		threefold		throng	
those		threescore		throttle	
thou		threesome		through	
though		thresh		throughout ⊙	
thought		thresher		throughway	
thoughtful		threshold		throw	
thoughtfully		threw		throwaway	
thoughtfulness		thrice		throwback	
thoughtless		thrift		thrower	
thoughtlessly		thriftier		throwing	
thoughts		thriftiest		thrown	
thousand		thrifty		throws	
thousands		thrill		thrum	
thousandth		thrilled		thrush	
thrall		thriller		thrust	
thralldom		thrilling		thrustful	
thrash		thrills		thud	
thrasher		thrips		thug	
thrashing		thrive		thuggery	
thread		thrives		thumb	

thumbing	tickets	tight
thumbnail	tickle	tighten
thumbprint	tickled	tightening
thumbs	tickler	tightens
thumbstall	ticklish	tighter
thumbtack	ticks	tightly
thump	tidal	tightrope
thunder	tidbit	tightwire
thunderbolt	tiddlywinks	tile
thunderburst	tide	tiled
thunderclap	tidegate	tiler
thunderer	tideland	tiles
thunderhead	tiderace	till
thunderous	tidewater	tillable
thus	tideway	tillage
thwart	tidier	tiller
thy	tidiness	tillite
thyme	tidings	tilt
thymol	tidy	tilth
thyroglobulin	tie	timbal
thyroid	tieback	timber
thyroidal	tied	timberhead
thyroidectomy	tiepin	timberland
thyroxine	tier	timberlands
thyself	ties	timberman
tick	tiff	timbers
ticker	tiffany	timberwork ⊙
ticket	tiger	time ○
ticketed	tigerish	timecard ⊙
ticketing	tigers	timed ⊙

timekeeper ☉	tinge	tirade
timekeeping ☉	tingle	tire
timeless ☉	tinier	tired
timelessly ☉	tiniest	tiredness
timelessness ☉	tink	tireless
timeliness ☉	tinker	tirelessly
timely ☉	tinkering	tires
timepiece ☉	tinkle	tiresome
timepieces ☉	tinkling	tiring
timer ☉	tinkly	tissue
timers ☉	tins	tissues
times ☉	tinsel	titanic
timesaver ☉	tinsmith	titanium
timesaving ☉	tint	titanous
timeserver ☉	tinted	titer
timeserving ☉	tintinnabulary	tithable
timetable ☉	tints	tithe
timetables ☉	tintype	tither
timework ☉	tinware	tithers
timeworn ☉	tinwork ☉	titian
timid	tiny	title
timidity	tip	titled
timidly	tipcart	titleholder
timing ☉	tipped	titles
timings ☉	tipper	titter
tin	tipple	titular
tincture	tips	to
tinder	tipsy	toad
tinderbox	tiptoe	toadfish
tine	tiptop	toadflax

---

timidity	tincture	tinge	tint	tintinnabulary	tintype	tinware	tiresome	titanic	titanium	titian	titular
təmidətē	tingkchər	tinj	tint	tintənabülerē	tintip	tinwār	tīrsəm	tītanik	tītānēəm	tishən	tichŭlər

toadstool	toilsome	tomboy
toady	toilworn	tombstone
toadyism	tokamak	tomcat
toast	token	tome
toaster	tokenism	tomfool
toastmaster	tokens	tomograph
toastmasters	tolan	tomorrow
toasts	told	tomorrows
tobacco	tolerable	ton
toboggan	tolerably	tonal
toccata	tolerance	tonalist
tocology	tolerances	tonalite
tocsin	tolerant	tonality
today	tolerate	tonally
todays	tolerated	tone
toddle	toleration	toned
toddler	toll	toneless
toddy	tollage	toner
toe	tollgate	tones
toenail	tollhouse	tong
toes	tollman	tonga
toffee	tolls	tongue
together	tollway	tonic
togetherness	toluene	tonically
toggle	tomahawk	tonight
toil	tomatin	tonka
toiler	tomato	tonkin
toilet	tomatoes	tonnage
toiletry	tomb	tonneau
toilless	tombolo	tons

tobacco   toccata   toiletry   tokamak   tolerance   tolerant   toluene   tombolo   ton   tone   tonga   tongue   tonneau
təbakō   təkätə   toilitrē   tōkəmak   tolərəns   tolərənt   tolūēn   tombəlō   tun   tōn   tonggə   tung   tunō

tonsil	topfull	torment
tonsillectomy	topic	tormented
tonsils	topical	tormentor
tonsorial	topicality	torn
tonsure	topics	tornado
too	topknot	tornadoes
took	topmaker	toro
tool	topman	toroid
tooled	topmast	toroids
toolholder	topmost	torpedo
tooling	topographic	torpedoman
toolmaker	topographical	torpid
toolroom	topographically	torpidity
tools	topography	torpor
toolshed	topped	torque
toot	toppings	torr
tooth	topple	torrefy
toothache	tops	torrent
toothbrush	topsail	torrential
toothbrushes	topside	torrid
toothbrushing	topsoil	torsade
toothpaste	topstitch	torsibility
toothpick	topwork ⊙	torsion
toothpowder	topworking ⊙	torsional
top	toque	torsionless
topaz	torch	torso
topazolite	torchlight	tort
topcoat	tore	tortfeasor
topcoats	toreador	tortoise
tope	torera	tortuous

torture	tougher	towers
torturesome	toughest	towhead
toss	toughness	towing
tossable	toupee	towline
tosspot	tour	town
total	toured	townhouse
totaled	touring	towns
totaling	tourism	townsfolk
totalitarian	tourist	township
totalitarianism	tourists	townships
totality	tournament	townsite
totally	tournaments	townsman
totals	tournay	townsmen
tote	tourney	townspeople
totem	tourniquet	townward
totemic	tours	towrope
totter	tousle	toxic
tottery	tout	toxicology
touch	touter	toxin
touchable	tow	toxoid
touchback	towage	toy
touchdown ⊙	toward	toyland
touched	towardly	toymaker
touches	towards	toys
touchily	towboat	trace
touching	towed	traceable
touchline	towel	traced
touchstone	towels	tracer
touchy	tower	trachea
tough	towerman	tracheal

trachoma	trading	traineeship
tracing	tradition	traineeships
tracings	traditional	trainer
track	traditionalism	trainers
trackage	traditionalist	training
trackhound	traditionalistic	trainload
tracking	traditionalize	trainman
tracklayer	traditionally	trainmaster
trackless	traditions	trains
trackman	traduce	traintime ⊙
tracks	traducement	traipse
tract	traffic	trait
tractable	tragedian	traitor
tractably	tragedies	traitorous
tractile	tragedy	traits
traction	tragic	traject *v.; n.*
tractive	tragical	trajectory
tractor	tragically	tram
tractors	trail	tramline
tracts	trailblazer	trammel
trade	trailer	tramp
traded	trailerite	trample
trademark	trailers	trampoline
trademarked	trailership ⊙	trampolines
trademarks	trails	tramroad
trader	train	tramway
traders	trainability	trance
trades	trained	trancedly
tradesman	trainee	tranquil
tradespeople	trainees	tranquility

tranquilize	transearth	transire
tranquilizer	transfer	transistor
trans	transferable	transistorize
transact	transferal	transistorized
transacted	transferee	transistors
transaction	transference	transit
transactions	transferor	transition
transacts	transferred	transitional
transatlantic	transferring	transitions
transborder	transfers	transitory
transcend	transfigure ☉	translatable
transcendence	transfigurement ☉	translate
transcendent	transfix	translated
transcendental	transfluent	translating
transcendentalism	transform ☉	translation
transcendentalist	transformation ☉	translations
transcension	transformational ☉	translator
transcontinental	transformed ☉	transliterate
transcribe	transformer ☉	transliteration
transcribed	transformers ☉	translocate
transcriber	transforming ☉	translucence
transcribers	transfuse	translucency
transcribing	transfuser	translucent
transcript	transfusion	translunary
transcription	transfusions	transmake
transcriptions	transgress	transmissible
transcriptive	transgression	transmission
transcripts	transgressor	transmissions
transduce	transience	transmit
transducer	transient	transmittal

transmitted	transposal	travels
transmitter	transpose	traversable
transmittible	transposition	traverse
transmitting	transship ⊙	traversing
transmural	transshipment ⊙	travesty
transmutable	transubstantiate	trawl
transmutation	transversal	trawler
transmute	transversally	trawlerman
transnational	transverse	trawlers
transocean	transversely	tray
transoceanic	trap	trayful
transom	trapeze	trays
transpacific	trapezoid	treacherous
transparencies	trapped	treachery
transparency	trapper	treacle
transparent	trapping	tread
transpiration	trappings	treadle
transpire	trapshooter	treadmill
transpired	trash	treason
transpiring	trashery	treasonable
transplant	trauma	treasonably
transplantable	traumatic	treasure
transplanted	traumatically	treasured
transpolar	travail	treasurer
transport	travel	treasurers
transportation	traveled	treasures
transportations	traveler	treasuries
transported	travelers	treasury
transporting	traveling	treat
transports	travelogue	treatable

treated	tremulous	tributaries
treaties	tremulously	tributary
treating	trench	tribute
treatise	trenchant	tricarpellary
treatment	trenches	trice
treatments	trend	trichina
treats	trends	trichinella
treaty	trepan	tri-cities
treble	trespass	tri-city
trebled	trespasser	trick
tree	trespassers	trickier
treeing	tress	trickiness
trees	trestle	trickle
treescape	trestlework ☉	trickly
treetop	triacid	trickster
trefoil	triad	tricky
trek	trial	tricolor
trekker	trials	tricorn
trellis	triamcinalone	tricot
trelliswork ☉	triangle	tricycle
tremble	triangular	tricyclist
trembler	triatomic	tried
trembling	tribal	tries
trembly	tribe	trifle
tremendous	tribesman	trifler
tremendously	tribesmen	trifocal
tremolando	tribulation	trifoliate
tremolant	tribulations	triform ☉
tremolo	tribunal	trig
tremor	tribune	trigger

triggered	trip	trolley
triggerman	tripartite ⊙	trolleyman
triglot	tripe	trombone
trigon	triple	trombonist
trigonal	tripled	tromometer
trigonometry	triplet	troop
trigraph	tripletail	trooper
trijet	triplicate *a., n.; v.*	troopers
trilinear	triplication	troops
trilingual	triply	troopship ⊙
trill	tripod	trope
trillion	tripped	trophies
trilobite	trips	trophy
trilogy	trisect	tropic
trim	trite	tropical
trimester	tritiate	tropist
trimmed	tritium	tropology
trimmer	triumph	trot
trimmers	triumphant	trotline
trimming	triumphantly	trotlines
trimmings	triumphs	trotter
trimonthly	trivalence	troubadour
trimotor	trivalent	trouble
trims	trivia	troubled
trinity	trivial	troublemaker
trinket	triviality	troublemakers
trinodal	triweekly	troubles
trinomial	troche	troublesome
trio	trodden	trough
triolet	troll	troughs

trounce		truelove		truth	
troupe		truer		truthful	
trouper		truest		truthfully	
trouser		truffle		truthfulness	
trousers		truism		try	
trousse		truly		trying	
trousseau		trump		tryout ⊙	
trout		trumpet		trysail	
troutless		trumpeter		tub	
trove		trumpetweed		tuba	
trowel		truncate		tubal	
troy		truncation		tube	
truancy		trundle		tuber	
truant		trunk		tubercular	
truanted		trunkful		tuberculate	
truantry		trunks		tuberculation	
truce		truss		tuberculosis	
truck		trusses		tubes	
truckdriver		trust		tubing	
trucker		trustee		tubular	
truckers		trustees		tuck	
trucking		trusteeship		tucker	
truckload		trustful		tuft	
trucks		trustfully		tug	
truculence		trusting		tugman	
truculent		trustingly		tugs	
trudge		trusts		tuition	
trudgen		trustworthiness ⊙		tuitional	
trudger		trustworthy ⊙		tulip	
true		trusty		tulipomania	

trousse	trousseau	truculence	truculent	trump	truncation	trundle	truss	tube	tuber	tubercular	tubular
trüs	trüsō	trukūləns	trukūlənt	trump	trungkāshən	trundl	trus	tüb	tübər	tübėrkūlər	tübūlər

tulipwood	tunnel	turndown ☉
tulle	tunnels	turndowns ☉
tullibee	tunny	turned
tumble	tuppence	turner
tumbler	turban	turning
tumblerful	turbinal	turnip
tumblers	turbinate	turnkey
tumbleweed	turbine	turnoff
tumbrel	turbines	turnoffs
tumefy	turbocar	turnout ☉
tumid	turbocharge	turnouts ☉
tumor	turbocharger	turnover
tumors	turboelectric	turnovers
tumular	turbojet	turnpike
tumulary	turbopower	turnpikes
tumult	turbopowered	turns
tumultuous	turbulence	turnstile
tumulus	turbulent	turnstiles
tun	turf	turntable
tuna	turfiness	turpentine
tundra	turfy	turpitude
tune	turgid	turquoise
tuneful	turkey	turret
tunefulness	turkeys	turrethead
tuneless	turmoil	turtle
tunelessly	turmoils	turtleback
tungsten	turn	tusk
tunic	turnabout ☉	tussle
tunicle	turnaround	tussock
tuning	turncoat	tutor

tutorial	twisted	typewriting
tutoring	twister	typewritten
tutors	twisty	typhoid
tuxedo	twit	typhoidal
twaddle	twitch	typhoidin
twang	twitter	typhonic
twangle	twittery	typhoon
tweak	two	typhus
tweed	twofold	typical
tweedy	twos	typicality
tweezers	twosome	typically
twice	tycoon	typify
twig	tying	typing
twilight	type	typist
twill	typecast	typists
twin	typed	typographic
twine	typer	typographical
twinge	types	typography
twinkle	typescript	typology
twinkling	typeset	tyrannical
twins	typesetting	tyrannize
twirl	typewrite	tyranny
twirler	typewriter	tyrant
twist	typewriters	tyrosine

U

ubiquitous	ultranationalism	unadjusted ⊙
ubiquity	ultraradical	unadorned
udder	ultrarightist	unadulterated
ugliness	ultrasonic	unadvised ⊙
ugly	ultraviolet	unaffected ⊙
ukulele	ululate	unafraid
ulcer	ululation	unaided
ulcerate	umbel	unallocated
ulceration	umber	unalterable
ulcers	umbery	unalterably
ulna	umbilical	unambiguous
ulster	umbilication	unambiguously
ulterior	umbra	unamiable
ultimate	umbral	unamused
ultimately	umbrella	unanalyzed
ultimatum	umbrellalike	unanimity
ultimo	umlaut	unanimous
ultra	umpire	unanimously
ultracentrifuge	unabashed	unannounced ⊙
ultrafiche	unabated	unanswered
ultrafine	unable ⊙	unanticipated
ultramicrometer	unabridged	unapplied
ultramodern	unacceptable ⊙	unappointed
ultranational	unaccompanied ⊙	unappreciated ⊙
	unaccountable ⊙	unapproved
	unaccountably ⊙	unarm
	unaccredited	unasked
	unaccustomed ⊙	unassembled
	unacknowledged	unassigned
	unacquainted	unassisted

unassuming	unblinkingly	uncertainties
unattached	unblushing	uncertainty
unattainable	unborn	uncertified ⊙
unattended	unbought	unchallenged
unattractive	unbound	unchangeable ⊙
unauthorized	unbrace	unchangeably ⊙
unavailability	unbraid	unchanged ⊙
unavailable	unbreakable	unchanging ⊙
unavailing	unbridle	unchangingly ⊙
unavoidable	unbroke	uncharge
unavoidably	unbroken	uncharted
unaware	unbuckle	unchecked
unawareness	unbundle	unchristian
unbalance	unburden	uncivil
unbalanced	unburned	unclad
unbear	unbusinesslike ⊙	unclaimed
unbearable	unbutton	unclamp
unbeatable	uncalled	unclasp
unbeaten	uncandid	uncle
unbelief	uncannily	unclean
unbelievable	uncanny	uncleanly
unbelievably	uncap	unclear
unbelieving	uncart	uncles
unbend	uncase	uncloak
unbent	uncashed	unclog
unbiased	uncaused	unclose
unbid	unceasing	unclosed
unbidden	unceasingly	unclothe
unbind	uncertain	uncloud
unblemished	uncertainly	unclutter

uncluttered	uncontested	undefeated
uncock	uncontradicted	undefended
uncoil	uncontrol ☉	undefined
uncollected	uncontrollable ☉	undeliverable ☉
uncollectible	uncontrollably ☉	undelivered ☉
uncolored	uncontrolled ☉	undemocratic
uncomely	unconventional ☉	undeniable
uncomfortable	unconventionally ☉	undeniably
uncomfortably	unconvince	undependable
uncomforted	uncooperative	undepicted
uncommitted	uncork	undepressed
uncommon	uncorrected	under
uncommunicative	uncostly	underachieve
uncomplainingly	uncountable ☉	underachievement
uncomplimentary	uncounted ☉	underarm
uncompressed	uncouple	underbid
uncompromising	uncouth	underbrush
unconcern	uncover	underbuild
unconcerned	uncovered	underbuy
unconditional ☉	uncrate	undercapitalize
unconditionality ☉	uncritical	undercarriage
unconditionally ☉	uncross	undercast
unconditioned ☉	uncrown	undercharge
unconnected	unction	underclass
unconquerable	uncurl	underclassman
unconscious	uncut	underclothe
unconsciously	undamaged	underclothing
unconsidered ☉	undated	undercoat
unconstitutional	undaunted	undercover
unconstitutionally	undecided	undercurrent

undercut	underhandedness	underprivilege
underdeveloped ☉	underinsured ☉	underprivileged
underdevelopment ☉	underlaid	underproduce
underdo	underlay	underproduction ☉
underdog	underlease	underpromote
underdose	underlie	underrate
underdrain	underlies	underrated
undereducated ☉	underline	underrating
underemphasis	underlined	underreport ☉
underemployed ☉	underling	underrepresent ☉
underemployment ☉	underlining	underrepresented ☉
underequipped ☉	underload	underripe
underestimate	underlying	underrun
underestimated	underman	underscore
underexpose	undermine	underscores
underfeed	undermost	undersea
underfinanced	underneath	undersecretary ☉
underfoot	undernourish	undersell
underframe	underpaid	underselling
undergo ☉	underpart ☉	undershirt
undergoes ☉	underpass	undershoot
undergoing ☉	underpay	undershore
undergone	underpayment	underside
undergraduate ☉	underpin	undersign
undergraduates ☉	underplant	undersigned
underground ☉	underplay	undersize
undergrown	underpopulate	undersized
undergrowth	underpopulated	underslung
underhand	underprice	undersold
underhanded	underpriced	understand ☉

understandability ⊙	undervaluation ⊙	undistributed ⊙
understandable ⊙	undervalue ⊙	undisturbed
understandably ⊙	underwater	undivided
understanding ⊙	underway	undo
understandingly ⊙	underwear	undoing
understandings ⊙	underweight	undone
understands ⊙	underwent	undoubtedly
understate ⊙	underwood	undoubting
understated ⊙	underwork	undress
understatement ⊙	underworld	undressed
understates ⊙	underwrite	undue
understating ⊙	underwriter	undulate
understock	underwriters	unduly
understocked	underwrites	unearned
understood	underwriting	unearth
understudy	underwritten	unease
undersupply	undeserved ⊙	uneasily
undertake	undesirable	uneasiness
undertaken	undetected	uneasy
undertaker	undetermined	uneconomic ⊙
undertakes	undeveloped ⊙	uneconomical ⊙
undertaking	undid	uneducated ⊙
undertakings	undiminished	unelected ⊙
underthings ⊙	undirected ⊙	unemotional
undertime ⊙	undisciplined	unemployability ⊙
undertone	undisclosed	unemployable ⊙
undertones	undisguised	unemployables ⊙
undertook	undisputed	unemployed ⊙
undertow	undistinguishable ⊙	unemployment ⊙
underutilize	undistinguished ⊙	unending

unenforceable	unfair	unfortunately
unenthusiastic ⊡	unfairly	unfounded ⊙
unequal	unfaith	unfree
[1]unequaled	unfaithful	unfreeze
[2]unequalled	unfalteringly	unfrequent
unequally	unfamiliar	unfriendly
unequivocal	unfasten	unfrozen
unequivocally	unfavorable	unfruitful
unerring	unfeasible	unfulfilled
unerringly	unfed	unfunny
unethical	unfeeling	unfurl
unethically	unfeelingly	unfurnish
uneven	unfenced	unfused
unevenly	unfetter	ungainly
uneventful ⊙	unfiled	ungentle
uneventfully ⊙	unfilled	unglue
unexcelled	unfinished	ungodly
unexcitable	unfired	ungovernable ⊙
unexpected ⊙	unfit	ungovernably ⊙
unexpectedly ⊙	unflagging	ungoverned ⊙
unexpectedness ⊙	unflattering	ungracious
unexpended	unfold	ungrateful
unexpired	unfolding	ungratified
unexplainable	unfoldment	ungrounded ⊙
unexplained	unforeseeable	unguided
unexplored	unforeseen	ungum
unexposed	unforgettable	ungummed
unexpressed	unformed ⊙	unhand
unfailing	unformulated ⊙	unhandily
unfailingly	unfortunate	unhandy

unhappiest	unified	unintelligible
unhappily	uniform ⊙	unintended
unhappiness	uniformed ⊙	unintentional
unhappy	uniformity ⊙	unintentionally
unharmful	uniformly ⊙	uninterest ⊙
unharness	uniforms ⊙	uninterested ⊙
unhasty	unify	uninteresting ⊙
unhealthy	unilateral	uninterestingly ⊙
unheard	unilaterally	uninterrupted
unheated	unimaginable	uninterruptedly
unheeded	unimaginative	uninvited ⊙
unhesitant	unimpaired	uninviting ⊙
unhesitatingly	unimpeachable	uninvitingly ⊙
unhitch	unimportance ⊙	union
unholy	unimportant ⊙	unionist
unhonored	unimportantly ⊙	unionization
unhook	unimposing	unionize
unhoped ⊙	unimpressed	unionized
unhopeful ⊙	unimpressive	unions
unhorse	unimprovable ⊙	unique
unhurried	unimproved ⊙	uniquely
unhurriedly	unincorporate △	uniqueness
unhurt	unincorporated △	unison
unhygienic	uninformative ⊙	unissued ⊙
unicellular	uninformed ⊙	unit
unicorn	uninhibited	unite
unicycle	uninitiate	united
unidentifiable	uninjured	unitize
unidentified	uninsurable ⊙	unitized
unification	uninsured ⊙	units

unhygienic	unicellular	unicorn	unify	unilateral	uninhibited	uninjured	union	unionization	unique	unite
unhĳēenik	ūnəselūlər	ūnəkôrn	ūnəfī	ūnəlatərəl	uninhibətid	uninjərd	ūnyən	ūnyənəzāshən	ūnēk	ūnīt

unity	unlicensed	unmercifully
universal	unlighted	unmindful
universality	unlikable	unmistakable
universally	unlike	unmistakably
universe	unlikelihood	unmixed
universities	unlikely	unmolested
university	unlimited	unmoved
unjust ☉	unlined	unnamed
unjustifiable ☉	unlink	unnatural
unjustifiably ☉	unlisted	unnaturally
unjustified ☉	unload	unnecessarily ☉
unjustly ☉	unloaded	unnecessary ☉
unkempt	unloader	unneeded
unkind	unloading	unnerve
unkindly	unlocated	unnoticeable ☉
unknowingly	unlock	unnoticeably ☉
unknown	unlocked	unnoticed ☉
unlace	unloose	unnumbered ☉
unladylike	unlove	unobjectionable
unlaid	unlovely	unobligated
unlamented	unluckily	unobservant ☉
unlash	unlucky	unobserved ☉
unlatch	unmailable	unobtainable
unlawful	unmanageable	unobtrusive
unlawfully	unmarked	unobtrusively
unleash	unmarried	unoccupied
unleavened	unmask	unofficial
unled	unmatched	unofficially
unless	unmentionable	unopened
unlevel	unmerciful	unopposed

unordered ☉	unpredictably	unreasonably
unorganized ☉	unprepared	unrecognizable ▫
unorthodox	unpresentable ☉	unrecognized ▫
unpack	unprintable	unreconstructed ☉
unpacked	unproductive ☉	unrecorded ☉
unpacking	unproductiveness ☉	unrecounted ☉
unpaid	unprofessional	unrecoverable
unpaired	unprofitable	unredeemable
unparalleled	unpromising	unrelated
unpardonable	unprompted ☉	unreleased
unpark	unprotected	unrelenting
unpatentable	unproven	unreliability
unpatriotic	unpublished ☉	unreliable
unpaved	unqualified	unrelieved
unperformable ☉	unqualifiedly	unremarkable
unperformed ☉	unquestionable ☉	unremitting
unpleasant	unquestionably ☉	unrentable
unpleasantly	unquestioned ☉	unrepentant
unpleasantness	unquestioningly	unrepresentative ☉
unpleased ☉	unravel	unreserve ☉
unpleasing ☉	unreadable	unreservedly ☉
unpleasingly ☉	unreadily	unresolved
unpleasurable	unready	unresponsive ☉
unplowed	unreal	unrest
unpopular	unrealism	unrestricted
unpractical	unrealistic	unrevealingly
unprecedented	unrealistically	unrewarding
unprecise	unreality	unripe
unpredictability	unreason	unroll
unpredictable	unreasonable	unromantic

unruffle	unsheltered	unsteady
unruly	unship ☉	unstick
unsafe	unshipped ☉	unstop
unsaid	unshown	unstressed
unsalable	unsightly	unstrung
unsalted	unsigned	unstuck
unsatisfactorily ☉	unsinkable	unsubscribed
unsatisfactory ☉	unskilled	unsubsidized
unsatisfied ☉	unskillful	unsuccess
unsatisfyingly ☉	unsmilingly	unsuccessful ☉
unsaturated	unsnap	unsuccessfully ☉
unsavory	unsnarl	unsuitable
unscathed	unsold	unsung
unscientific	unsolder	unsupported
unscrew	unsolicited	unsure ☉
unscrupulous	unsolved	unsurmountable
unseal	unsophisticate	unsurpassed
unsealed	unsound	unsuspecting
unsecured	unsoundly	unswerving
unseen	unspeak	unsympathetic
unselfish	unspeakable	unsystematic
unselfishly	unspecialized ☉	untarnished
unserviceable ☉	unspecific ☉	untaxable
unset	unspecified ☉	untaxed
unsettle	unspent	untenable
unsettled	unspoken	unthankful ☉
unsettling	unstable	unthink ☉
unshaven	unstained	unthinkable ☉
unsheathe	unstatesmanlike ☉	unthinking ☉
unshed	unsteadily	unthinkingly ☉

untidy	unwarranted	upgraded
untie	unwaveringly	upgrading
until	unwed	upheaval
untimed ⊙	unwelcome	upheld
untimely ⊙	unwell ⊙	uphill
untiring	unwilling ⊙	uphold
unto	unwillingly ⊙	upholding
untold	unwillingness ⊙	upholds
untouched	unwind	upholster
untoward	unwise	upholstered
untrained	unwisely	upholstering
untrammeled	unwittingly	upholstery
untrim	unworkable ⊙	upkeep
untrimmed	unworkmanlike ⊙	upland
untrue	unworthily ⊙	uplands
untruth	unworthiness ⊙	uplift
unturned	unworthy ⊙	upon
untutored	unwrap	upper
unusable	unwrinkle	uppermost
unuse	unwritten	uppers
unused	unyielding	upraise
unusual	up	upright
unusually	upbeat	uprightly
unutilized	upbringing	uprise
unutterable	upcoming	uprisings
unuttered	update	uproar
unvalued ⊙	updated	uproarious
unveil	updates	uproariously
unwanted ⊙	updating	uproars
unwarrantable	upgrade	uproot

ups	urged	uses
upset	urgency	usher
upsets	urgent	using
upshot	urgently	usual
upside	urges	usually
upstairs	urging	usurious
upstanding ☉	urinalysis	usurp
upstart	urinary	usury
upstate ☉	urine	utensil
upstater ☉	urn	utensils
upstream	urologist	utilitarian
upstroke	urologists	utilities
upsurge	urology	utility
upswing	us	utilization
uptake	¹usable	utilize
uptown	usage	utilized
upturn	use	utilizes
upturns	²useable	utilizing
upward	used	utmost
upwards	useful	utopia
uranium	usefully	utopian
urban	usefulness	utopianism
urbanism	useless	utter
urbanization	uselessly	utterance
urbanize	uselessness	uttered
urethane	user	uttering
urge	users	utterly

V

vacancies

vacancy

vacant

vacate

vacation

vacationer

vacationers

vacationist

vacationists

vacationland

vacations

vaccinate

vaccination

vaccine

vacillate

vacillation

vacuity

vacuolate

vacuolation

vacuous

vacuum

vacuumize

vacuums

vagabond

vagary

vagrancy

vagrant

vague

vaguely

vagueness

vaguest

vail

vain

vainly

valance

vale

valedictorian

valedictory

valentine

valet

valiant

valiantly

valid

validate

validated

validating

validation

validities

validity

validly

valley

valleys

valor

valorization

valuable ⊙

valuables ⊙

valuation ⊙

valuations ⊙

value ⊙

valued ⊙

valueless ⊙

values ⊙

valuing ⊙

valve

valves

vamp

vampire

van

vandal

vandalism

vandalize

vane

vanguard

vanilla

vanillin

vanish

vanity

vanload

vans

vantage

vapor

vaporization

vaporize

vaporizer

vaporizers	vary	vehicle
vaquero	varying	vehicles
variability	vas	vehicular
variable	vasa	veil
variables	vascular	veilless
variance	vase	vein
variances	vast	veinous
variant	vastly	veinstone
variate	vat	veinule
variation	vatful	velar
variations	vaudeville	velarize
varicolored	vaudevillian	vellum
varicose	vault	velocimeter
varicosis	vaults	velocity
varied	vaunt	²velour
variegate	vaunter	¹velours
varies	veal	velvet
varieties	vealy	velvety
variety	vector	venal
variform ⊙	vectorial	venatic
variolate	veer	vend
variolation	vegetable	vendee
variorum	vegetables	vending
various	vegetal	vendor
variously	vegetarian	vendors
varitype	vegetate	veneer
varitypist	vegetation	veneered
varnish	vehemence	venerability
varnishes	vehement	venerable
varsity	vehemently	venerably

vaquero	variance	variate	variolate	variorum	varitype	vascular	vaunt	vegetable	vegetarian	vehement	velar
väkärō	vãrēəns	vãrēāt	vãrēəlāt	vãrēôrəm	vãrētip	vaskūlər	vônt	vejtəbl	vejətãrēən	vēəmənt	vēlər

venerate	verb	vermiculation
veneration	verbal	vermilion
vengeance	verbalization	vermin
venial	verbalize	vermouth
venire	verbally	vernacular
venison	verbatim	vernacularize
venom	verbena	vernal
venomous	verbiage	vernally
vent	verbose	vernier
ventage	verdancy	versatile
vented	verdant	versatility
ventilate	verdict	verse
ventilated	verdure	versed
ventilating	verdureless	versicle
ventilation	verge	version
ventilator	verger	versions
ventilators	veriest ⊙	versus
ventral	verification	vertebra
ventricle	verified	vertebrae
ventricular	verifier	vertebral
ventriloquist	verifies	vertebrate
ventriloquy	verify	vertex
vents	verifying	vertical
venture	verily	vertically
ventured	verisimilar	vertigo
venturesome	verisimilitude	vertiport
venue	veritable	vervain
veracious	verity	verve
veracity	vermeil	very ○
veranda	vermiculate	vesicle

vesiculate	viagraph	video
vesiculation	vial	videophone
vesper	vibrance	videotape
vesperal	vibrancy	videotaped
vessel	vibrant	videotapes
vessels	vibrantly	videotaping
vest	vibrate	vie
vested	vibration	view
vestibular	vibrator	viewed
vestibule	vicar	viewer
vestige	vicarage	viewers
vestigial	vicarious	viewing
vesting	vice	viewpoint
vestment	viceless	viewpoints
vestments	vicennial	views
vestry	viceroy	vigil
vests	viceroyship	vigilance
vetch	vicinities	vigilant
veteran	vicinity	vigilante
veterans	vicious	vignette
veterinarian	viciousness	vigor
veterinary	vicissitude	vigorous
veto	victim	vigorously
vex	victimize	vile
vexatious	victims	vileness
vexing	victor	vilification
via	victorious	vilify
viability	victoriously	villa
viable	victory	village
viaduct	victual	villager

villages	violent	viscoelasticity
villain	violently	viscose
villainous	violet	viscosimeter
villainy	violetlike	viscosimeters
vim	violin	viscosity
vimful	violinist	viscount ⊙
vindicate	viper	vise
vindication	viperine	visibility
vindictive	virgin	visible
vindictively	virginal	visibly
vindictiveness	virginity	vision
vine	virile	visionary
vinegar	virility	visit
vineland	virtual	visitation
vinery	virtually	visitations
vineyard	virtue	visited
vineyards	virtues	visiting
vinology	virtuosity	visitor
vintage	virtuoso	visitors
vinyl	virtuous	visits
vinyls	virulence	visor
viola	virulent	visors
violate	virus	vista
violated	visa	visual
violating	visage	visualization
violation	visas	visualize
violations	viscera	visually
violator	visceral	visuals
violators	viscid	vita
violence	viscoelastic	vitae

vital	vocation	voltaic
vitality	vocational	volts
vitalize	vocationally	volubility
vitalizing	vociferous	voluble
vitally	vociferously	volume
vitamin	vogue	volumes
vitamins	voguish	volumetric
vitiate	voice	volumetrically
vitiated	voiceless	voluminous
vitric	voiceprint	voluntarily
vitrify	voices	voluntarism
vitriol	void	voluntary
vitriolic	voidable	volunteer
vituperate	volant	volunteered
vivacious	volar	volunteering
vivacity	volatile	volunteers
vivid	volatilize	voluptuous
vividly	volcanic	vomit
vividness	volcano	vomited
vivify	volcanology	vomiting
vivo	vole	voodoo
vocabularies	volition	voodooism
vocabulary	volitional	voracious
vocal	volley	voraciously
vocalic	volleyball	vortex
vocalism	volplane	vortical
vocalist	volplanist	vote
vocalization	volt	voted
vocalize	voltage	voter
vocally	voltages	voters

votes		vowel		vulgarize	
voting		vowels		vulnerability	
vouch		vows		vulnerable	
vouched		voyage		vulpine	
voucher		voyager		vulture	
vouchers		vulcanize		vying	
vouchsafe		vulcanizer			
vow		vulgar			

W

wad	wainscot	walkover
wadable	wainwright	walks
waddle	waist	walkway
waddler	waistband	walkways
wade	waistcloth	wall
wader	waistcoat	wallboard
wafer	waistline	walled
wafery	wait	wallet
waffle	waited	wallets
wafflelike	waiter	wallop
wag	waiters	wallops
wage	waiting	wallow
waged	waitress	wallpaper
wager	waitresses	walls
wages	waive	walnut
waggish	waived	walrus
waggle	waiver	waltz
waging	waivers	wampum
wagon	waiving	wan
wagoner	wake	wand
wagons	wakeful	wander
waif	wakefulness	wanderer
wail	waken	wanderers
wailful	walk	wandering
	walked	wanderings
	walker	wanders
	walkie	wane
	walking	wangle
	walkout ○	wangler
	walkouts ○	want ○

wanted ⊙	warlock	wart
wanting ⊙	warm	wartime ⊙
wantless ⊙	warmer	warty
wantlessness ⊙	warmest	wary
wanton	warming	was ⊙
wantonly	warmish	wash
wants ⊙	warmly	washability
war	warmonger	washable
warble	warmth	washbasin
warbler	warn	washboard
ward	warned	washbowl
warden	warner	washcloth
wardrobe	warning	washed
wardroom	warningly	washer
wards	warnings	washers
ware	warns	washing
warehouse	warp	washings
warehouseman	warpage	washout ⊙
warehousemen	warplane	washroom
warehouses	warrant	washstand ⊙
warehousing	warranted	wasn't ⊙
wareroom	warranting	wasp
warerooms	warrantor	waspish
wares	warrants	wastage
warfare	warranty	waste
warhawk	warren	wastebasket
warhead	warrior	wasted
warily	wars	wasteful
wariness	warship ⊙	wasteland
warlike	warships ⊙	wastepaper

W

wastes	waterproof	waybills	
wasting	waters	waylaid	
wastrel	watershed	waylay	
watch	watersheds	ways	
watchband	waterside	wayside	
watchdog	watertight	wayward	
watched	waterway	waywardly	
watcher	waterways	we	
watchers	waterworks ⊙	weak	
watches	watery	weaken	
watchful	WATS	weakened	
watching	watt	weakens	
watchmaker	wattage	weaker	
watchmakers	watts	weakest	
watchman	wave	weakly	
watchmen	waved	weakness	
watchtower	waver	weaknesses	
water	waves	wealth	
watercraft	wavy	wealthier	
waterer	wax	wealthiest	
waterfall	waxed	wealthy	
waterflow	waxen	wean	
waterfowl	waxes	weanling	
waterfront	waxing	weapon	
watering	waxwork ⊙	weaponless	
waterleaf	waxworks ⊙	weaponry	
watermark	waxy	weapons	
watermelon	way	wear	
watermelons	waybill	wearability	
waterplane	waybilled	wearer	

watch	water	waterfront	watermark	waterway	watery	WATS	watt	wattage	wave	wax	waxen	waxy	wealth	weapon
woch	wôtər	wôtərfrunt	wôtərmärk	wôtərwā	wôtərē	wots	wot	wotij	wāv	waks	waksn	waksē	welth	wepən

weariest		wedlock		weight	
wearily		wee		weighted	
weariness		weed		weighting	
wearing		weedkiller		weightless	
wearisome		weeds		weightlessness	
wears		weedy		weights	
weary		week		weighty	
weasel		weekday		weird	
weather		weekdays		weirdly	
weatherbeaten		weekend		welcome	
weathercast		weekender		welcomed	
weathercondition ⊙		weekenders		welcomes	
weathered		weekends		welcoming	
weathering		weeklong		weld	
weatherman		weekly		welded	
weatherproof		weeknight		welder	
weatherworn		weeknights		welders	
weave		weeks		welding	
weaver		weep		weldment	
weaving		weepily		welfare	
web		weepy		welfarism	
webbing		weevil		well ⊙	
webbings		weevily		we'll ⊙	
webwork ⊙		weigh		wellborn ⊙	
wed		weighbridge		wellhead ⊙	
we'd ⊙		weighed		wellhole ⊙	
wedding		weighing		wells ⊙	
weddings		weighman		wellspring ⊙	
wedge		weighmaster		welt	
wedges		weighs		welted	

welter		what's ☉	whereby ☉
went		whatsoever ☉	wherefore ☉
wept		wheat	wherefrom ☉
were		wheatcake	wherein ☉
we're ☉		wheaten	whereinto ☉
weren't		wheatland	whereof ☉
west		wheedle	whereon ☉
westerly		wheel	wheresoever ☉
western		wheelbarrow	whereupon ☉
westerns		wheelbarrows	wherever ☉
wests		wheelbase	wherewith ☉
westward		wheeled	wherewithal ☉
wet		wheeler	whet
wetland		wheeling	whether
wetness		wheelless	whetstone
wettable		wheels	whetting
wetter		wheelspin	whey
we've ☉		wheelwork ☉	wheyface
whack		wheeze	which ☉
whale		wheezy	whichever ☉
whaleback		whelp	whichsoever ☉
whaleboat		when ☉	whiff
whalery		whence ☉	whiffle
wharf		whenever ☉	while ☉
wharfage		where ☉	whim
wharfside		whereabout ☉	whimper
wharve		whereabouts ☉	whims
what ☉		whereafter ☉	whimsical
whatever ☉		whereas ☉	whimsy
whatnot ☉		whereat ☉	whine

whinny	whiteness	why ⊙
whip	whitewall	wick
whipcord	whiteware	wickedly
whiplash	whitewash	wickedness
whippet	whitewood	wicker
whipping	whitish	wickerwork ⊙
whippoorwill	whittle	wicket
whips	whittles	wide
whipsaw	whiz	widely
whipstitch	whizzer	widen
whir	who	widened
whirl	whoever ⊙	widener
whirlabout ⊙	whole	widening
whirlaway	wholeness	wider
whirlpool	wholesale	widespread
whirlwind	wholesaler	widest
whisk	wholesalers	widow
whisker	wholesales	widower
whiskerless	wholesaling	widowhood
whiskey	wholesome	widows
whisper	who'll ⊙	width
whisperings	wholly	widths
whistle	whom	wield
whistles	whomever ⊙	wielded
whistling	whomsoever ⊙	wielder
whit	whoop	wiener
white	whorl	wienerwurst
whitecap	who's ⊙	wife
whiteface	whose	wifely
whiten	whosoever ⊙	wig

wiggery	wills ○	wine
wiggle	wilt	winehouse
wiggles	wily	winery
wiggly	wimble	wines
wigwag	win	wing
wigwam	wince	wingless
wild	winch	wingman
wildcat	wincingly	wings
wildcatter	wind *n., v.; n., v.*	wingspan
wilder	windage	wink
wilderness	windbag	winkle
wildest	windbreak	winless
wildfire	winder	winner
wildfires	windfall	winners
wildlife	windgall	winning
wildly	windiness	winnings
wildness	winding	winnow
wile	windless	wins
wiles	windmill	winsome
will ○	window	winter
willed ○	windowless	winterbloom
willful ○	windowpane	winterfeed
willfully ○	windows	wintergreen
willfulness ○	windpipe	winterize
willing ○	windrow	winterizing
willingly ○	winds *n., v.; n., v.*	winterkill
willingness ○	windshield	winters
willow	windstorm	wintertime ○
willowy	windward	wintry
willpower ○	windy	winze

wipe	wistfully	wives
wiper	wit	wizard
wipers	witch	wobble
wipes	with ⊙	wobbler
wire	withdraw ⊙	wobbly
wired	withdrawable ⊙	woe
wiredraw	withdrawal ⊙	woebegone ⊙
wireless	withdrawals ⊙	woeful
wireman	withdrawing ⊙	woefully
wires	withdrawn ⊙	woke
wirework ⊙	withdraws ⊙	wold
wireworker ⊙	withdrew ⊙	wolf
wiring	wither	wolves
wiry	withers	woman
wisdom	withheld ⊙	womanhood
wise	withhold ⊙	womanly
wiseacre	withholding ⊙	women
wisely	withholdings ⊙	womenfolk
wiser	withholdment ⊙	won ⊙
wish	within ⊙	wonder
wished	without ⊙	wondered
wisher	withstand ⊙	wonderful
wishers	withstands ⊙	wonderfully
wishes	withstood ⊙	wondering
wishful	witness	wonderland
wishing	witnessed	wonders
wisp	witnesses	wondrous
wispy	wits	wondrously
wisteria	wittingly	won't
wistful	witty	woo

wood	wordlessly	workout ☉
woodbine	words	workouts ☉
woodborer	wordy	workplace ☉
woodcarver	wore	workroom ☉
woodcock	work ☉	works ☉
woodcut	workability ☉	workshop ☉
woodcutter	workable ☉	workshops ☉
wooded	workaday ☉	worktable ☉
wooden	workbasket ☉	workweek ☉
woodhouse	workbench ☉	world
woodland	workbook ☉	worldly
woodlands	workbooks ☉	worlds
woodpecker	workbox ☉	worm
woodpile	workday ☉	wormed
woods	worked ☉	wormhole
woodside	worker ☉	wormy
woodsman	workers ☉	worn
woodsmoke	workhorse ☉	worried
woodsy	workhouse ☉	worriedly
woodwork ☉	working ☉	worries
woodworker ☉	workingman ☉	worrisome
woodworking ☉	workings ☉	worry
woody	workingwoman ☉	worrying
wool	workless ☉	worse
woolen	workload ☉	worsen
woolly	workloads ☉	worship
word	workman ☉	worshiper
worded	workmanlike ☉	worshipful
wording	workmanship ☉	worst
wordless	workmen ☉	worsted
		v.; a., n.

worsteds		wrath		wristband	
worth ○		wrathful		wristlock	
worthier ⊙		wreak		wrists	
worthiest ⊙		wreath		writ	
worthiness ⊙		wreck		write	
worthless ⊙		wreckage		writer	
worthlessness ⊙		wrecked		writers	
worthwhile ⊙		wrecker		writes	
worthy ⊙		wrecks		writhe	
would ○		wrench		writing	
wouldn't ⊙		wrenches		writings	
wound		wrest		written	
n., v.; v.		wrestle		wrong	
wounded		wrestling		wrongdoer	
wove		wretch		wrongful	
woven		wretchedness		wrongly	
wrack		wriggle		wrote	
wrangle		wring		wroth	
wrangler		wringer		wrought	
wrap		wringers		wrung	
wrapped		wrinkle		wry	
wrapper		wrinkles		wryly	
wrapping		wrinkling			
wrappings		wrist			
wraps					

wound	wound	wove	woven	wrangler	wrathful	wreck	wrest	wretchedness	wrinkle	writhe	wrongdoer	wrung
wünd *n., v.*	wound *v.*	wōv	wōvən	rangg+ lər	rathfəl	rek	rest	rechidnis	ringkl	rīth	rôngdüər	rung

xanthein		yanks		yell	
xanthic		yap		yelled	
xenia		yard		yellow	
xenon		yardage		yellowbird	
xenophile		yardarm		yellowfin	
xenophobe		yardman		yellowish	
xerographic		yardmen		yellowtail	
xerography		yards		yellowthroat	
xerox[1]		yardstick		yelp	
x-ray[2]		yardsticks		yen	
x-rays		yarn		yeoman	
xylan		yarns		yeomanry	
xylem		yarrow		yes	
xyloid		yaw		yesterday	
xylophone		yawl		yesterdays	
yacht		yawn		yet	
yachting		yawnful		yield	
yachtsman		yea		yielded	
yachtsmanship		year		yielding	
yachtsmen		yearbook		yields	
yak		yearbooks		yip	
yam		yearling		yipe	
yank		yearly		yiped	
yanking		yearn		yiping	
		yearned		yipping	
		yearningly		yodel	
		yearnings		yoga	
		years		yogi	
		yeast		yogurt	
		yeastiness		yoke	

xanthein	xenon	xenophobe	xerography	xylan	xylem	xyloid	yearn	yip	yipe	yoga	yogi	yogurt
zanthēin	zēnon	zenəfōb	zērogrəfē	zīlan	zīlem	zīloid	yérn	yip	yīp	yōgə	yōgē	yōgért

yokel	yowl	zincify
yokels	yowler	zing
yolk	yucca	zip
yolks	yule	ZIP
yonder	yuletide	zipper
yore	zag	zippers
york	zamia	zippy
yorker	zander	zircon
you	zaniness	zirconic
you'd ☉	zany	zodiac
you'll ☉	zeal	zodiacal
young	zealot	zombi
younger	zealous	zone
youngest	zealously	zoned
youngish	zebra	zones
youngster	zebrine	zoning
youngsters	zebroid	zoo
your ○	zenith	zookeeper
you're ☉	zenithal	zoologist
yours ☉	zeolite	zoology
yourself ☉	zeolitic	zoom
yourselves ☉	zero	zooming
youth	zeroed	zoos
youthful	zest	zucchini
youthfully	zesty	zyme
youthfulness	zig	zymoid
youths	zinc	zymology
you've ☉	zincic	zymotic

yokel	you	youth	yowl	yule	zamia	zealot	zenith	zenithal	zero	zest	zinc	zing	zodiac	zoology	zymology
yōkl	ū	ūth	youl	ūl	zāmēə	zelət	zēnith	zēnəthəl	zērō	zest	zingk	zing	zōdēak	zōoləjē	zimoləjē

X - Y

Z

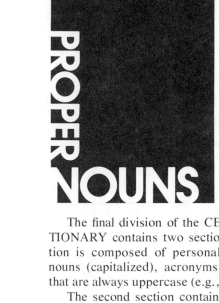

PROPER NOUNS

The final division of the CENTURY 21 DICTIONARY contains two sections. The first section is composed of personal and geographic nouns (capitalized), acronyms, and trademarks that are always uppercase (e.g., Addressograph).

The second section contains tables of abbreviations including the International Metric system with official symbols as they are written in longhand and in CENTURY 21.

Proper nouns
Personal names and geographic proper nouns come from two sources: (1) the CENTURY 21 texts and (2) the reference book entitled *6,000 Most-Used CENTURY 21 Shorthand Outlines*.

Three guidelines were used for minimizing the number of duplicate entries while preserving the basic outline for each proper noun:

- Names ending in *s* were deleted when the name without the *s* was present (*Adams* was deleted; *Adam* retained).
- Names were not repeated as adjacent duplicates (*Ashley* was deleted; Ashley-Lowell retained).
- Names appearing lowercase in the main vocabulary division were deleted in the proper noun section (*White* and *Baker* deleted when *white* and *baker* appeared as lower case vocabulary entries).

Personal names — particularly surnames — and city names are not differentiated (e.g., Mr. Mansfield and Mansfield, Ohio). In those few cases where a Postal Code abbreviation for a state had a personal name equivalent, the identical personal name retained its theory outline. For example, the girl's name Virginia is not represented by the ZIP code VA in longhand or in shorthand.

Special information
All abbreviated cities, names, and states are marked with the code shown in the Dictionary Legend, page xiv, of the User's Guide. This time-saving procedure removes any need for guessing about the theory or classification of a given outline.

In addition, superior figures are used to footnote an alternate way of:

- Spelling of names in CENTURY 21 texts (see *Allen*[1])
- Pronouncing of a foreign name (see *Jacinto*[2])

Differences in the spelling and pronunciation of names provide ample evidence that preciseness in the dictation, recording, and transcription of names is critical to the learner in the classroom and the stenographer/secretary in the occupational world.

Century 21 authors recommend that students and secretaries obtain confirmation of coined names (e.g., *TelePrompTer*), infrequent personal names (e.g., *Jacinto*), as well as names with optional spellings (e.g., *Allen, Allan,* and *Alan*) in order to assure accurate usage.

Special abbreviations
Since experienced CENTURY 21 secretaries are going into thousands of offices where the terminology varies in terms of its frequency — as does the active vocabulary of dictators — no attempt has been made to construct abbreviations for the hundreds of different occupational areas. All Century 21 abbreviations have been coded and/or summarized for the user's convenience.

As the metric system becomes more and more a part of daily awareness in the United States, the need for understanding and using metric measures and symbols becomes apparent.

The Century 21 metric table contains the most common metric terms along with a supplement of the less frequent multiple and fractional prefixes. The present list, along with CENTURY 21 official symbols, provides an excellent working vocabulary in this area of emerging importance.

a

Aagard	Alice	Arabic
Aaron	Allen[1]	Arborcrest
Abbott	Allentown	Arcadia
Abilene	Altman	Archie
Abington	Altoona	Archwood
Acapulco	Alvin	Arden
Ackerson	Amanda	Argentina
Adam	Amarillo	Arizona △
Addressograph	America △	Arkansas △
Adkins	American △	Arlene[4]
Aiken	Americana △	Arlington Heights
Akron	Americans △	Arlo
Al	Ames	Armstrong
Alabama △	Amos	Arnold
Alamo	Amtrak	Arthur
Alaska △	Amy	Asher
Albany	Anchorage	Asheville
Albert	Anderson[2]	Ashland
Alberta	Andrea	Ashley-Lowell
Alberta △	Andrew	Ashton
Albright	Andy	Asia
Albuquerque	Angelica	Asian
Alcorn	Ann[3]	Aspen Grove
Alcott	Anson	Astrojet
Alex	Antex	Athens
Alexander	Anthon	Atkins
Alexandria	Anthony	Atlanta
Alfred	Antonio	Atlantic City
ALGOL	Apollo	Atwood
	Appleton	Audrey

---

[1]Also: Alan, Allan   [2]Andersen   [3]Anne   [4]Arlyne

Augusta		Barnaby		Bellingham	
Austin		Barnard		Bellino	
Australia		Barnes		Belmont	
Australian		Barney		Ben	
Austria		Barnhart		Benedict	
Avery		Barrett		Benner	
Axelson		Barron		Bennett	
Aycock		Barry		Bennion	
Aztec		Barstow		Benson	
		Bart		Bentley	
		Barton		Benton	

b

Bailey		Bassett		Bergin	
Bakersfield		Batavia		Bergsen	
Baldwin		Bateman		Berkeley	
Ballard		Baton Rouge		Berlin	
Ballentine		Battle Creek		Berman	
Ballinger		Baumholder		Bernard	
Baltimore △		Baxter		Berney	
Bancroft		Bayman		Bertha	
Bangkok		Bayview		Bertrand	
Bankhead		Beamis		Bessie	
Banncock		Beardall		Bestor	
Barale		Beason		Bestway	
Barbara		Beaumont		Bethel	
Barcelona		Beaverdam		Bethlehem	
Barclay		Becker		Betts	
Bardell		Becky		Betty	
Barkley		Bedford		Beverly Hills	
		Beesley		Biehle	
		Belgium		Bigelow	

Billroth	Bowling Green	Brigham
Biloxi	Boyack	Bringhurst
Binet	Boyd	Brinkerhoff
Bingham	Boyle	Brinkley
Binghamton	Boynton	Brisco
Birmingham △	Bozeman	Britain
Blackburn	Braddock	British
Blackstone	Bradenton	British Columbia △
Blackwell	Bradford	Broadway
Blaine	Bradley	Brockbank
Blair	Bradshaw	Brockman
Blake	Bradstreet	Brockton
Bloomfield	Brady	Brookings
Blythe	Braille	Browne
Bohn	Brailsford	Bruce
Boise	Brandenburg	Brunner
Bolivar	Brandley	Brussels
Bolton	Brandon	Bryan[1]
Bombay	Brazil	Bryant
Bonner	Breedlove	Bryce
Boone	Breen	Bryson
Boothe	Breiner	Buchanan
Bordelon	Brent	Budapest
Borden	Brett	Buena Vista
Borderman	Brewerton	Buenos Aires
Borland	Brewster	Bruner
Boshard	Bricker	Burbank
Boston	Bridgeport	Burke
Boswell	Bridger	Burt
Bowden	Briggs	Burton

[1]Also: Brian, Bryon

Busch

Bushman

Buss

Busselberg

Butterfield

Butterworth

Buxton

Byers

C

Cairo

Cal

Calcutta

Caldwell

Calfrey

Calgary

Calhoun

California △

Callwood

Calvert

Calvin

Cameron

Campbell

Canada

Canal Zone △

Canfield

Canoga Park

Cape Cod

Capitoland

Capri

Cardston

Cardwell

Carl

Carlsbad

Carlson

Carlton

Carolann

Carolyn

Carr

Carroll[1]

Carson

Casey

Casper

Cassidy

Catherine

Catholic

Cathy

Cecil

Cedar Falls

Cedar Rapids

Cedarstrom

Cedarville

Celsius

Centrex

Chadwick

Champaign

Chapman

Charles

Charleston

Charlie

Charlotte

Charlottesville

Chattanooga △

Chatterley

Cherrington

Cheryl

Chester

Chevrolet

Cheyenne

Chicago △

Childs

Chile

China Lake

Chris

Christ

Christensen

Christian

Christmas

Cincinnati △

Claremont

Clarence

Clark[2]

Clarkson

Clarks Summit

Claude

Clayton

Clearwater

Clements

[1]Also: Carrol   [2]Clarke

Clermont		Coos Bay		Daniel	
Cleveland △		Corbello		Dansie	
Clifford		Corpus Christi		Danvers	
Cliffwood		Corrington		Danville	
Clifton		Council Bluffs		Darleen	
Clinton		Coyne		Darnell	
Clyde		Craig		Darrell	
Coalville		Cramer		Darvon	
COBOL		Crandall		Dave	
Cody		Crawford		Davenport	
Coggins		Creighton		David	
Cohen		Crenshaw		Davidson	
Coleman		Crestview		Davies	
Colledge		Crowther		Davis	
Collier		Croxton		Dawson	
Collins		Cuba		Dayton	
Colorado △		Cumberland		Daytona Beach	
Colorado Springs △		Cummings		Debra	
Colson		Cunningham		Decatur	
Colton		Curtis		Delaware △	
Columbia △		Custer		Delhi	
Columbus △		Cynthia		Delmar	
Compton				Demerol	
Conlee				Dempsey	
Connecticut △		**d**		Demsey	
Conners				Denhardt	
Connie		Dacron		Dennis	
Conover		Dallas		Densworthy	
Conrad		Dan		Denver	
Conway		Danforth		Derricott	

Deseret	Dorothy	Eastwood
Des Moines	Dotson	Eaton
Des Plaines	Douglas	Ed
Detroit △	Dover	Edgar
Devaney	Dow	Edgemont
Devereaux	Dowdle	Edgewood
Dewey	Doxey	Edith
Diana	Doyle	Edmonton
Diane	Driggs	Edmund
Dick	Drummond	Edward
Dickey	Dry Creek	Edwin
Dickinson	Duane	Egypt
Dickson	Dudley	Eileen
Dillon	Duluth	Ekstrom
Dimick	Dunbar	Elaine
District of Columbia △	Duncan[1]	El Camino
Dittmer	Dunn	Eleanor
Dixie	Durango	Elgin
Dixieland	Durham	Elizabeth
Dixon	Dutson	Elkhart
Djakarta	Dutton	Elkington
Dobbs	Duval	Ellen
Dobson	Dwayne	Ellenbecker
Dodd	Dwight	Ellington
Doke	Dyke	Elliott[2]
Dolan		Ellis
Donald		Elmer
Donaldson		Elmo
Donna	**e**	El Paso
Dorny	Easter	Elrod

Elsie	Ezra	Floyd
Elvin		Foley[3]
Elwood		Fontenot
Ely	# f	Forest Springs
Emerson		Formica
Emil	Fahrenheit	Formosa
Enders	Fairbanks	Forrest
England △	Fairfield	Forsberg
English △	Fairmeadows	FORTRAN
Englishman △	Fallows	Fountain Valley
Englishmen △	Fall River	Foxlane
Enke	Fannie	Frampton
Enloe	Fargo	Fran
Enright	Farley	France
Eric[1]	Farmington	Francis[4]
Erickson[2]	Farnsworth	Frandsen
Erie	Fay	Franklin
Erin	Fayetteville	Frazier
Ernest	Fazzio	Fred
Essen	Felix	Frederick
Estelle	Fenley	French
Ethan	Fenton	Fresno
Euclid	Ferguson	Friden
Eugene	Fillmore	Friedman
Europe	Fitch	Ft. Lauderdale △
European	Fitchburg	Ft. Smith
Evan	Fleming	Ft. Wayne
Evansville	Fletcher	Ft. Worth
Everett	Florence	Fulton
Evers	Florida △	Funliner

g

Gail		Gilbert	Granville
Galbraith		Giles	Grayson
Galen[1]		Gillespie	Greece
Gallagher		Gilmer	Greek
Galveston		Gitlow	Greeley
Gans		Givan	Green Bay
Gant		Gladstone	Greene
Garber		Gladys	Greenfield
Garcia		Glasgow	Green Island
Gardena		Gleason	Greenlee
Gardner[2]		Glenn	Greensboro
Garfield		Glenna	Greenshields
Garlock		Goble	Greenville
Gary		God	Greg
Georganne		Goddard	Gregory
George		Goldberg	Greymountain
Georgia		Goldstein	Gridley
Georgia △		Golightly	Griffin
Gerald		Gomez	Griffith
Gerhard		Goodman	Grossman
German		Goodrich	Guam △
Germany		Gordon	Guatemalan
Gibbonsville		Gorton	Gulfport
Gibraltar		Gowan[3]	Gunn
Gibson		Grand Island	Gunnison
		Grand Junction	Gunther
		Grand Rapids	Gurney
		Grandview	Gus
		Grantland	Gutzman
		Grants Pass	Guymon

[1] Also: Gailen   [2] Gardiner   [3] Gowen

h

Hadfield	Harold	Helen
Hadley	Harper	Helena
Hadlock	Harrell	Helman
Hafen	Harris	Helquist
Hagen	Harrisburg	Henderson
Hal	Harrison	Hendrickson
Halleck	Harroway	Henley
Halliday	Harry	Henretty
Halloween	Harston	Henry
Halsey	Hart	Henson
Halstead	Hartford	Herbert
Hamburg	Hartley	Herman[2]
Hamilton	Harvey	Herndon
Hamlin	Haslam	Hertz
Hammond	Hatfield	Hess
Hampshire	Hathaway	Hibbert
Hampton	Hauser	Hicks
Hancock	Havana	Higgins
Hanes	Hawaii △	High Point
Haney	Hawkins	Hillsdale
Hanford	Hawthorne	Hilton
Hanna	Hayden	Hinkel
Hanover	Hayes	Hippocrates
Hanscom	Haynes	Hodgkin
Hanson[1]	Hayward	Hoff
Hardin	Headley	Hoffman
Harker	Healey	Holdaway
Harkness	Heber	Holden
Harmon	Hedley	Holland
	Heiner	Hollandale

Holling	Huffman	Iowa △
Hollist	Hugh	Ira
Hollister	Hughes	Iran
Hollywood	Hulbert	Ireland
Holman	Hulterstrom	Irving
Holmes[1]	Humphrey	Istanbul
Holt	Hungary	Italia
Holyoke	Huntingdon	Italian
Homebuilder	Huntington	Italy
Homer	Huntley	Ivie
Hondo	Huntsville	
Hong Kong	Hyatt	
Honolulu △	Hyde	
Hooley	Hyrum	# j
Hooper		Jacinto[2]
Hoopes	# i	Jackson City
Hoover		Jacksonville
Hopewell	Ida	Jacob
Hopkins	Idaho △	Jacobsen
Horace	Illinois △	Jacoletti
Hornby	Imhoff	Jake
Horst	Imlay	James
Horton	Inca	Jamison
Houston	India	Jan
Howard	Indian	Jane
Howell	Indiana △	Janet
Howes	Indianapolis △	Janice[3]
Hoyt	Indio	Janith
Hubert	Indonesia	Jansen
Hudson		Japan

---

[1]Also: Holms [2]Sometimes pronounced: həsintō [3]Janis

Japanese	Jonathan	Kearns
Jarvis	Jones	Keats
Jarwoski	Jordan	Keck
Jason	Jorgenson	Keith
Jeff	Jose	Keithman
Jefferson	Joseph	Keller
Jeffries	Joyce	Kellermeyer
Jemez[1]	Juab	Kelly[8]
Jenkins-Foley	Judd	Kelsey
Jennifer	Judy	Kempton
Jennings	Julian	Ken
Jensen	Julianne	Kendall
Jeppson	Julio[4]	Kennedy
Jerry		Kenneth
Jersey City		Kent
Jewish	**k**	Kentucky △
Jews		Kerby
Jiles	Kalamazoo	Kermit
Jill	Kane[5]	Kern
Jim	Kansas △	Kerper
Jimmy	Kansas City △	Kerr
Joan	Karen	Kessler
Joanne	Karl	Ketchum
Joe[2]	Kate	Ketrow
Johannesburg	Katherine[6]	Kidd
John[3]	Kathleen	Kim
Johnson	Kathy	Kingbridge
Johnston	Kaufman	Kingston
Johnstown	Kay[7]	Kingstone
Jolley	Kayleen	Kinsey

[1]Sometimes pronounced: hāməs   [2]Also: Jo   [3]Jon   [4]Sometimes pronounced: hūlyō   [5]Kain   [6]Kathryn   [7]Kaye   [8]Kelley

Kirby	Landry	Lemar[7]
Kirk	Landstrom	Lemhi
KlearVu	Lang[2]	Len
Klein[1]	Langford	Leningrad
Knapp	Langley	Leo
Knott	Lankford	Leominster
Knox	Lansing	Leon
Knoxville	Laron	Leonard
Kolstad	Larry	Leroy
Korea	Larson[3]	Les
Korean	LaSalle[4]	Leslie
Kramer	La Scala	Lester
Krause	Lassiter	Lethbridge
Kress	Las Vegas	Levanger
Kristine	Latin	Lewis
	Latman	Lexington
	Laura	Liberty Center
La Boheme	Lawrence[5]	Lilly
Labrador △	Lawson	Lima[8]
Lackland	Lawton	Lincoln
Laferty	Leath	Linda
Lake Charles	Leavenworth	Lindsey[9]
Lakepoint	Lee	Ling
Lakewood	Leesburg	Linwood
Lambert	Leever	Lionel
Lana	Leff	Little Rock
Lancaster	LeGrand[6]	Liverpool
Lander	Leigh	Livingston
	Leland	Lloyd
	Lelis	Lockman

Locksley	Lundgren	Manitoba △
Logan	Lustro	Mankato
Lois	Lydia	Mann
London	Lyle	Mansfield
Long Beach	Lyman	Manship
Long Island City	Lynden[1]	Manville
Longley	Lynn	Manwaring
Longview	Lyons	Maplecrest
Lorenson		Margaret
Los Alamos		Margetts
Los Angeles △		Margie
Los Gatos		Marguerita
Lottman	**m**	Marian[2]
Lou	Mabel	Marie[3]
Louis	Mabey	Marilyn
Louise	Mace	Markham
Louisiana △	Mack	Marleen
Louisville	Macon	Marshall
Loveland	Macy	Martin
Lovingston	Madison	Martinez
Lowell	Madras	Marty
Luana	Madrid	Mary
Lubbock	Magna	Maryland △
Lucas	Mahaffrey	Marylou
Lucerne	Maine △	Maslow
Lucille	Malcolm	Mason City
Ludelle	Malone	Massachusetts △
Ludwig	Malstrom	Massey
Luke	Manchester	Massillon
Lundblad	Manhattan	Matilda

Matlock	Mecham	Middleton
Matthew	Meckling	Midvale
Maude	Medex	Midville
Maurice	Medford	Midwest
Max	Medici	Mike
Maxey	Meeks	Mikesell
Maxfield	Mel	Mikkelson
Mayberry	Melbourne	Milan
Maynard	Melissa	Milberg
Mayo	Melvin	Mildred
Mazanillo	Memphis	Milford
Mazatlan	Menlove	Millard
McAllister[1]	Mennen	Millersburg
McCarthy	Mercer	Milo
McCoy	Meriden	Milton
McCreary	Merkley	Milwaukee △
McDaniel	Merlin	Minneapolis △
McDonald	Merrimac	Minnesota △
McGee	Mesa	Minnie
McGraw	Metcalf	Minster
McGuire	Mexican	Mississippi △
McKinnon	Mexico △	Missoula
McKnight	Mexico City △	Missouri △
McMann	Meyer	Mitchell
McNair	Miami △	Mobile
McNary	Miami Beach △	Mobley
McQuarrie	Michael	Modernline
McRae[2]	Michigan △	Modesto
McReynolds	Mick	Moline
Meade	Middlefield	Monroe

n

Montague		Newhouse
Montana △		New Jersey △
Monterey Park	Nancy	Newland
Montgomery △	Naples	New London
Montreal	NASA	Newman
Mooney	Nash	New Mexico △
Moore	Nashville	New Orleans
Moorestown	Nathan	Newport News
Moreland	Nathaniel	New York △
Morgan City	Navarro	New York City △
Morley	Neal	Niagara Falls
Morris	Neaman	Nichols
Morrison	Nebeker	Niles
Morrow	Nebraska △	Nina
Morse	Neeley	Niven
Morton	Neff	Noblesville
Morwood	Negro	Noffsinger
Moscow	Neil	Nolan
Moses	Nelson	Nordgren
Moyer	Nephi	Norfolk
Mt. Lebanon	Nevada △	Norman
Mt. Prospect △	Newark	Norris
Mt. Vernon	New Bedford	North America △
Mullin	New Britain	Northbrook
Mumford	New Brunswick △	North Carolina △
Muncie	Newburgh[1]	North Dakota △
Murdock	New England △	North Hollywood
Murphy	Newfoundland △	Northwest Territories △
Murray	New Hampshire △	Norwich
Muskegon	New Haven	Nova Scotia △

[1]Also: Newburg

O

Oakland
Oakley
Oak Ridge
Oberlin
O'Brien
O'Connor
Ogden
O'Hare
Ohio △
Oklahoma △
Oklahoma City △
Oldershaw
O'Leary
Oliver
Olson
Omaha
Ontario △
Openshaw
Oran
Oregon △
Orlando
Orlon
Ormsbee
Osaka
Osborn
Oscar
Overland Park
Overman
Overson

Owen
Oxnard
Oyler

p

Packard
Padersen
Paducah
Palmer
Palo Verde
Pamela
Papanicolaou
Parcell
Paris
Parkhurst
Parkwood
Patricia
Patrick
Patterson
Patton
Paul
Paula
Pawtucket
Paxton
Payne
Pearson
Peking
Pelton

Pennsylvania △
Pennyhurst
Penrod
Pensacola
Peoria
Pepperdine
Percy
Perez
Perkins
Perry
Peru
Pete
Peter
Petersburg
Peterson
Petrochem
Petrograd
Pettijohn
Phelps
Phil
Philadelphia △
Philippines
Phillip
Phipps
Phoenix
Photocolor
Phyllis
Piedmont
Pierson
Pinedale

Pittsburgh	Protestant	Rand
Pittsfield	Providence △	Randall
Plain City	Provo	Randy
Plainfield	Pryor	Rankin
Pleasant Grove	Pueblo	Rasmussen
Pleasant Hill	Puerto Rico △	Rawlings
Plunkett	Puerto Vallarta	Rawson
Plymouth	Purcell	Raymond
Pocatello	Purdy	Reaves
Pohlman	Pyne	Rebecca
Poland	Pyrex	Redd
Polk		Redform
Polson		Redmond
Pomeroy		Reese[1]
Poplar Bluff	**q**	Reid
Popperwell		Remington
Port Arthur	Quackenbush	Reno
Porterfield	Quebec △ (Province)	Renshaw
Portland △	Quincy	Rex
Portsmouth △	Quinn	Reynolds
Portugal		Rhode Island △
Posey		Rhodes
Poughkeepsie		Richard
Powell	**r**	Richardson
Pratt		Richins
Preston	Racine	Richland
Prince Edward Island △	Radcliffe	Richmond △
Princeton	Raleigh	Rickey
Priscilla	Ralph	Ridgeville
Probert	Ramona	Rigby
	Ramsey	
	Rancho del Rey	

Riggs		Roscoe	
Riley		Roselyn	
Rinehart		Rosenman	
Ringling		Rosenquist	
Rio de Janeiro		Rosie	
Ripley		Ross	
Ripplinger		Rossiter	
Rita		Roswell	
Riviera		Roth	
Roanoke		Roundy	
Robbins		Rowland	
Robert		Roxanne	
Roberta		Roy	
Robertson		Rulon	
Robetta		Russell	
Robinson		Russia	
Robison		Russian	
Rochester		Rust City	
Rockford		Ruston	
Rock Island		Ruth	
Rodney		Ryan	
Rodsley			
Roger			
Rollins		**S**	
Rome			
Romero		Sacramento	
Ron		Saginaw	
Ronald		Saigon	
Roosevelt		Sainsbury	
Roquefort		Salamon	

Salazar	
Salem	
Salt Lake City △	
Sam	
Samson	
Samuel	
San Antonio △	
San Bernardino △	
San Diego △	
Sandra	
Sanford	
San Francisco △	
San Jose	
Santa Ana	
Santa Barbara	
Santa Claus	
Santa Cruz	
Santa Fe	
Santiago	
Sao Paulo	
Sarah[1]	
Sarasota	
Saskatchewan △	
Sattler	
Saturn	
Savannah	
Sayles	
Scarborough	
Schaller	
Scharp	

---

[1]Also: Sara

Schatzer	Shelby	Socrates
Schenectady	Shelley	Sorenson
Schlinker	Shelton	Sorrento
Schmidt	Sheridan	Soules
Schmutz	Sherman	South Africa
Schneider	Sherwood	South America △
Schoenwald	Shimmin	South American △
Schoff	Shipley	South Bend
Schooler	Shirley	South Carolina △
Schultz	Shreveport	South Dakota △
Scotland	Sibille	Southerner
Scott	Sid	Southington
Scranton	Sidney	Southview
Seagraves	Silver City	Southworth
Seattle	Simmons	Spain
Seeley	Simms	Spalding
Selman	Simone	Spanish
Seneca	Simons	Spanswick
Seoul	Simkins	Spencer
Sevey	Simpson	Spokane
Sevier	Sims	Springfield
Seville	Sioux City	Springville
Shakespeare	Sioux Falls	Sprinkel
Shane	Skagit	Stacy
Shanghai	Skylab	Stan
Shannon	Slade	Stanford-Binet
Sharon	Slatter	Stanley
Shaw	Sloan	Stanton
Sheffield	Smedley	Stardust
Sheila	Snyder	Starley

Statler	Swanson	Ted
St. Charles	Sweeney	Tedesco
Steele	Sweetwater	Tehran
Steen	Swor	Teldon[2]
Steiner	Sydney	TelePrompTer ⊙
Steubenville	Sykes	Telford
Steve	Sylvia	Telstar
Steven[1]	Symons	Templeton
Stewart	Syracuse	Tennessee △
St. George		Terre Haute
Stilson		Terrence[3]
St. Louis		Tew
St. Matthews	†	Texas △
Stockton		Texas City △
Stokeley		Texturite
STOL		Thailand
St. Paul		Thelma
St. Petersburg	Tacoma	Theodore
Strate	Taft-Hartley	Thermos
Straughan	Taipei	Thiensville
Straus	Taiwan	Thomas
Streeter	Talman	Thompson
Strunk	Tampa	Thornburgh
Stucky	Tara	Thorne
Sugarloaf	Tashimoto	Thornton
Sullivan	Tastee	Thorstenson
Sumpter	Tate	Thurmon
Super-Matic	Taylor	Tibbits
Susan	Taylorsville	Tibet
Suzy	Teasdale	Tim

Timothy		
Tobler		
Toby		
Tokyo		
Toledo		
Tolley		
Tolliver		
Tom		
Tommy		
Tony[1]		
Topeka		
Toronto		
Townsend		
Tracy[2]		
Trans-Canadian		
Travis		
Trenton		
Trevino		
Trimble		
Triplett		
Tripp		
Tucson		
Tulane		
Tulsa		
Turnerville		
Tuscaloosa		
Twin Falls		
Ty[3]		
Tyler		
Tyson		

U

United States		
Updike		
Upper Darby		
Upper St. Clair		
Urbana		
Utah △		
Utica		
Utley		

V

Valenti		
Valetti		
Van Buren		
Vance		
Vancouver		
Van Horn		
Van Huss		
Varney		
Ventura		
Vera		
Verl		
Vermont △		
Vernon		
Verona		
Vic		
Victoria		
Vienna		

Vietnam	
Viewmont	
Vincent	
Vinson	
Virgil	
Virginia	
Virginia △	
Virginia Beach △	
Virgin Islands △	

W

Wacker	
Waco	
Waddell	
Wagner	
Waite	
Wakefield	
Wallace	
Wallman	
Wally	
Walsh	
Walter	
Walton	
Wanship	
Warnick	
Warnock	

[1]Also: Toni [2]Tracey [3]Tye

Warsaw	Westfield	Willard
Wasatch	Westgate	William
Washington △	Westglen	Williamsburg
Washington D.C. △	West Hempstead	Williamson
Waterbury	Westlake	Willis
Waterloo	Westmead	Wills
Watkins	Westminster	Wilmer
WATS	Weston	Wilmington
Watson	West Orange	Wilson
Waverly	Westover	Wingate
Wayman	West Palm Beach	Winnemucca
Wayne	West Virginia △	Winslow
Waynesboro	Westwind	Winson
Webb	Westwood	Winston-Salem
Weber	Weymouth	Winthers
Webster	Whitehorse	Wirthlin
Weems	Whitfield	Wisconsin △
Weirton	Whitney	Witherspoon
Welby	Wichita Falls	Wong
Welch	Wickel	Woodrow
Welker	Widdison	Woodward
Wellington	Wiesbaden	Woonsocket
Wells	Wiggins	Worcester
Wendell	Wight	Workman
Wentz	Wilbur	Worth
Werner	Wilcox	Wright
Wes	Wilkes-Barre	Wrigley
Wesley	Wilkins	Wyatt
Westerner	Wilkinson	Wynn
Westernfield	Williamette	Wyoming △

xyz

Xerox	Yates	Yuen
X ray	Yellowstone	Yukon
Yale	Yiddish	Yukon Territory △
Yancey	Yonkers	Yuma
Yang	York	Zeeman
Yankee	Yosemite	Zimmerman
Yarborough	Yost	ZIP
Yardley	Youngstown	Zoffer
	Yucca Flat	

CORRESPONDENCE FORMS

Salutations

Dear Madam	
Dear Miss	
Dear Mr.	
Dear Mrs.	
Dear Ms.	
Dear Sir	
Gentlemen	

Complimentary

Very truly yours	
Yours cordially	
Yours respectfully	
Yours sincerely	
Yours truly	
Yours very sincerely	
Yours very truly	

Closings

Cordially	
Cordially yours	
Most sincerely	
Respectfully yours	
Sincerely	
Sincerely yours	
Very sincerely yours	

DAYS OF THE WEEK / MONTHS OF THE YEAR

Days

Sunday	
Monday	
Tuesday	
Wednesday	
Thursday	
Friday	
Saturday	

Months

January		July	
February		August	
March		September	
April		October	
May		November	
June		December	

SPECIAL ABBREVIATIONS

a.m. (*ante meridiem — before noon*)		etc. (*et cetera — and so forth*)		No. (number)	
bcc (blind carbon copy)		f.o.b. (free on board)		o'clock	
billion		[fractions]	½ 3/4 5/8	OK (approved)	
cc (carbon copy)		hundred		[ordinal numbers]	
cent		hundred dollars		percent	
cents		hundred thousand		p.m. (*post meridiem — after noon*)	
Co. (company)		hundred thousand dollars		P.O. Box (post office box)	
C.O.D. (cash/collect on delivery)		Inc. (incorporated)		P.S. (*post scriptum — postscript*)	
dollar		million		thousand	
dollars		million dollars		thousand dollars	
[dollars and cents]		Mr.		TV (television)	
Dr. (doctor)		Mrs.		U.S. (United States)	
et al. (*et alii — and others*)		Ms.		U.S.A. (United States of America)	

Metric Terms and Official Symbols – CENTURY 21

Length			Capacity			Weight		
meter	m	10	liter	l	10	gram	g	10
centimeter	cm	10	centiliter	cl	10	centigram	cg	10
decameter	dkm	2	decaliter	dkl	2	decagram	dkg	2
decimeter	dm	10	deciliter	dl	10	decigram	dg	10
hectometer	hm	3	hectoliter	hl	3	hectogram	hg	3
kilometer	km	7	kiloliter	kl	7	kilogram	kg	7
millimeter	mm	10	millimeter	ml	10	milligram	mg	10
candella	cd	1	ampere	a	½0	mole	mol	1
Celsius	C	70	second	s	10	tonne	t	